Antique
Automotive
C⊙LLECTIBLES

Jack Martells

Contemporary Books, Inc.
Chicago

Library of Congress Cataloging in Publication Data

Martells, Jack.
    Antique automotive collectibles.

    Includes bibliographical references and index.
    1. Automobiles—Collectors and collecting.
2. Automobiles—Equipment and supplies—Collectors and
collecting.   I. Title.
TL7.M37   1980   629.2   80-65924
ISBN 0-8092-7205-9

Published by Contemporary Books, Inc.
180 North Michigan Avenue, Chicago, Illinois 60601
Manufactured in the United States of America
Library of Congress Catalog Card Number: 80-65924
International Standard Book Number: 0-8092-7205-9

Published simultaneously in Canada by
Beaverbooks
953 Dillingham Road
Pickering, Ontario L1W 1Z7
Canada

Table of Contents

Foreword

WHY does man collect? A modern day philosopher once said, "Two reasons, insecurity or the desire to build a monument to oneself." In some cases that statement probably has a ring of truth to it, but I must take exception. What kind of a monument does a pile of rusty car parts make? A nostalgia buff finds a certain fascination in the mechanical simplicity of old-car components, the beauty of fine lithography in old tins and advertising, or the rich look of long since discontinued brass, not to mention the fun of reading old advertising claims about beauty, power, speed, mileage, and a quality built or more reliable car.

No matter what you collect today, it most likely has some value. Cecil Heidelberger of Andover, Minnesota, provided the validity of this statement with his thirty-year accumulation of old tires, twelve million in all, covering forty acres. After charging people a fee to dump these tires over the years, he then sold them for a cool seven million to a firm that reclaimed carbon black, high tension wire, oil, and a variety of other secondary products. Old Cecil's philosophy is: "A little of something is not worth much, but tons of it is!" So the next time you see someone stock piling something ridiculous such as motorcycle doors, don't laugh although you might stare in wonderment about whether that pile is his monument, security, or perhaps his lunacy.

Collecting holds a fascination for all ages. From the five-year-old whose pockets bulge with marbles to the millionaire acquiring another priceless treasure, truly millions of people collect. Years ago the adult usually collected something having a tangible, readily recognizable value such as stamps, coins, guns, antiques, etc. On the other hand, youngsters usually collected nonvaluable items like baseball cards, bottle caps, butterflies, cereal-box premiums, marbles, etc.

Times have changed considerably in that people of all ages are collecting anything imaginable. You name it, and there is someone who will collect it. Items like thimbles, beer cans, mouse traps, swizzle sticks, and light bulbs may sound ridiculous to one who collects auto nostalgia, but so might spark plugs and hubcaps evoke a laugh from a comic book collector. No matter what you collect you are not alone. The announcement of some supposedly new collectible seems to bring people out of the woodwork. They may have been collecting an item for years, thoroughly convinced of being the only one involved.

Those who have collected for many years have found, much to their frustration, that a once inexpensive hobby has in most cases grown out of proportion and has become cost prohibitive. Baseball cards that were once free with a penny pack of bubble gum now sell for anywhere from ten cents to two thousands dollars each. Beer cans, once basically a throw away item, are treasured by thousands, and certain rare cans have reached astronomical values. Old cars that we now lovingly call antiques and classics were once basically a throwaway item, designed with planned obsolesence in mind. Having lived out their ten-to-fifteen-year average life span, they were abandoned to the north forty or sent to the scrap heap. Again, the collector or old car buff emerges to buy up everything in sight. Naturally, the law of supply and demand prevails, and with these increasing values our beloved hobby has gone one step further. Wealthy investors looking for a hedge against inflation have bought up many of the fine old autos we love, only to resell them in the near future to the highest bidder, who more often than not has never seen the car. What a waste of beautiful machinery, to be treated like shares of common stock! This action has put the price of most antique cars out of reach for the average enthusiast.

Frustrated, looking for a way to continue involvement in the hobby, many have turned to just saving pieces of cars. Although this facet of the hobby is not new, few people were collecting ten years ago. With the tremendous increase in flea markets and car-part swaps, the means have now been provided to obtain these collectibles. Although not plentiful, one never knows where a collectible might show up. A quality found in most collectors is the obsession to acquire a complete collection (one of every kind). This offers a tremendous challenge but is not very realistic when pursuing antique auto parts. With coins and stamps there is a record of every one ever issued, resulting in a relatively easy task, providing funds don't run out. Trying to acquire every hubcap or license plate becomes an almost impossible task, because there are no really valid records of what has been produced over the years or the varieties that might exist. Inadvertently, during your quest, you may become somewhat of an expert at your particular endeavor.

Another problem facing collectors of auto parts is deciding what to collect—a little bit of each item or everything ever made pertaining to one subject. This decision only you can make; however, space and finances usually play a big role in this choice.

No matter what you collect it is always interesting to collect all associated material. To collect just hubcaps can make an interesting hobby. But why not include other items associated with the wheel? Hubcap wrenches, valve stem covers, tire gauges, associated advertising, etc., abound in large quantities. Here is an idea I have not seen, but I am sure someone has done. Cut six- or eight-inch sections out of early balloon tires, and display the various tread patterns—like the many round suction cups on one brand or the words *Non Skid* raised all over the tread pattern on another.

Whatever you decide to collect, it is my hope that this book will assist in your quest.

Acknowledgments

THE making of any historical or collectors' book requires input from other collectors and informational sources.

I would like to give special thanks to Bill Bond, founder of Spark Plug Collectors of America, for much technical information and many photographs of his collection. Bruce Ledingham of Vancouver, B.C., supplied much technical information and over 140 pictures of early hubcaps. He provided an unparalleled cross section of material for this chapter. Lee Hartung graciously opened his License Plate and Automobile Museum to my camera and provided many interesting tidbits of information. Joe Korosa of "Little Joe's Antique Cars" provided access to many fine photographs of mascots and emblems. Thanks to Bill Williams for the loan of a few of his fine mascot photographs from his book. Carl Zahm was quite helpful with dating of emblems and provided a few examples for the book.

Thanks also to the following for their important contributions: Jerry Gill for World's Fair; Bill Franzen, advertising; Carl Montegna, miscellaneous collectibles; Disabled American Vets; United States Air Force Museum; and International Harvester Company.

Introduction

A FASCINATING encounter for any collector is stimulating conversation with an old timer who remembers old cars and readily reminisces over their quirks and idiosyncrasies. Many of us grew up in the fifties, a period when cars were uppermost in the minds of the young. From grandiose plans to build a hot rod or custom car to dreams of buying a factory-new, high-performance car, we all had wheels on our minds. Because of this constant association in the past, we can at a glance today, recognize a 1957 Chevy, a 1955 T-Bird, or a Studebaker Golden Hawk. It was this same love of cars on a smaller scale that produced the old-timer who at a glance can identify a 1927 Whippet hubcap or a 1925 Star radiator medallion. Conversation with one of these gentlemen can truly be an educational or at the least an entertaining experience. Unfortunately, as time passes, there are fewer of these gentlemen around, and with all due respect to age and experience, sometimes memories fade. Therefore, we must rely more on museums or present-day collectors who are knowledgeable about their hobby to acquire this type of information. A wise collector today endeavors to acquire as much reference material as possible in the form of old manuals, magazines, advertisements, trade journals, and photographs. Material such as this produced during the days when these old cars were new is much more likely to be accurate than currently produced information. Admittedly, this book is bound to have some errors as well.

There are probably those who collect dipsticks, bumper brackets, drain-oil specimens, rear-door hinge pins, or anything else that abounds in more than two varieties, but this book deals with more popular aspects of automotive collectibles.

Little has been written in the area of automotive collectibles; however, some articles are being featured in monthly automotive magazines. I feel that this book, although not a complete work, will fill a gap in our hobby. Unfortunately, a book on collecting can never be complete. An undertaking such as that would be impossible. New finds are always turning up, to say nothing of the tremendous amount of material already in private collections, some of which are inaccessible.

The following alphabetical list will give you an idea of the more popular possibilities of automotive collectibles:

After-Market Accessories
Antitheft Devices
Avon Cars

Banks
Books
Brass Carburetors
Brass Lamps
Bud Vases
Buttons

Calendars
Carbide Generators
Chauffeur Badges
China Plates
Clocks
Club Badges

Dashboard Emblems
Dealers' Models
Door Handles
Drain Cocks

Emblems (Radiator)

Felt Pennants

Ford Script
Ford Tools
Ford—World's Fair 1934

Gadgets & Gimmicks
Gas-Pump Globes
Gas-Station Accessories
Gearshift Knobs

Headlamp Lenses
Horn Buttons
Horns
Hubcaps

Indy 500 Souvenirs
Instruments

Jacks

Key Fobes
Keys
Knives

Lamps
License Plates
Literature

Lubricators

Magazine Ads
Mascots
Matchbooks
Medals—Coins
Models
Motor Meters
Music, Sheets, Records

Nameplates

Oilcans
Oilers
Owner's Manuals

Paperweights
Pencils & Pens
Photographs
Pins
Plates—Glass, China,
   Metal
Postcards
Posters
Primer Cups

Racing Souvenirs
Radiator Caps
Radiator Shells
Running-Board Step
   Plates

Scripts
Shift Knobs
Signs
Smoking Accessories
Spark Plugs
Speedometers
Stamps with Cars
Stoplights — Lenses

Taillight Lenses
Tie Tacks
Tins
Tire Ads
Tire Gauges
Tire Pumps

Valve-Stem Covers

Wall Posters
Watch Fobs
World's-Fair Auto
   Souvenirs

My purpose in writing this book is to stimulate would-be collectors and to inspire experts to write specialized, in-depth books on the subject. In fact, I understand that an in-depth work on spark plugs has already been begun.

For the beginner this book will offer much general information. Even the advanced collector will find items he has not seen before. That's the way it is with collecting: Just when you think you have seen everything in your particular hobby, something new crops up.

Collectors like technical information, but even more they like to see what is available.

Automotive collectibles can turn up just about anywhere, but since many people are out looking for these treasures, competition is stiff. If your time is precious, and you are unable to scrounge for treasures, your best bet is to visit the many part-swap meets taking place around the country. On any given weekend, especially during the summer, there are two or three swap meets within a hundred miles of most cities.

Some collectors are not innovative when it comes to restoring or displaying collections, because they are content to accumulate their treasures in boxes or to hang them promiscuously on nails in the barn or garage. Some do not have the time or ability, but for those who do, restoration and attractive displays can be self-rewarding. There are two schools of thought on restoration. One group scoffs at the idea of restoration, believing that the "as is" condition reflects the history of the piece. On the other hand, there are those who advocate restoration, because when the item was new, it was not chipped, dented, scratched, or rusty. For the latter I have revealed a few tricks for restoration to be used where applicable.

CHAPTER 1

What's in a Name?

THE automobile name game is an intriguing and a most interesting one. From *A.B.C.* to *Zvezda* and over 3,000 names, somewhere in between there are a wealth of history and just plain interesting facts. Automobiles have been named after presidents, famous people, birds, animals, trees, planets, gemstones, places, insects, cities and towns, and companies known for products other than automobiles (such as *Dupont, Pullman, Messerschmitt, Alco, Deere, Westinghouse, Maytag,* etc.), but most of all, cars were named after their designers and builders. Some of the more prominent you will recognize: Henry Ford, John and Horace Dodge, Walter P. Chrysler, Louis Chevrolet, Ransom E. Olds, and Frederick S. Duesenberg, just to name a few. If these famous men could adorn their vehicles with their names, Germany's *Kleinschnittger* and Holland's *Schimmelpennick* could so adorn their autos in the same manner. However, I would not expect to hear names like these used as a household word such as *Ford* or *Chevy!* But all names were not that complicated. Over thirty had three-letter names, and perhaps the makers of *A.B.C.* were looking to be listed first in the phone book. Then there was *Jack's Runabout;* Jack must have been proud parking his car in front of Fred's Bank or having lunch with Dr. Bill. Other simple names of the early days lacked imagination or panache: *Zip, Vim, Zust, Foos, Peep, Dort, Bird, Imp, Fish, Duck,* or *Do Do,* but who could knock *Mom.* Then there were the confusing names. If you boasted of owning a *Dan Patch* or *Clydesdale,* you might be asked how much you paid for your horse. Or if you owned an *Alldays* and *Onions, Liver,* or *American Chocolate,* you may have been constantly reminded of something good to eat. Who knows what people might have thought if they heard you talk about your *Pic Pic, Pungs Finch, Hyslop, Gurgle,* or *Seven Little Buffaloes.* They might have slowly slipped out of the room to avoid contracting whatever it was you had. Then again you might not feel too comfortable riding in a *Klink, Havoc, Blood, Hazard,* or *Coffin.* Your pride may have been bolstered with cars like *Economy, Old Reliable, Best, All Steel, Rapid,* or *Jumbo,* as these manufacturers were probably trying to instill confidence in the motoring public. Then there was the *Fwick, Twombly,* and the *Twyford,* which were most certainly not named by Elmer Fudd, as they would have been called the *Cwazy Wabbit* and *Cwazy Wascal!* How about the *Dewabout?* Henny Youngman, King of the One Liners, would have had fun with this one, "Oh, it will do about forty!" There was even a *Barbarino;* I wonder if John Travolta owns one. Three famous Rs sure, you got it, *Rockne, Roosevelt, Rickenbacker!* If you are Polish, don't feel slighted, because there are a couple for you: *Grabowski* and *Piscorski.*

Things really have not changed much over the years. You don't have to go far today to find an amusing or funny car name: *Le Car, Thing, Brat, Luv, Gremlin, Swinger,* and *Rabbit*—mostly new names. But you might remember the *Apperson Jack Rabbit,* and even the little *Volkswagen* we lovingly call *Bug* had an ancestoral namesake in the *Autobug* or *Bugmobile.*

All things considered there was once the ultimate vehicle name, *Traffic*! If they only had known back then!

Early auto makers were not looking for a catchy or exotic name that would be impressed on the minds of the public through national advertising campaigns since most were small regional car builders and could not handle such volume. Today, with communication and transportation what it is, the advertising people are much more sophisticated and tend to promote names that suggest exotic places and animals, such as *Seville, Eldorado, Monte Carlo, Riviera, Bonneville, Catalina,* and where the heck is *Grandville*? It must be just down the road a piece from *Greatburg.* Great who?

While General Motors was using exotic places, Ford was running the gamut with animals and birds for example, *Falcon, Thunderbird, Bobcat, Pinto, Mustang, Maverick,* and *Bronco.* I wonder if the next horse in Ford's corral will be called *Stud*? Chrysler advertising people were riding high on the speed and macho image with names like *Fury, Charger, Roadrunner, Barracuda,* and *Magnum.*

The nostalgia craze has opened up a new front for the name game. Coupe, two-door and four-door sedan just no longer have any flair. So along came secondary descriptive names, reminiscent of the classic cars of the early thirties: *Phaeton, Landau, Brougham, Salon,* and *Towncar.* Even the traditional workhorse of large families and small businesses is no longer a station wagon; it is a *Ranch Wagon* or an *Estate Wagon.* Car makers have even brought back names they dropped years earlier in an effort to recapture old memories of class or quality. Buick revived their *Limited,* and American Motors tried the *Hornet* again. Ford as early as 1951 brought back the *Victoria* after a seventeen-year absence but dropped it again after six years in favor of the *Fairlane.* More recently, Ford has returned the *Zephyr* and *Monarch* to stardom. Even a current rock group has revived a long forgotten auto name, *R.E.O. Speedwagon.*

The following you might recognize as a list of modern-day car models. But actually these names were all used over fifty years ago by other car makers, and due to the long time lapse, there was apparently no infringement on copyright.

Apollo	Buick	*Continental*	Lincoln	*Marmon*	Truck	*There have been ten
Arrow	Plymouth	*Dart*	Dodge	*Mustang*	Ford	different companies
Colt	Dodge	*Eagle**	AMC	*Phoenix*	Pontiac	using *Eagle.*
Comet	Mercury	*Falcon*	Ford	*Regal*	Buick	
Concord	AMC	*Invicta*	Buick			

In the ninety-year tenure of the automobile's existence, over five thousand makes of cars and trucks have been sold in the world.

The following list of 3,005 should prove there are endless possibilities for automotive collectibles to be had. It was compiled from many sources and provides a respectable representation.

A.B.C.
Abarth
Abenaque
Abendroth & Root
Abbott
Abbott-Cleveland
Abbott-Detroit
Abbott-Downing
A.C.
Acadia
Acason
Ace
A.C.F.
A.C.M.A.
Acme
Acorn
Adams
Adams-Farwell
Adelphia
Ader
Adette
Adland
Adler
Adria
Adrian
Advance
A.E.C.
Aero
Aero-Car
Aero-Minor
Aerotype
Aero-Willys
Ahrens Fox
Air Scout
Air Way
Ajax 1901
Ajax 1925
Ajax Electric
A.J.S.
Akron
Alamobile
Aland
Albanus
Albany
Albatross
Albert
Albion
Alco
Alco Berliet
Aldo
Alden-Sampson
Alena
Alfa
Alfa-Romeo
Alfasud
All American
Allard
Alldays & Onions
Allegheny
Allen
Allen & Clark
Allen Cyclecar
Allen Kingston

Allen Steam
Allith
Allis Chalmers
All State
All Steel
Alma
Alpena
Alsace
Alta
Alter
Altha
Altham
Altman
Alvis
Alxo
Amalgamated
Ambassador
Amco
America
American
American Austin
American Bantam
American Beauty
American Benham
American Berliet
American Chocolate
American Clouthard
American Electric
American Fiat
American Gas
American La France
American Mors
American Mercedes
American Napier
American Populaire
American Carriage
American Simplex
American Steam Car
American Steamer
American Sterling
American Traveler
American Tri Car
American Underslung
American Vorturette
American Willys
Ames
Amesbury
Amex
Amilcar
Amphibian
Amplex
A.M.S.-Sterling
A.M.X.
Anchor
Anderson
Anger
Anglia
Anglo-Dane
Angus
Anheuser Busch
Anhut
Ansaldo

Ansted
Anthony
Apeth
Apex
Apollo
Appel
Apperson
Apple
Appleton
Aquila
Arbenz
Arcadia
Ardsley
Argo Borlund
Argo Case
Argo Electric
Argo Gas
Argonne
Argyll
Ariel
Aries
Aristos
Armac
Armleder
Armstrong-Siddeley
Arnold Electric
Arnolt-Bristol
Arrol-Johnston
Arrow
Arrow Cyclecar
Artzberger Steamer
Aspen
Aster
Aston-Martin
Astor
Astra
Astre
Atco
Atlantic
Atlas
Atlas Knight
Atterbury
Atvidaberg
Auburn
Audi
Auglaize
Aultman
Austenuo Steam
Austin 1903
Austin 1930
Austin Bantam
Austin-Healey
Austin-Sprite
Austin Steam
Australian
Austro Daimler
Austro Fiat
Auto Acetylene
Autobarn
Auto Bug
Autobuggy
Auto Car

Auto Cycle
Auto Dynamic
Auto Fore Carriage
Auto Go
Auto Loco Steam
Automatic
Automaton
Automobile Forecar
Automobile Vorturette
Automote
Automotor
Autonacional
Autoplane
Auto Tri Car
Auto Two
Auto Union
Auto Vehicle
Aurora
Available
Avanti
Avery
Aviette

Babcock
Babcock Electric
Bachelle Electric
Backhus
Bacon
Badger
Bailey Electric
Baker & Elberg
Baker Electric
Baker Steam
Balboa
Baldner
Baldwin
Ball
Ball Steam
Ballot
Balzer
Banker
Banker Bros.
Banker Electric
Banner
Bantam
Barbarino
Barley
Barlow
Barnes
Barnhart
Barracuda
Barrett & Parret
Barrow Electric
Bartholomew
Barver
Bat
Bateman
Bates
Bauer
Bauroth
Bayard
Bay State 1906
Bay State 1922
Beach
Beacon Flyer
Bean
Beardmore
Beardsley

Beau Chamberlin
Beaver
Beck
Beck-Hawkeye
Bedelia
Bedford
Bee
Beggs
B.E.L.
Belden
Belfontaine
Belgica
Bell 1907
Bell 1915
Bellamy
Belmont
Belsize
Belsize Bradshaw
Belvedere
Bemmel & Burnham
Bendix
Bendix Ames
Benham
Ben Hur
Benjamin
Benner
Benson
Bentley
Benton Harbor Motor
Benz
Berg
Bergdoll
Berkley
Berkshire
Berliett
Berna
Bernardi
Bertolet
Berwick Electric
Berz
Bessemer
Best
Bethlehem
Betz
Beverly
Bewis
Bewman
Beyster
Beyster Bi Autogo
B.F.S.
Bianchi
Biddle
Biddle Murray
Biederman
Bignan
Bimel
Binford
Binney-Burnham
Birch
Bird
Birmingham
Birnel
Biscayne
Bjering
Black
Black Crow
Black Diamond
Blackhawk 1903

Blackhawk 1929
Blair
Blaisdell
Blakeslee
Blanchard
Blazzer
Bliss
Blitz
B.L.M.
Block Bros.
Blomshons
Blomstrom
Blood
Bluebird
Blumberg
B.M.M.
B.M.W.
B.N.C.
Bobbi Car
Bob Cat
Boggs
Boisselot
Bollee
Bollstrom
Boltz
Bonneville
Borbein
Bogward
Borland
Borland-Grannis
Boss
Boston
Boston & Amesbury
Boston Hayes Apperson
Boston Hayes Wheel
Bour Davis
Bournoville
Bourville
Bouton & Bates
Bovy
Bowman
Boynton
Bradfield
Bradley
Bramwell
Bramwell-Robinson
Brasie
Brat
Brazier
Brecht
Breer
Breeze & Lawrence
Breman
Brems
Brennabor
Brennan
Brenner
Brew & Hatcher
Brewster
Brewster Knight
Bridgeport
Briggs
Briggs & Stratton
Briggs Detroiter 1902
Briggs Detroiter 1912
Brighton
Brightwood
Brintel

Brinton
Briscoe
Bristel
Bristol
British Salmson
Brixia-Zust
B.R.M.
Broc Electric
Brock
Brockville Atlas
Brockway
Brodesser
Brogan
Bronco
Brook
Brooks
Brough-Superior
Brounce
Brower
Brown
Brown-Burtt
Brownell
Brownie Kar
Brown-Luverne
Brunn
Brunner
Brunswick
Brush
Bruss
Bryan
B.S.A.
Buc
Bucciali
Buchet
Buck
Buckeye
Buckeye Gas Buggy
Buckles
Buckmobile 1903
Buckmobile 1907
Buffalo
Buffalo Electric
Buffington
Buffman
Buffum
Buford
Bugatti
Buggyaut
Buggycar
Bugmobile
Buick
Burdick
Bundy
Burg
Burman
Burney
Burns
Burroughs
Burt
Bus
Bush
Busser
Bussing
Buzmobile
Byrider

Cadillac
Calais

Calcott
California
California Cycle Car
Californian
Calvert
Camaro
Cameron 1903
Cameron 1914
Campbell
Canada
Cannon
Cantone
Capitol
Capps
Capri
Caprice
Carbon
Carcovan
Car De Luxe
Cardway
Carhart
Carlisle
Carlson
Car Nation
Carpenter
Carqueville-McDonald
Carrison
Carroll 1908
Carroll 1913
Carter
Cartercar
Carter Mobile
Carter Twin Engine
Carthage
Cartone
Casco
Case
Casear
Cass
Cassel
Castle
Castro
Cato
Cavac
Cavalier
Caward-Dart
C.B.
C-Del
Ceco
Cederholm
Ceirano
Celtic
Cemsa-Caproni
Centaur
Central
Century
Century Tourist
C.F.
C.G. Gay
C.G.V.
Chadwick 1905
Chadwick 1911
Chalfant
Challenger
Chalmers
Chalmers-Detroit
Champion 1909
Champion 1919

Champion Electric
Chandler
Chandler-Cleveland
Chapman
Charger
Charron
Charron-Laycock
Charter Car
Charter Oak
Chase
Chatham
Checker
Chelsea
Chenard & Walcker
Chevelle
Chevette
Chevrolet
Chicago
Chicago Commercial
Chicago Electric
Chicago Motor Buggy
Chicago Slim
Chief
Childs
Chiribiri
Christiansen
Christie
Christman
Christopher
Chrysler
Church
Church-Field
Cincinnati
Cinco
Cino
Cisitalia
Citation
Citroen
Citroen-Kegresse
Clapps Motor Carriage
Clark
Clark Carter
Clark Electric
Clark Hatfield
Clarkmobile
Clarkspeed
Clark Steamer
Clarkson
Classic
Clear & Dunham
Cleburne
Cleburg
Cleeg
Clement
Clement-Bayard
Clement-Talbot
Clement-Panhard
Clendon
Clermont 1903
Clermont 1922
Cleveland 1902
Cleveland 1919
Climber
Clinton
Cloughley
Club Car
Clyal
Clyde

Clydesdale
Clymer
Clyno
Coates
Coates Goshem
Coey
Coey Flyer
Coffin
Cogswell
Colburn
Colby
Cole
Coleman
Colla
Collier
Collinet
Collins
Collins-Electric
Colly
Colonial
Colonial Electric
Colt 1907
Colt 1978
Columbia 1897
Columbia 1916
Columbia-Dauman
Columbia Electric
Columbia Knight
Columbia Motor Carriage
Columbian Electric
Columbus
Columbus Electric
Comet
Comet Cyclecar
Commander
Commerce
Commercial
Commodore
Commonwealth
Compound
Coneat
Concord
Conda
Condor
Conestoga
Conklin Electric
Connersville
Conover
Conrad Stam
Consolidated
Continental 1907
Continental 1914
Continental 1933
Continental 1940
Cook
Cooley
Copper
Coppock
Corbin
Corbitt
Cord
Cordoba
Core
Corinthian
Corl
Cormedian
Cornelian
Cornish Friedberg

Coronet
Correja
Corressus
Cortez
Corvair
Corvette
Corweg
Corwin
Coscob
Cosmopolitan
Cotay
Cotta
Cottinet
Cottin et Dequttes
Cougar
Cotton
Country Club
Couple Gear
Courier 1904
Courier 1909
Courier 1922
Coventry-Climax
Covert
Covert Motorette
Coward-Dart
Coyote
C.P.
Craig-Hunt
Craig Toledo
Crane
Crane & Breed
Crane-Simplex
Crawford
Crescent
Crest
Crestmobile
Cricket
Criterion
Croesus Jr.
Crock
Crodus
Crompton
Crosley
Cross Steam Carriage
Crossley
Crother Duryea
Crouch
Crough Steamer
Crow
Crow Elkhart
Crowdus
Crown
Crown High Wheel
Crown Magnetic
Crowther Duryea
Croxton
Croxton-Keeton
Cruiser
Crusader
Cuemobile
Cull
Culver 1905
Culver 1917
Cumbria
Cummins
Cunningham
Cunningham Steamer
Curtis

Custer
Custom
Cutlass
Cutting
C.V.I.
Cycle Car
Cyclemobile
Cyclone
Cycleplane
Cycloplane

D.A.C.
D.A.F.
Dagmar
Daihatsu
Daimler
Daimler-Benz
Daley
Dalton
Daniels
Dan Patch
Dansk
Darby
Darling
Darracq
Darrin
Darrow
Dart
Dartmobile
Datsun
Dauville
Davenport
Davids
DaVinci
Davis 1910
Davis 1947
Davis-Daubille
Dawson
Day
Day Elder
Day Utility
Dayton-1909
Dayton-1913
Dayton Electric
Dayton Steam
Deal
Dean
Dearborn
Debonair
Decan
Decauville
Decker
De Cross
De Curney Belleville
De Dietrich
De Dion Bouton
Deemaster
Deemotor
Deere
Deere Clark
Deering Magnetic
Defiance
DeKalb
Delahaye
Delage
Delaunay-Belleville
De La Vergne
Delcar

De Leon
Delhore
Delling Steam
Del Mar
Delmore
Delta 88
Deltal
DeLuxe
De Mars Electric
De Martini
De Mot
De Motte
Denby
Denzel
De Page
De Parn
Dependable
Derain
Derby
Desberon Steam
De Shaum
De Shaw
DeSoto 1915
DeSoto 1928
De Tamble
De Tomaso
Detroit 1900
Detroit 1922
Detroit Air Cooled
Detroit Chatham
Detroit Dearborn
Detroit Electric
Detroit Speedster
Detroit Steam
Detroiter
De Vaux
De Ville
Dewabout
Dewcar
Dey Griswold Electric
Diabolo
Dial
Diamler
Diamond
Diamond Arrow
Diamond Red
Diamond Reo
Diamond T
Dianna
Diehl
Diexel
Differential
Dile
Dill
Direct Drive
Disbrow
Dispatch
Divco Twin
Divoy
Dixi
Dixie
Dixie Flyer
Dixie Tourist
Dixton
D.K.W.
Doane
Doble Detroit
Doble Steam Car

Dodge
Dodge Graham
Dodge Steam Car
Dodgeson
Dodgeson & Empire
Do Do
Dolo
Dolphine
Dolson
Dong-Feng
Dorris
Dort
Douglas
Dover
Dowagiac
Downing
Dowing Detroit
Dragon
Dragon Steam
Drake
Dreadnought
Drexel
Driggs
Drubon
Drummond
Duck
Dudgeon
Dudley Bug
Duebon
Duel
Duer
Duesenberg
Dufaux
Dumont
Dunn
Duo
Duplex
Du Pont
Duquesene
Durable
Durant 1921
Durant 1927
Durant Dorr
Durkopp
Durmont
Durocar
Duryea 1895
Duryea 1905
Duryea 1914
Duryea Gem
Duryea Light Car
Dusseau
Duster
Dux
Dyke
Dymaxion
Dynamobile

Eagle 1905
Eagle 1979
Eagle Electric
Eagle Macomber
Eagle Rotary
Earl 1907
Earl 1921
Eastern Dairies
Eastman
Eastman Steam

Easton
Easton Electric
Eaton
Eck
Eclair
Eclipse
Economy 1906
Economy 1915
Economy Car
Eddy Electric
Edison
Edsel
Edwards Knight
Egg
E.H.V.
Eichsteadt
Eisenhuth
Eisenhuth Compound
E.J.M.
Elberon Steam
Elbert
Elcar
Elco
Eldorado
Eldridge
Electra
Electric Vehicle
Electric Wagon
Electrobat
Electrocar
Electromatic
Electronomic
Elgin
Elinor
Elite
Elite Steamer
Elk
Elkhart
Elliott
Ellis Electric
Ellsworth
Elmore
Elrich
Elston
Elwell Parker
Elysee
Emancipator
Emerson
Emerson Fisher Motor
E.M.F.
Empire 1898
Empire 1910
Empire State
Empress
Endurance Steamer
Enfield-Allday
Enger
Englehardt
Engler
Enterprize
Entiro
Entyre
Entz
Erie
Ernst
Erskine
Esco
Essex 1901

Essex 1919
Essex Steam Car
Euclid
Eureka
Evans
Evans Steam
Evansville
Everitt
Everybody's
Ewing
Excalibur
Excelsior
Executive

F-85
Facel-Vega
Facto
Fageol
Fairbanks Morse
Fairlane
Fairmont
Fairmount
F.A.L.
Falcar
Falcon 1914
Falcon 1922
Falcon 1959
Falcon Knight
Famous
Fanning Electric
Fargo
FarMac
Farman
Farmobile
Farner
Fauber
Fay
Fedelea
Federal
Federal Steamer
Fee
Fenton
Fergus
Ferrari
Ferris
F.I.A.T. (American)
Fiat
Fiat Simca
Field Steam
Fiesta
Fifth Ave. Coach
Findley
Firebird
Firestone Columbus
Fischer
Fish
Fisher
Fitch
Fitzjohn
Flagler
Flanders
Flanders Electric
Fleetwood
Flexbi
Flexible
Flint 1902
Flint 1924
Florenzia
Flyer

F.N.
Fonck
Foos
Ford
Ford Steam
Forest
Forest City
Forschler
Forster Six
Forster Steam
Fort Pitt
Foster
Fostoria
Fournier
442
Four Traction
Four Wheel Drive
Fox
Frankfurt
Franklin
Frayer
Frayer Miller
Frazer
Frazer Nash
Frederickson
Fredonia
Freeman
Freemont
French
Friedman
Friend
Fritchie Electric
Frontenac
Front Drive
Frontmobile
F.R.P.
F.S.
Fuller
Fulton
Fury
F.W.D.
Fwick

Gabriel
Gadabout
Gaeth
Gaithmobile
Gage
Galaxie
Gale
Galloway
Galt
Gamage
Gardner
Gardner-Serpolet
Garford
Garvin
Gary
Gas-Au-Lec
Gas Engine
Gasmobile
Gasoline Motor Carriage
Gatts
Gawley
Gaylord
Gearless
Geer Steam
Gem

Gendron & Drance
General
General Cab
General Electric
General Vehicle
Genesee
Geneva
Gens
Georges-Irat
German American
Geronimo
Gersix
Ghent
Giant
Gibbs Electric
Gibson
Gifford-Pettitt
Gifford Vittet
Gill
Gillet
G.J.G.
Gleason 1912
Gleason 1913
Glide
Globe
Glover
G.M.C.
Gnome
Goethe
Goethemobile
Golden Eagle
Golden State
Golden West
Goodspeed
Goodyear
Gorson
Gotfredson
Grabowsky
Graf & Stift
Graham 1905
Graham 1930
Graham-Fox
Graham Paige
Gramm
Gramm-Bernstein
Gramm-Logan
Grand
Grand Prix
Granite Falls
Grannis Electric
Grant
Grant Ferris
Grass-Bremer
Grass Premier
Graves-Condon
Graves-Gordon
Gray
Gray Dort
Great Arrow
Great Eagle
Great Smith
Great Southern
Great Western 1900
Great Western 1909
Greely
Gregoire
Gregory
Gregory Front Drive
Grensfelder

Greuter
Gremlin
Greyhound
Gride
Grinnel Electric
Griswold
Grout
Grout Steamer
G.S.G.
G.T.C.
G.T.O.
Guilder
Gurgel
Gurley
Guy Vaughn
Gyroscope

Hackett
Hagenlocher
Hahn
Hale
H.A.L.
Hal-Fur
Hall
Halladay
Halsey
Halton
Hambrick
Hamilton
Hamlin Holmes
Hammelvognen
Hammer
Hammer-Sommer
Handley
Handley Knight
Hands
Hanger
Hannah
Hanomag
Hanover
Hansa Lloyd
Hansen
Hanson
Harding
Hardy
Hare
Harper
Harrie
Harrigan
Harris
Harrisburg
Harrison
Harroun
Hart Kraft
Hartley
Hartley Steamer
Hartman
Hartnett
Harvard
Harvey
Hasbrouck
Haseltine
Haslerouck
Hassler
Hatfield
Hathaway
Haupt
Havers
Haviland

Havoc
Hawkeye
Hawley
Hay-Berg
Haydock
Haynes
Haynes Anderson
Haynes Apperson
Hayward
Hazard
H. Brothers
H.C.S.
Healey
Hearsey
Hebb
Heifner
Heilman
Heine Velox
Heinis
Helios
Handel
Henderson
Hendrickson
Henley Steam
Henney Hearse
Henrietta
Henry
Henry J
Hercules
Hercules Electric
Herff-Brooks
Hermes
Herreshoff Detroit
Herreshoff-Troy
Herschmann
Hershell-Spilman
Hertel
Hertz
Hess Steam
Hewitt
Hewitt-Lindstrom
Heyman
Hicks
Hidgon & Hidgon
    Horseless
Highlander
Highway-Knight
Hill
Hill Locomotor
Hillman
Hillman-Minx
Hillsdale
Hinde-Dauch
Hines
Hispano-Suiza
Hobbie
Hochenhull
Hoffman
Hoffman Steam
Holden
Holland Steam
Holley
Hollier
Holly
Holmes
Holmes Gastricycle
Holsman
Hol Tan
Holtzer Cabot

Holyoke
Holyoke Steam
Homer
Homer-Laughlin
Honda
Hoover
Hopkins
Hoppenstand
Horch
Horizon
Hornet
Horsey Horseless
    Carriage
H.O.S.
Hoskins
Hossier Scout
Hotchkiss
Houghton
Houghton Steamer
Houpt
Houpt Rockwell
House
House Steamer
Howard
Howard Gasoline Wagon
Howey
H.R.G.
H.R.L.
Hudson
Hudson-Franklin
Hudson Steam Car
Huffman
Huffman Steam
Hug
Humberette
Humber-Hawk
Hunter
Huntington
Hupmobile
Hupp-Yeats Electric
Hurlburt
Huron
Hurricane
Hurtu
Hustler Power Car
Hutton Napier
Hydro Carbon
Hydromotor
Hylander
Hyslop

Ideal
Ideal Electric
I.H.C.
Illinois Electric
Imhoff
Imp
Impala
Imperia
Imperial 1900
Imperial 1907
Impetus
Independence
Independent
Indiana
Indianapolis
Ingersoll Rand
Ingrame Hatch
Innes

International
International Buggy
International Car
International Harvester
Inter-State
Intrepid
Invicta
Iowa
Iris
Iroquois
Iroquois Buffalo
Iroquois-Seneca Falls
Ishakawajima
Isis
Iso
Isotta Fraschini
Italia
Iverson
Izzer

Jackson
Jacks Runabout
Jacquet Flyer
Jaguar
James
Janney
Jarrett
Javelin
Jarvis Huntington
Jaxon Steam
Jay
Jay-Eye-See
Jeannin
Jeep
Jeffery
Jem Special
Jenkins
Jennis
Jensen
Jewell
Jewett 1906
Jewett 1922
J & J
Joel
Johnson
Johnson Steamer
Jones
Jones Corbin
Jones Steam Car
Jonz-Kansas City
Jonz New Albany
Jordan
Jowett
Joy
J.P.L.
J.T.
Judkins
Julian Brown
Julien
Junior
Junz
Jumbo
Justicialista
Juvenile Electric

Kaiser
Kalamazoo
Kane Pennington
Kankakee

Kansas City
Karbach
Karavan
Karvin
Kato
Kauffman
K.D.
Kearns
Keasler
Keating
Keene Electric
Keene Steam
Keeton
Keller Chief
Keller Kar
Kelley-Springfield
Kellogg
Kelly
Kelsey
Kenmore
Kennedy
Kensington
Kent
Kentworthy
Kenworth
Kermath
Kermet
Kerns
Kerosene Surrey
Kessler
Keystone
Keystone Steamer
Kiblinger
Kidder
Kimball
Kimball Electric
King
King Midget
King Remick
King Zeitler
Kingston
Kinnear
Kinney
Kirk
Kissel
Kissel-Kar
Kleiber
Klemm
Kline
Kline-Car
Kleinschnittger
Kling
Klink
Klock
Klondike
Knickerbocker
Knight & Kilbourne
Knight Special
Know
Knox
Knox Landsen
Knox Switsen
Kobusch
Koco
Koehler
Komet
Konigslow
Konollman
Kopp

Koppin
Korn et Latil
Kraft Steam
Krall
Krastin
Krebs
Kreuger
Krit
Kron
Krupp
Kunz
Kurtis
Kurtis-Kraft
Kurtz
Kyma
K.Z.

Laconia
Lada
Lad's Car
Lafayette 1920
Lafayette 1934
Lagonda
Lafitte
La France-Republic
La Marne
La Marne Junior
Lambert
Lamborghini
Lamphen
Lampher
Lamson
Lancamobile
Lancaster
Lancer
Lancer Delambon
Lanchester
Lancia
Lane Steam
Langan
Lange
Lanpher
Lansden Electric
La Petite
Larchment Steam
Lark
Larrabee Deyo
Larroumet & Lagarde
Larson
La Salle
La Salle Niagara
La Semeuse
Lasky
Latil
Laughlin
Laurel
Lauth-Gergens
Lavergne
Law
Lawler Steam
Lawter
L.C. Erbes
L & E
Leach
Leach Biltwell
Leader
Lea Francis
Lear

Lebanon
Le Baron
Le Car
Legnano
Lehigh
Lehr
Le Mans
Le Moon
Lende
Lennon
Lenox
Lenox Electric
Leon Bollee
Leonruboy
Le Roy
Le Sabre
Lescina
Leudinghaus
Lewis 1901
Lewis 1913
Lewis 1923
Lexington
Leyland
Le Zebre
Liberty
Liberty Brush
Licorne
Lima
Limited
Lincoln
Lincoln Zephyr
Linn
Lindsley
Lion
Lippard-Stewart
Little
Little Kar
Little Mac
Littlewol
Liver
L.M.C.
Loche Steamer
Lococar
Locomobile
Locomotor
Locomotrice
Logan
Lohr
Lola
Lomax
Lomis
London
Lone Star
Long
Long Distance
Longest
Loomis
Lorraine 1900
Lorraine 1920
Los Angeles
Lotis
Lotus
Louisiana
Lovejoy
Lowbed
Lowell
Lowell American
Lozier

L.P.C.
L.T.D.
Luedinghaus
Leudinghaus Esperichied
Lutzmann
Lutz Steam
Luv
Luvenae
Luverne
Lux
Luxer Cab
Luzion
Lyman
Lyman & Burnham
Lyman & Burton
Lyon Steam
Lyons Atlas
Lyons Knight

Maccar
MacDonald
Mack
Mackle-Thompson
MacNaughton
Macomber
Macon
Macy-Roger
Madison
Madou
Magic
Magnolia
Magnum
Mahoning
Mailbohm
Maiocchi
Mais
Majestic
Malbomb
Malcolm
Malcolm Jones
Malden
Mallby
Malverun
Man
Manexall
Manon
Manhattan
Manistee
Maplebay
Marathon
Marauder
Marble-Swift
Marcus
Marelock
Marendez
Marion
Marion-Handley
Mark Electric
Mark I
Mark II
Mark III
Mark IV
Mark V
Mark VI
Marlboro Steam
Marmon
Marmon-Herrington
Marquette 1909

Marquette 1929
Marquis
Marr
Marrel
Marron
Marsh 1905
Marsh 1920
Marshall
Marshall Steam
Martin
Martin Wasp
Martini
Marvel
Marwin
Maryland
Mascotte
Maserati
Mason
Mason Steamer
Mass
Massachusetts Steam
Massilon
Master
Matador
Mather
Matheson
Mathews
Mathewson
Mathis
Matra
Maumee
Mavag
Maverick
Maxim
Maxim-Goodridge
   Electric
Maxim Motortricycle
Maxwell
Maxwell Brisco
Maybach
Mayer
Mayes
Mayfair
Maytag
Mazda
McCarron
McCrea
McCue
McCullough
McCurdy
McDonald
McFarlan
McGill
McIntyre
McKay Steam
McLaughlin
McLean
Mead
Mearo
Mecca
Med-Bow
Medcraft
Media
Meech Stoddard
Meiselbach
Melbourne
Mel Special
Menard

Menges
Menominee
Mercedes
Mercer 1906
Mercer 1931
Merchant
Mercury 1904
Mercury 1914
Mercury 1938
Merit
Merkel
Merselback
Mertz
Merz
Meserve
Messerer
Messerschmitt
Messier
Metallurgique
Metcar
Meteor 1906
Meteor 1919
Metor
Metropol
Metropolitan 1922
Metropolitan 1956
Metz
Metzger
MG
MG Morris
Michigan
Michigan Electric
Michigan Hearse
Middleby
Midgley
Midland
Midwest
Mier
Miesse
Mighty Michigan
Milac
Milburn Electric
Milburn Steam
Militaire
Miller
Miller Special
Miller Steam
Mills Milwaukee
Milwaukee Steam
Minerva
Minneapolis
Mino
Mission
Mitchell
Mitchell Lewis
Mobile
Mobile Steam
Mock
Model
Modern
Modex Magic
Modilette
Modoc
Moehn
Mogul
Mohawk
Mohler
Moline

Moline Knight
Moller Cab
Mom
Monaca
Monarch 1906
Monarch 1914
Moncrief
Mondex-Magic
Monitor
Monroe
Monte Carlo
Montego
Monterey
Montgomery Ward
Monza
Moody
Mooer
Moon
Moore 1906
Moore 1917
Moorspring Steam
Mora
More
Moreland
Morelock
Morgan
Morison Electric
Morresy
Morris
Morris-Cowley
Morris London
Morris-Oxford
Morriss
Morrissey
Mors
Mors-Kittenwagen
Morse
Morse Steam
Mort
Moto Bloc
Motorcar
Motorette
Motor Truck
Mover
Moyea
Moyer
M.P.M.
Mt. Pleasant
Mueller
Mueller Benz
Mueller Trap
Muir Steam
Mulford
Multiplex
Muncie
Munson
Muntz
Murdaugh
Murray
Murray Mac Six
Muskegon
Mustang
Mustang II
Mutual
Myer, B & F

Nadez
Nagant-Liege

Nance
Napier
Napoleon
Nardi
Nash
National
National Electric
National Sextet
Nebraska
Nielson
Nelson
Nelson & Le Moon
Nester Electric
Netco
Neustadt-Perry Steam
Neville
Nevin
Newark
Newberg
Newcomb
New Departure
New England Electric
New England Steam
New Era
New Haven
New Home
Newman Electric
New Perry
New Pittsburg
Newport
New York
New York & Ohio
New Yorker
Niagara
Nichols
Nichols Shepard
Niles
Nippy
Noble
Noma
Norma
Northern
Northway
Northwestern
Norton
Norwalk
Norwalk Underslung
Nova
Novarn
N.R.G.
Nyberg

Oakland
Oakman
Oakman-Hertel
O.B.
Obertine
O'Connell
Octoauto
Odelot
Offenhauser
Ogden
Ogren
Ohio
Ohio Electric
Ohio Falls
Ohio Gas
Ohio Packard

O.K.
Okey
Oldfield
Old Hickory
Old Mill
Old Reliable
Olds Electric
Oldsmobile
Olds Steam Car
Oliver
Olsen
Olympian 1897
Olympian 1917
Olympic
Omaha
Omni
Omort
Oneida
Onlicar
Only
Opel
Oregon
Orient
Orient-Auto Go
Orion
Orleans
Orlo
Ormond
Orson
Oshkosh
Otto
Ottokar
Ottomobile
Overhold Steam
Overholt
Overland
Overman Steam
O-We-Go
Owen
Owen Magnetic
Owen Shoenick
Owen-Thomas
Oxford Steam

Pacer
Pacific
Packard
Packett
Packer
Page
Page Toledo
Paige
Paige Detroit
Pak-Age-Car
Palm
Palmer
Palmer-Moore
Palmer-Singer
Pan
Pan American 1903
Pan American 1917
Panda
Panhard
Panther
Paragon
Paramount Cab
Parenth
Parenti

Parker	Plymouth 1928	Railsback	Rigsthat Run
Parkin	P.M.C.	Railton	Riker
Parry	Pneumobile	Rainier	Riker Electric
Parson Electric	Pobieda	Ralco	Rikmobile
Partin	Polara	Raleigh	Riley
Partin Palmer	Polo	Rambler	Riley & Cowley Steam
Pastoria	Pomeroy	Rambler Harvey Steam	Rilsbach
Paterson	Ponder	Rambler Steam	Riper
Pathfinder	Pontiac 1908	Rand & Harvey Steam	Ritz
Patriot	Pontiac 1926	Randall	Riveria
Patterson Greenfield	Pope	Randolph Steam	R & L Electric
Patton Gas Electric	Pope Hartford	Ranger	R.M.C.
Pawtucket Steamer	Pope Motor	Ranlet	R.O.
Pax	Pope Robinson	Rapid	Roach
Payne Modern	Pope Toledo	Ras Electric	Roadabee
Peabody	Pope Tribune	Rassler	Road Cart
Peck	Pope Waverly Electric	Rauch & Lang	Roader
Peep	Popp Car	Raulang Electric	Roadmaster
Peerless	Poppy Car	Rayfield	Road Plane
Peerless Steam	Porkorney	R.C.H.	Roadster
Pegaso	Proter	R.D.C.	Roamer
Pellitier	Porter Steam	Read	Robe
Peninsular	Port Huron	Reading 1901	Roberts
Penn	Portland	Reading 1912	Robey
Penn Thirty	Poss	Real	Robinson
Pennigton	Postal	Rebel	Robson
Pennsy	Powercar	Red Arrow	Roche
Pennsylvania	Prado	Red Bug	Rochester Steamer
Peoples	Praga	Red Jacket	Rochet-Schneider
Perfect	Pratt	Red Seal	Rocket
Perfection	Pratt-Elkhart	Red Wing	Rockette
Perfex	Praul	Reed	Rockaway
Perry	Preferred	Rees	Rock Falls
Peru	Prefex	Reeves	Rock Hill
P.E.T.	Premier	Reeves Octo	Rockliff
Peterbilt	Premocar	Reeves Sexto	Rockne
Peter Pan	Prescott Steam	Regal 1908	Rockway
Peters	Preston	Regal 1974	Rockwell
Petrel	Pridemorn	Regas	Rodenhousen
Peugeot	Prigeot	Rehberger	Rodgers
Phelerne	Primo	Reid	Roebling
Phelps	Prince	Reiland & Bree	Roger
Phianna	Princess	Reinertsen	Rogers
Philbern	Princeton	Relay	Rogers & Hanford
Phipps	Prodal	Reliable	Rogers Steam
Phoenix	Prospect	Reliable Dayton	Rohr
Pickard (Pic-Pic)	Protos	Reliance	Rollin
Piedmont	Prunel	Remel Vincent	Rolls-Royce
Pierce	P & S Magic	Remington 1901	Roman
Pierce Arrow	Publix	Remington 1915	Romer
Pierce-Motorette	Pullman 1905	Renault	Roosevelt
Pierce-Racine	Pullman 1907	Reno	Roots
Pierron	Puma	REO	Roper Steam
Piggins	Pungs Finch	Republic	Rosengart
Pilgrim	Pup	Revere	Ross
Pilgram	Puritan Steam	Revere Steam	Ross Steam
Pilloid	Pyramid	Rex	Rotarian
Pilot		Reya	Rotaris
Pinto	Quadrant	Reynolds	Rotarius
Pioneer	Queen	Rhodes	Rotary
Pipe	Quick	Richard	Rovena
Piscorski	Quinlan	Richelieu	Rover
Pitcher	Quo Vadis	Richmond	Rovern
Pittsburgh		Rickenbacker	Rowe
Planche	Rabbit	Ricketts	Royal Electric
Plass Motor Sleigh	R.A.C.	Riddle	Royal Tourist
Playboy	Racine	Rider Lewis	Rubay
Plymouth 1914	Rae	Riess Royal	Rugby

Ruggles
Ruggmobile
Ruler
Rumley
Rumpf
Rumpler
Runabout
Rush
Rushmobile
Ruston-Hornsby
Russell
Russo-Baltique
Rutenberg
Ruth
R & V Knight
Ruxton
Ryder

Saab
Sabra
Saf T Cab
Saginaw
Salisbury
Salmson
Salter
Salvador
Sampson
Samuels Electric
Sandlow
Sandow
Sandusky
Sanford
Santos Dumont
Satellite
Saurer
Savage
Sawyer
Saxon
Saxon Duplex
Sayers
Sayers & Scotville
Scania
Scarab
Scat
Schacht
Schaum
Schebler
Schimmelpennic Electric
Schleicher
Schlosser
Schnader
Schoening
Schwartz
Scootmobile
Scott
Scott Newcomb Steam
Scout
Scripps
Scripps Booth
Seabery
Seabrook
Seagrave
Searchmont
Sears Motor Buggy
Sebring
Secqueville-Hoyau
Sekine
Selden

Sellers
Selly Steam
Selve
Senator
Seneca
Serpentina
Serf
Serrifile
Service
Servitor
Seville
Seven Little Buffaloes
Severin
Sextoauto
S.G. Gay
S.G.V.
Shad-Wyck
Shain
Sham
Sharon
Sharp Arrow
Sharp Steam
Shatswell Steam
Shaum
Shavers Steam
Shaw
Shawmut
Shaw Wick
Shelby
Shepherd
Sheridan
Shoemaker
Short
Sibley
Sibley-Curtis
Siddeley
Siegel
Sigma
Signal
Signet
Silent
Silent Knight
Silent Northern
Silver Knight
Simca
Simms
Simmons
Simmons Steam
Simplex
Simplex Crane
Simplex Steam
Simplicity
Simplo
Sinclair Scott
Singer
Single Center
Sinica
Sinpar
Sintz
S.J.R.
Skelton
Skene
Skeock
Skoda
Skylark
Slack
Slater
S & M

Smith
Smith & Malby
Smith Motor Buggy
Smith Motor Wheel
Smith Spring Motor
S.N.
Snyder
Soames
Soller
Sommer
Soules
South Bend
Southern
Southern Six
Sovereign
S.P.A.
Spache
Spartan
Spaulding 1900
Spaulding 1910
Special
Speedy
Speedway
Speedwell
Speery
Spencer
Spencer Steam
Sperling
Sphinx
Spicer
Spiker
Spiller
Spinnell
Spirit
Spitz
S.P.O.
Spoerer
Sponer
Sprague
Springer Steam
Springfield Electric
Springfield Steam
Sprint
Sprite
Spyker
Squire Steam
S.S.
S.S.E.
S & S Hearse
Stack
Stafford
Stag
Staiger
Standard
Standard Electric
Standard Steamer
Standard Vanguard
Stanhope
Stanley
Stanley Steamer
Stanley Whitney
Stanmobile Steam
Stanton Steam
Stanwood
Staple
Star 1908
Star 1922
Star Flee

Starin
States 1910
States 1916
Static Super Cooler
Staver
Staver Chicago
St. Cloud
Steamobile
Steam Vehicle
Stearing
Stearns
Stearns Knight
Stearn Steam Car
Steco
Steel-Swallow
Stegeman
Steiger
Steinhart Jensen
Stein Koenig
Stelka
Stella
Stemmetz
Stephens
Stephens-Salient
Sterling 1909
Sterling 1916
Sterling Knight
Sterling Steam
Sternberg
Stetson
Stevens
Stevens-Duryea
Stew
Stewart
Stewart Coats Steam
Steyr
Stickney Motorette
Stigler
Still
Stilson
Stirling
St. Joe
St. John
St. Louis 1899
St. Louis 1922
Stoddard
Stoddard Dayton
Stoddard Knight
Stoewer
Stolle
Stolz
Stonebow
Storck Steam
Storey
Storm Electric
Story
Stoughton
Stout
Stout Scrab
Stranabuss
Stranahan
Strathmore
Stratton
Stratton-Premier
Strauss
Strauss Steam
Streator
Stringer Steam

Strobel & Martin Electric
Strong & Rodger
Strouse
Struss
Stuart
Studebaker
Studebaker Electric
Studebaker GMF
Studebaker Garford
Sturgis
Sturgis Electric
Sturtevant
Stutz
Stutz H.C.
Stuyvesant
S-U
Suburu
Suburban
Success
Sullivan
Sultan
Suminde
Summit
Sun
Sunbeam
Sunbeam Talbot
Sunset
Super Car
Super Chief
Superior
Super Steamer
Super Two
Supreme
Surry
Suttle Steam
Sutton
Sweany Steam Carriage
Swenson
Swift
Syndusky
Synnestevdt Steam
Syracuse Electric
Szawe

Tait Electric
Talbert
Talbot
Talbot-Lago
Tally-Ho
Tama
Tarkington
Tarrant
Tasco
Tatra
Taunton
Taunus
Taurinia
Taylor
Tayto
Teco
Tempest
Templar
Temple
Templeton-Durbrie
Tempo
Tennant
Terraplane
Terrot

Terwilliger Steam
Tex
Texan
Texas
Texmobile
T.G.E.
Thames
Theiss
Thermot-Monohan
Thing
Thomas
Thomas-Detroit
Thomas Flyer
Thomond
Thompson
Thompson Electric
Thomson Steam
Thor
Thornycroft
Thorobred
Threasher Electric
Thrige
Thunderbird
Tic Tac
Tiffany
Tiffin
Tiger
Tillie
Times
Tincher
Tinkham
Tiny
Titan
Tjaarda
Toboggan
Tobrensen
Toledo
Toledo Steamer
Tollin
Tonawanda
Topolino
Toquet
Torbensen
Torino
Tornado
Tornax
Toronado
Torpedo
Touraine
Tourist
Tower
Towne Shopper
Toyopet
Toyota
Trabold
Tracta
Tractomobile Steam
Traffic
Train
Trans Am
Transport
Trask-Detroit
Traveler
Traylor
Trebert
Triangle
Tribune
Tri Car

Tricolet
Trimo
Tri Motor
Trinity Steam
Triumph
Triunfo
Troll
Troy
Trojan
Trumbull
Tuar
Tuck
Tucker
Tudhope
Tulsa
Turbo
Turicum
Turner
Twin City
Twin Coach
Twombly
Twyford
Tyne

Uaz
Ulster
Ultimate
Unic
Union
United Motor
Unito
Universal
University
Univim
Unwin
Upton
Urban Electric
Ursus
U.S.
U.S. Electric
U.S. Long Distance
U.S. Motor Vehicle
Utile

Vabis
Vale
Valiant
Valley Dispatch
Van
Vanderbuilt
Vandergrift
Van Dyke
Vanell Steam Carriage
Vanette
Van L
Van Wagoner
Vaughan
Vauxhall
V.E.C.
V.E. Electric
Veerac
Vega
Vehicle Equipment Co.
Velie
Vera
Verett
Veritas
Vernon

Versalle
Vespa
Vestal
Victor
Victor Steamer
Victoria
Victory
Victory Steam
Viking 1908
Viking 1929
Vim
Vim Cyclecar
VIP
Vinot & Deguingand
Viqueot
Virginian
Vivinus
Vixen
Vocur
Vogue
Voisin
Voiturette
Volarie
Volga
Voltz
Volkswagen
Volpini
Volvo
Vulcan
Vulkan

Wachusette
Waco
Wagenhalls
Wahl
Walden
Waldron
Walker-Electric
Walker-Johnson
Wall
Walter
Waltham
Waltham Orient
Walther
Walton
Walworth
Wanamaker
Wanderer
Ward Electric
Ward La France
Ward Leonard
Ware
Warren
Warren Detroit
Warren Lambert
Warwick
Washburn
Washington 1909
Washington 1921
Wasp
Waterloo-Duryea
Waterman & Chamberlin
Waters
Waterous
Watrons
Watson
Watt
Watt Steam

Waukeshaw
Waverly
Waverly Electric
Wayne
Webb Jay Steam
Weber
Weidley
Weidlez Entz
Welch
Welch Detroit
Welch & Lawson
Welch Marquette
Welch Pontiac
Werner
West
West & Burgett
Westcott
Western
Westfield
West Gasoline Vehicle
Westinghouse
Weston
W.F.S.
Whaley-Henriette
Wharton
Wheel
Wheeler
Whippet
White
White Hall
White Hickory
White Star
White Steamer
Whiteside
Whiting
Whitlock
Whitney
Wichita

Wick
Wilco
Wilcox
Wildcat
Wildman
Willard
Williams
Williams Electric
Wills St. Claire
Willys
Willys American
Willys Jeep
Willys Knight
Willys Overland
Willys Six
Wilson
Windsor
Windsor White
Wing
Winner
Winther
Winton
Wisco
Wisconsin
Witt Will
Wizard
Wolfe
Wolseley
Wolverine 1904
Wolverine 1918
Wolverine Detroit
Wonder
Wood
Woodill Wildfire
Wood-Loco
Woodruff
Woods 1901
Woods 1918

Woods Dual Power
Woods Electric
Woods Mobilette
Woodworth
World
Worth
Worthington Bollee
Worthington Runabout
Wright

Xenia
Xtra

Yale 1903
Yale 1916
Yank
Yankee
Yates
Yaxa
Yellow Cab
Yellow Coach
York
York Pullman

"Z"
Zar Car
Zbrojovka
Zedal
Zena
Zenith
Zent
Zentmobile
Zephyr
Zim
Zimmerman
Zip
Zucchi
Zust
Zvezda

Probably the most complete listing of world automobiles available is a book entitled *100 Years of the World's Automobiles,* originally by Floyd Clymer, noted auto expert, and revised by G. R. Doyle and G. N. Georgano. This book lists 5,000 makes of cars only (no trucks) and goes into much detail listing every company that used a common name. For example there were seven Clarks, five Continentals, ten Eagles, six Falcons, and thirteen Standards, to name a few. However, even this book is missing names of existing cars.

CHAPTER 2

Hubcaps

THOUGH people collect many unusual things these days, to reveal that you collect hubcaps can evoke some strange looks. Immediately one thinks of the huge silver discs that adorn our roadsides today, especially near large chuck holes. Unless you are over forty or are a car buff, you probably don't remember that hubcaps used to be exactly what the name implies. A device to cover the end of the wheel hub, keeping dirt out of the bearings and grease. For the sake of beauty and design, these relatively obscure parts, which once adorned the auto maker's name, have evolved into huge gaudy wheel covers, mostly without names. Once removed from their parent vehicle, most owners would not recognize them. Furthermore, each model today has several optional designs to choose from, so one cannot tell a 1979 *Gismobile* from a 1967 *Whatsamacar*! Oh, well, some of them make terrific frisbees.

The earliest caps were usually plain cast brass, machined all over and bearing no name or identifying marks, but as early as 1903 some auto makers cast their name in either raised or depressed letters on the face of the cap. Until approximately 1910 caps were predominantly cast brass, some quite heavy, and most wire wheel hubcaps were equipped internally with anti-back-off devices such as spring-loading latch pins or huge lock-ring arrangements. This type of wire-wheel hubcap provided two services—that of centering the wheel as well as actually holding the wheel on the axle. A few of the manufacturers like *National* and *Chalmers* used a locking ring on the outside of their standard hubcap around 1910. Right- and left-hand threads were also used as a double safety feature. Vibrations created by early rough roads loosened many things including hubcaps. Some auto names were etched in brass plates with a painted background and affixed to these heavy caps with two small pins or rivets. As some car makers continued this practice in later years, the medallions were crimped or sweated into place. The first change in cap production came with the use of thin brass sheet stock drawn over stamping dies forming the basic shape of the cap and raising the letters or script of the car maker's name on the face. These thin caps were much more prone to damage than the cast variety.

Around 1915 the era of the "Brass Car" ended as new materials and cost reduction brought forth the use of nickel plating for most of the bright metal trim on cars. The auto was being used more and more as a regular means of transportation rather than a weekend play toy or status symbol. The nickel was a much more durable surface, not nearly as susceptible to tarnish as brass. With the heavy use of coal in those days, the sulfur introduced in the air would attack the brass, creating a constant cleaning vigil for the owners. Although the base metal was still brass, most caps adorned the nickel plating. The use of brass came to a temporary end during World War I due to the requirement of brass for the war effort. Aluminum was widely used as a substitute for hubcap manufacture. Some companies used steel as a substitute and double plated it with copper and nickel. After the war some auto makers returned to the use of nickel-plated brass, but most stayed with aluminum. After the introduction of chrome plating in 1927, some companies chrome plated the aluminum caps to make them more durable. Caps were made out of various other materials, cast iron, cast steel, german silver, cast aluminum, and several varieties of pot metal. While the United States and Canadian manufacturers used an internal thread, it is interesting to note that European-built cars were smaller with external threads.

Ford was probably the first to change tradition by switching from a screw-on to a crimp-on type cap with the introduction of the Model "A" in 1928. This cap was inserted into the end of a welded steel wire wheel and then small tabs were bent over to hold it in place. If not installed properly, it was probably also the first hubcap to rattle!

Although some cars had accessory wood-spoke wheels, which used screw-on caps as late as 1933, most auto makers were into snap-on caps by 1930.

With the demise of the spoke wheel and the advent of the solid steel or welded wheel, some caps gradually lost identity. Although most still carried the name, they had increased in size to about ten inches, and most all of this snap-on variety had a common moon shape, which makes them much less desirable to collect compared to the screw-on, whose size ranged from two inches to seven-and-a-half inches in diameter. The weight factor was a different story, as some screw-ons weighed as much as seven pounds.

Hubcaps remained rather unattractive until about the mid-1950s, when somebody discovered that chrome and glitter would sell cars. Detroit looked to the wheel cover as an eye catcher, and that started the race for the best looking wheels rolling. This race led to the Mag and Turban wheels of today.

If you were raised in the fifties, you will remember that hubcaps were a real status symbol among the youth. If your car had a set of Baby Moons or Flippers or spun aluminum discs, you were considered to be *cool*. By the same token, if you owned a 1955 or 1956 Oldsmobile factory-equipped with Flippers, it was more likely than not you would lose them some night to hubcap thieves. A collector today might add one of these to his collection for sentimental reasons.

It is a wonder how any screw-on hubcap survived until today for the collector to have, as these little jewels usually protruded far out to the side of the wheel sometimes even beyond the protection of the running board. Hence they were vulnerable to damage by curbs, trees, poles, other cars, and occasionally a tall dog. And, of course, let's not forget the muddy road. Many a fine hubcap fell victim to the quagmire of yesteryear's unpaved roads. When the old flivver got stuck in six or eight inches of mud and would no longer yield to spinning tires, the driver would grab a board, branch, or piece of pipe and look for a place to pry while someone else tried to drive the car free. Of course, the most logical place to stick that pry bar was under that shiny little hubcap, sticking out almost beckoning to be bent out of shape in a sacrificial attempt to free the car. The brass caps usually held up better under these conditions than their aluminum counterparts.

The hubcap-replacement business must have been excellent since some aftermarket auto-part companies tooled up to produce look-alike caps to compete against original equipment sales. Due to trademark and copyright law the car name could not, in most cases, appear on the aftermarket version. One enterprising company in an effort to simulate Ford script used the word *Bool* on the face of the cap, and at a glance it would *Fool* most. Another innovative aftermarket item was a cap with a grease fitting in the center so the wheel bearings could be greased without removing the cap.

There is a bright note for beginning hubcap collectors in the recent resurgence of the small hubcap. This is due to the popularity of the Mag- or Rally-type wheel. These are not screw-on hubcaps; they are snap-on, but because of the colorful inserts and bright chrome plating, they make an attractive display. There are two types of Mag wheels: the original factory equipment with the car name or logo and the aftermarket versions such as *Craiger, American Racing, Keystone,* etc., which also have small caps with logos. Some collectors may choose to save only original manufacturers' caps.

Another source for collectible material is the bolt on center hubs on some modern wheel covers or the flat plastic insert recessed in the center. Most of these are in abundance in auto wrecking yards and scrap yards. We envy the old-timer who had the foresight to remove hubcaps from scrap vehicles thirty years ago, but in reality we have the same opportunity today to accumulate some of this modern trivia. Then, when we are old-timers, our grandchildren can look at our collections in awe and shower our ears with comments like, "Wow, look at that Mustang Horse and that Thunderbird simulated knock-off hub!" "I haven't seen one of those for years, ever since they started running cars on these magnetic suspension beams." "It's just a shame that the only place you can even see a wheel anymore is in a museum." A statement like that may sound incredible, but an eighty-year-old man today has progressed from horse and buggy days to space travel during his lifetime. Those modern hubcaps may be common today, but just add thirty years to them and see how many will still be around. With our society of built-in obsolescence, the time required for certain parts to become scarce is getting shorter. Add to this the salt factor in the northern cities, and most cars rot out before they reach the halfway point to antiquity. Years ago, unless an item was over one hundred years old, it had better not be referred to as an antique. In contrast today some states recognize a car as an antique if it is twenty years old. So then logically any part for such a car should also be considered antique.

Bruce Ledingham of Vancouver modestly admits he is not an expert on hubcaps. However, his diligent research for the past eighteen years has made him well versed on the subject. Back in 1962 he stumbled over a mysterious object in some tall grass. Upon close inspection, it turned out to be a *Gray Dort* axle. He unscrewed the hubcap and took it away to become the cornerstone of the largest known collection. He also keeps a brief history of each cap and how it was acquired. For example: From New Zealand came a 1912 *Clement-Talbot* manufactured in England. It came from the grandson of the homesteader who brought the car from England in 1913. Or how about the 1907 *Thomas Flyer* found under sagebrush alongside an abandoned road that had originally been the stage route to Carson City, Nevada.

Bruce has graciously offered his help in dating many of these caps and supplying pictures of many scarce caps. Following are more than two hundred pictures showing a good sampling of American screw-on hubcaps. Many manufacturers used the same cap for the life of the car, while others like *Huppmobile, Buick, Maxwell, Cadillac, Franklin,* and *Oakland* had a different cap for each year.

1. **Acme/1904–1910**
2. **Aerocar/1906**
3. **Allen/1914–1922**
4. **American/1905–1914**
5. **Apperson/1902–1926**
6. **Apperson/1917**

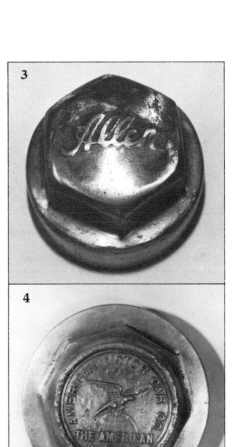

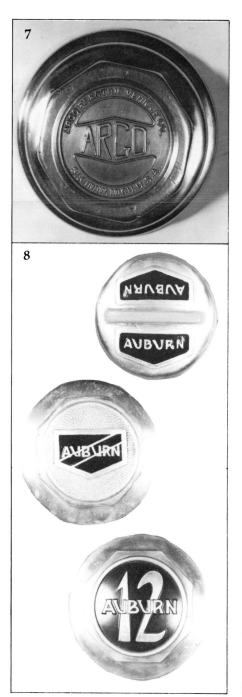

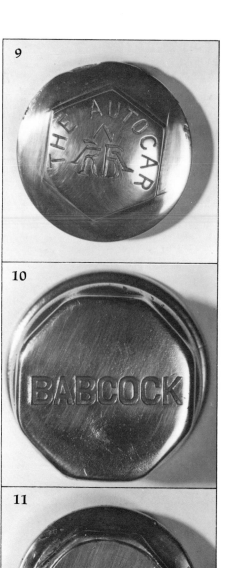

7. Argo/1912–1918
8. Auburn/1900–1937
9. Autocar/1903
10. Babcock Electric/1906–1912
11. Baker/1911
12. Baker Steamer/1917–1924
13. Bay State/1924
14. Bour-Davis/1915–1922

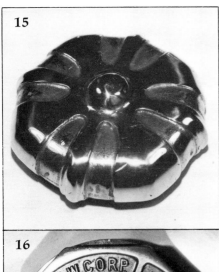

15

18

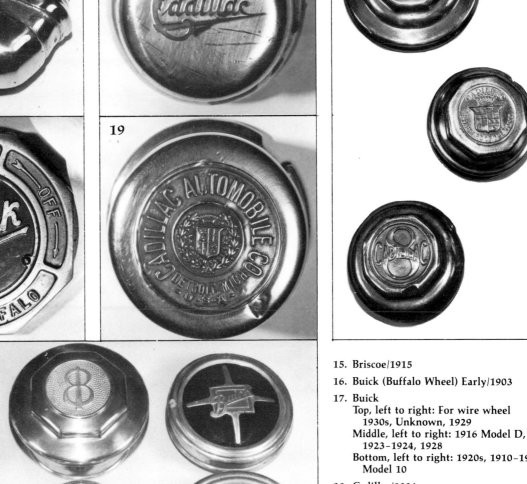

20

16

19

17

15. Briscoe/1915

16. Buick (Buffalo Wheel) Early/1903

17. Buick
   Top, left to right: For wire wheel
      1930s, Unknown, 1929
   Middle, left to right: 1916 Model D,
      1923–1924, 1928
   Bottom, left to right: 1920s, 1910–1913
      Model 10

18. Cadillac/1904

19. Cadillac/1906

20. Cadillac
   Top and center: 1920s front and rear cap
   Bottom: 1915

21

22

23

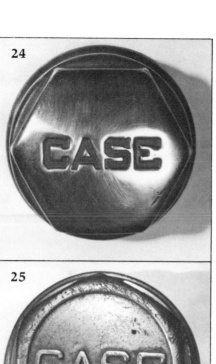

24

25

26

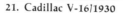

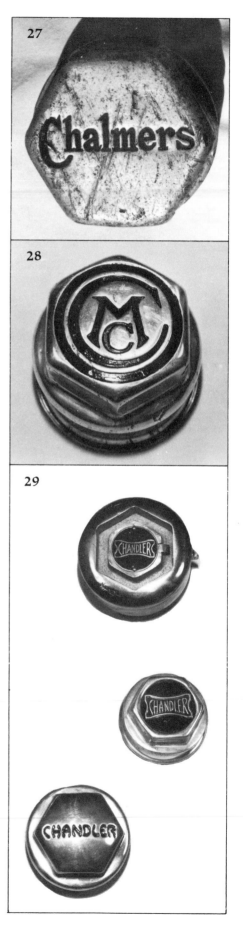

27

28

29

21. Cadillac V-16/1930
22. Cameron/1913
23. Cartercar/1907–1927
24. Case/1913
25. Case/1920
26. Chadwick/1904–1916
27. Chalmers/1908–1924
28. Chalmers/1924
29. Chandler
    Right: early wire wheel

30. Checker/1923–

31. Chevrolet
    Top five caps are minor varieties from
        1911 to the mid 1920s. Chevrolet did
        not change their cap often
    Bottom row are all 1929, left is factory,
        middle is aluminum replacement, and
        right is cheap chrome-plated steel
        replacement

32. Chrysler/1923–

33. Cleveland/1919–1926

34. Cole/1909–1925

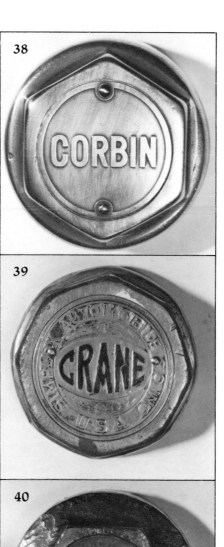

35. Columbia/1916–1924
36. Columbus/1909–1914
37. Conrad/1900–1903
38. Corbin/1909
39. Crane/1915–1924
40. Crawford/1905–1923
41. Crow Elkhart/1909–1922
42. Cunningham/1910–1936

43. Demot/1910

44. Desoto/1928–1960

45. Detroit/1907–1942

46. Dixie/1916–1923

47. Doble/1911–1932

48. Dodge/1914–
    Top row: late 1920s
    Bottom center: name disc from spare
        tire cover
    Bottom row: 1914 to mid-1920s

49. Dorris/1905–1926

50. Dort/1915–1924

51. Douglas/1918–1922
52. Duesenberg/1920–1937
53. DuPont/1920–1923
54. Durant/1921–1932
55. Earl/1921–1924
56. Elcar/1916–1931

57

58

59

60

61

62

63

64

57. Elgin/1916–1924
58. Elgin/1916–1924
59. Elmore/1900–1912
60. Empire/1913
61. Erskine/1928–1929
62. Essex/1918–1932
    Lower right is replacement 1929–1931
63. Everitt/1911
64. Falcon/1927–1928

65. Ford/1903
    For accessory Hayes wire wheel

66. Ford/1906
    For Model K

67. Ford
    Top center and top right: two
      aftermarket caps for Model T with
      grease zerks for easy lubrication of
      bearings
    Top left: brass Model T 1909–1927
    Middle row left and center: truck caps
    Middle row right: 1928–1929
      aftermarket attempt to copy Ford
      script with Bool; some had Fool
    Bottom row left: aluminum
      aftermarket Model T
    Bottom right: 1928–1929 factory cap
      which is the only snap-on shown in
      this chapter

68. Flint/1925

69. Fox/1921–1925

70. Franklin/1911

71. Franklin
    Top left: 1929–1931
    Top right: 1929–1930
    Bottom left: 1913–1920
    Bottom right: 1927–1928

72. Gardner/1926

73. Gardner/1929–1930

74. Graham Page
    Top left: Graham Bros. Truck,
    1925–1930
    Top right: 1928
    Lower left: 1929
    Bottom right: 1927

75. Grant/1913–1923

76. Hal 12/1918

77. Hatfield/1917–1924

78. Hayes—Accessory wire wheel

79. Haynes/1894–1926

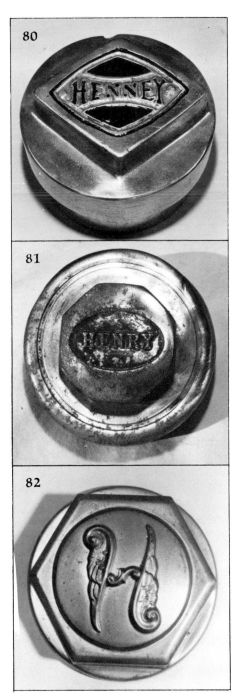

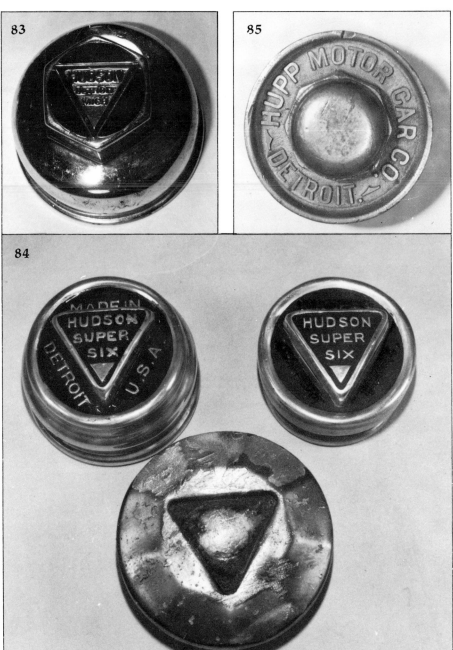

80. Henney/1924—Ambulance and Hearse

81. Henry/1910–1912

82. Holmes/1918–1923

83. Hudson/1910

84. Hudson
   Left: 1925
   Right: 1915–1921
   Bottom: replacement

85. Hupp Model 20/1910

86

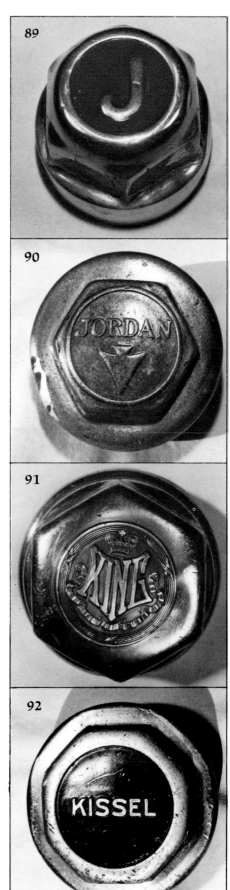

89

90

87

88

91

92

86. Huppmobile
    Left to right top: 1930–1932 Wood
      Wheel, 1929, Disc wheel Model A,
      and 1929 wood wheel Model A
    Middle row: 1926–1928 wood and disc
      wheel Model E, 1926–1928 wood and
      disc Model A, 1928 wood and disc
      Model M
    Bottom row: 1922–1925, 1925–1926
      wood and disc (name spelled out in
      cross bar of H), 1918–1922

87. Jones/1915–1920—with Accessory wire
    wheel by Hayes

88. International/1928–1930
89. Jewett/1923–1926
90. Jordan/1925–1927—For wood wheels
91. King/1910–1924
92. Kissel/1906–1931

93. Kissel Kar/1909
94. Kleiber/1925
95. Koehler/1910–1914
96. Kimball/1911
97. Krit/1909–1916
98. Lafayette/1920–1924
99. Lambert/1904
100. Lexington/1908–1926
101. Lincoln/1920–1922

102. Lincoln
 Left: 1925
 Right: Circa 1930.

103. Little/1912

104. Locomobile/1910

105. Lozier/1901–1917—Someone put grease fitting in face of cap.

106. Mailbohm/1916–1922

107. Marathon/1908–1915

108. Marion/1904–1914

109. Marmon/1929

110. Marquette/1930

111. Mason/1906–1910
112. Maxwell/1905
113. Maxwell/1905–1925—Notice script variations
114. Maxwell Briscoe/1905
115. McFarlan/1910–1928
116. Mercer/1910–1925
117. Meteor/1909–1927
118. Mitchell/1903–1924
119. Moline Knight/1904–1919—with accessory Houk wire wheel

120

123

121

126

122

124

125

127

120. Moon/1905–1930

121. Moon/1905–1930

122. Mort/1923

123. Nash
Left to right top: 1931, 1930 front, 1929
Bottom: 1930 rear, no name on replacement, 1927, and 1928

124. National/1906

125. National/1916

126. Northern/1902–1909

127. Norwalk/1911–1916

128. Oakland/1912

129. Oakland/1907–1932—Changed cap design many times

130. Ohio/1910–1918—Electric

131. Oldsmobile
Left column: 1926, 1924, 1920
Right column: two aftermarket replacements, and 1929 wood wheel

132. Overland/1912

133. Overland
Left: 1914
Right: 1928.

134. Owen Magnetic/1918

135. Packard/1899–1958—Accessory Buffalo
wire wheel

136. Packard
Bottom: wire and disc wheel 1920s
Top: wood wheel 1910–1928

137. Paige/1920s

138. Pan/1920

139. Pan American/1917–1922

140. Parry/1910

141

142

143

144

145

146

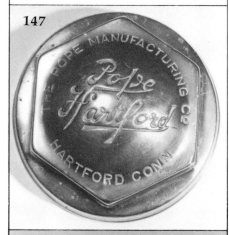

147

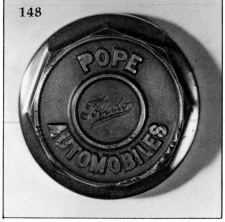

148

141. Peerless/1900–1932

142. Peerless/1900–1932

143. Pierce Arrow/1907

144. Pierce Arrow/1901–1938

145. Plymouth
 Bottom: 1928
 Top: 1929

146. Pontiac
 Left: 1926
 Bottom: 1930
 Top: 1929
 Right: 1929 wire wheel

147. Pope Hartford/1901–1914

148. Pope Toledo/1903

149

152

155

150

153

156

151

154

157

149. Pratt/1911-1917

150. Pullman/1906-1917

151. Rambler/1903

152. Rambler/1908

153. Rauch & Lang/1905-1923

154. Regal/1910

155. Reo/1910

156. Reo
Top: 1912-1915
Middle: "Flying Cloud" 1929-1930
Bottom: 1927-1929

157. Rickenbacker/1922-1927—Same all years

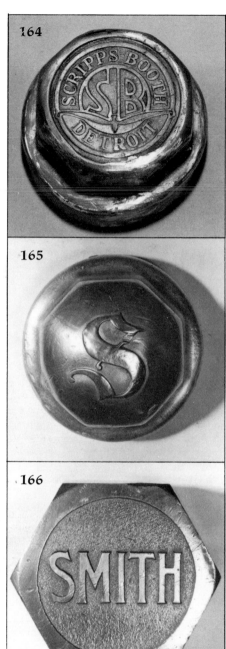

158. Rio/1927—Reo made for export to Spanish speaking countries.

159. Romer/1921

160. Roosevelt/1929

161. R.V. Knight/1924

162. Saginaw/1915

163. Saxon/1914–1923

164. Scripps-Booth/1914–1923

165. Sheridan/1921

166. Smith/1908

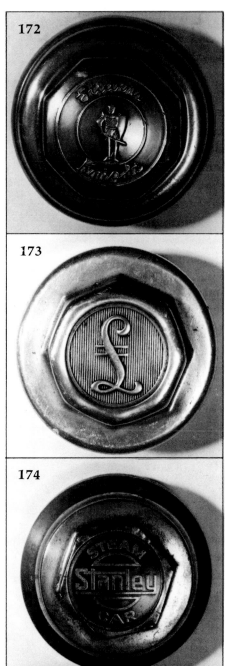

167. Standard/1920
168. Stanley/1920
169. Star/1922–1928
170. Stephens/1923
171. Stearns/1899–1930
172. Stearns—Knight/1900–1930
173. Sterling Knight/1923–1925
174. Stevens Duryea/1902–1926

175

178

181

176

179

182

180

183

177

175. Stoddard Dayton/1911

176. Studebaker/1902–1967

177. Stutz/1912–1935

178. Stutz/1912–1935

179. S.G.V./1911–1915

180. S & S (Sayers & Scovill)/1924–?

181. Thomas/1903

182. Thomas Flyer/1910

183. Trumbull/1899–1905

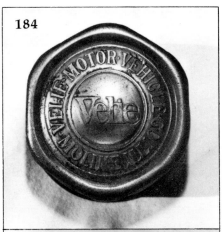

184

187

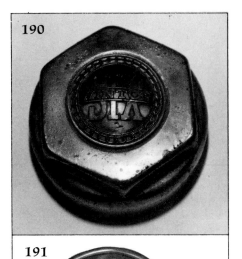

190

185

188

191

186

189

184. Velie/1920
185. Warren/1909–1914
186. Waverley/1898–1916
187. Wayne/1904–1908
188. Westcott/1910–1925
189. Winton/1904
190. Winton/1897–1924
191. Whippet

192. Wills St. Claire/1921–1927

193. Willys/1914–1955

194. Wolverine/1927

CANADIAN HUBCAPS

195. Brooks/1924

196. McKay/1912

197. McLaughlin Buick/1911

198. McLaughlin Buick/1908–1942

199. Gray-Dort/1917-1924
200. Pontiac/1929
201. Regal/1910
202. Russell/1905-1916

FOREIGN HUBCAPS

203. Benz/1895-1925—German
204. Chenard/1897-1939—France
205. Ferrari/1947-present—Italian
206. Italia/1909—Italian
207. Lancia/1906-present—Italian

208. Renault/1898–present—France
209. Rolls-Royce/1910—England
210. Rover/1914

TRUCK HUBCAPS

211. Divco
212. Harvey/1913–1933
213. Hendricks/1912
214. General Motors
215. Rush/1916–1918
216. White/1902–present
217. Yellow

Collecting carriage and buggy hubcaps is an interesting hobby; however, there are two drawbacks: There are very few other collectors to trade with, and secondly, the hubcaps are extremely scarce and hard to find.

The design of some of the really early automobile hubcaps closely resembled the design of the carriage caps. There must have been a fairly close liaison between carriage manufacturers as many U.S. builders used similarly designed hubcaps. These almost identical designs were used in several countries that I am aware of—Norway, Sweden, Britain, France, U.S.A., Canada, and Australia.

Cast brass was used exclusively and the caps were machined all over (tool marks can still be seen particularly on the inside), creating fine workmanship and beautifully finished products. About 50 percent used outside thread.

The name and address was usually stamped into the face; others had the name engraved; a few were hand engraved. The hubcap's average weight is about one pound each, and most measure about 3 inches outside diameter. Many are fitted with a leather washer on the inside to act as a grease seal.

There are 50 different carriage hubcaps in my collection from seven different countries, about 25 percent of them from France.

Bruce Ledingham

CARRIAGE HUBCAPS

218. Brewster
219. Cunningham
220. Chauncey Thomas
221. Flandrau
222. Hincks & Johnson
223. John H. Schmidt

224. An assortment of full-disc hubcap
centers removed from their base.
Largest is Buick at upper left about six
inches. All are of pot metal
construction. Oldsmobile at upper
right is simulated spoke wheel center.

225. More imitation of classic features.
Simulated knock-off hubs. These, too,
bolt on to full-disc caps.

226. Small hubcap emblems, roof and grille
emblems, and racing wheel caps. Most
are affixed with die-cast studs and
speed nuts.

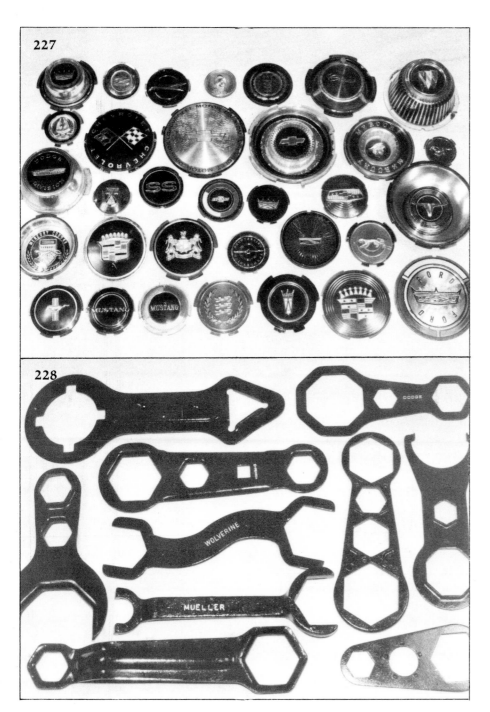

227. Very colorful plastic name discs are usually fastened to wheel disc with a snap ring, three bolts and steel ring, or glued on.

228. Hubcap wrenches supplied by auto manufacturers.

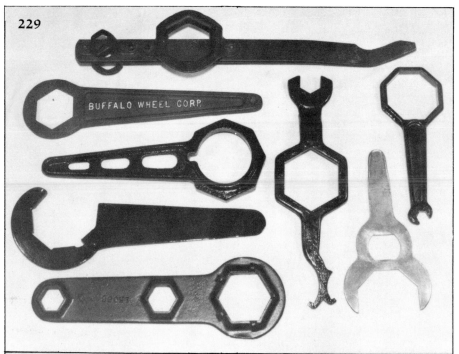

229

231

230

229. Accessory hubcap wrenches. Second from bottom has hinged end.

230. Finding matching caps and wrenches can be a challenge, as they were often lost or discarded. Very few had names or distinctive shapes like the Hudson, top left.

231. There was an automobile named Kent and one named Moore, but this wrench proved to be for neither one. A call to a Kent-Moore tool dealer who had old catalogs, revealed that this wrench was made for a 1929 Chevrolet. The opening allowed the wrench to be slipped on from the back as the face was larger than the octagonal flats.

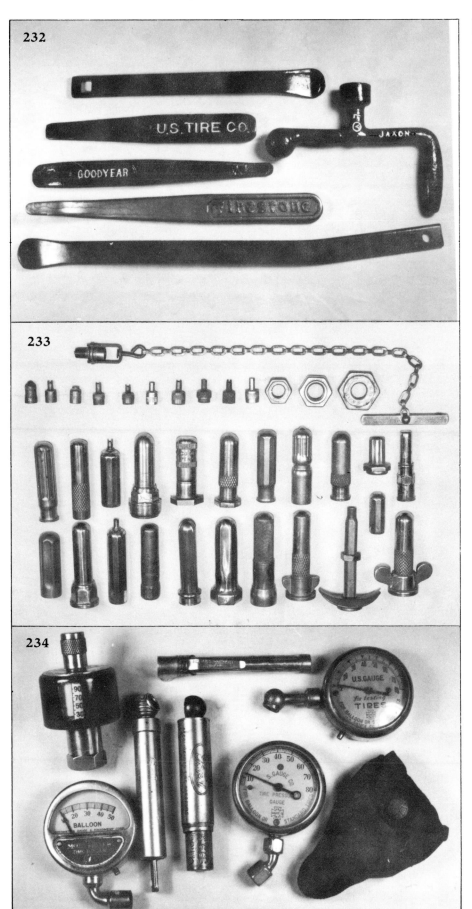

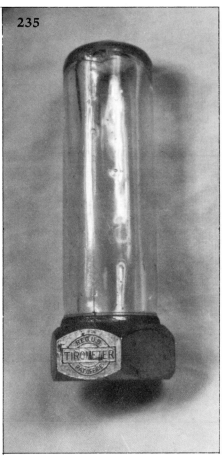

232. Factory and tire store tire irons. The T-shaped tool at right could be a lug nut wrench from a Jaxon steam car.

233. Valve stem covers used from the beginning of balloon tire era until the early 1930s make an interesting collection. Most have Schrader or Dill name; one even has the Michelin man on it.

234. An assortment of early tire gauges.

235. Tirometer. Fill this glass tube with water and screw it on the valve stem to detect leaks.

To restore or not to restore, that is the question. Appearance is the name of the game. There are those who prefer to leave their hubcap acquisitions in the condition they found them in, and there are those who prefer to restore them. The chief consideration here is usually time. If you have decided to restore your caps, I hope you find the following information helpful.

Most caps when acquired still contain a slug of axle grease, the bulk of which can be removed with a small putty knife. Afterward, a good soaking in kerosene or solvent will loosen most of the remaining grease. For stubborn bits of hardened grease try naphtha or lacquer thinner. One or the other will usually cut these with a little assistance from a stiff-bristled brush. Beware of the flammability of naphtha and lacquer thinner, and work in a well-ventilated area.

After the initial cleanup what you do next depends on your skill. If your restoring skills are limited, then try to acquire caps that are in fairly good condition. Minor cleanup and a little shining with steel wool will make them quite displayable. Also, be prepared to pay a little more for caps that are in good condition. Car restorers usually look for caps such as these and pass over those in poorer condition unless the brand is rare. Even caps in good condition get what a coin collector calls *bag nicks* from knocking around in boxes of parts from swap meet to swap meet. Gravel roads were also responsible for a lot of nicks and dings in an otherwise good cap.

The biggest mistake most people make with an aluminum cap is using a rotary wire brush. Although this is a quick method of removing most foreign matter, it can be somewhat destructive. If wire brushing is as far as you intend to go with your restoration, you may have to settle for a rough surface. A coarse brush on a bench-type motor has a tendency to undercut and pile the aluminum surface with ridges. Wire brushing also can destroy or smooth out raised letters or other more intricate surface detail such as the *Durant* dragon or the *Nash, Cadillac,* and *Cole* shields. Even brass caps can take on this appearance if sufficient pressure is exerted on the wire wheel. Should this happen, simply take 180 or 240 grit sandpaper (wet-or-dry type works best), and sand out the surface pile up and follow up with fine steel wool. It would be much less work, however, to skip the wire wheel and go directly to sandpaper to achieve the same final effect. Appearance will continue to improve as you work toward finer grit paper ending up with 400 or 600 grit. At this point the amateur would have a very nice displayable cap.

If you are a perfectionist, you will probably want a total restoration, and for a skilled machinist or an experienced restorer this would be simple. If you have never tried it before, a little time and patience will produce a collection of jewels that will dazzle even the best in the hobby.

You will need a few tools to start with:

Hammer—preferably "pointed" body type
Vise
Files—mill, rat tail, 3 corner
Bench Grinder with buffing attachment
Sandpaper—several grades
Punches and **Special Shaped Bars**—assortment (to be used as backing tools)
Lathe—optional
Acetylene Torch—optional

The first step after cleaning is removing dents. Although brass and aluminum are malleable, removing deep dents can split the metal if not done carefully. Brass is even more susceptible to cracking as it tends to harden with age, oftentimes cracking by itself. To witness this look at some unrestored radiator shells, headlight trims, or even the threaded portion of some hubcaps. Several thin cracks will be noticed around the edges. Unfortunately, most dents were inflicted in the largest diameter. Some cap designs prohibit easy access to the backside of the dent. For this task an assortment of old screwdrivers, tire irons, and bar stock can be bent, ground smooth, and reshaped to fit inside the various contours. In most cases it works better if you place a backing tool in the vise and slip the cap over it positioning the dent on the tip of the tool. Hold the cap firmly in one hand while tapping all around the dent with flat face of a body hammer. This is one task that a textbook could not teach you. You just have to develop a feel for how hard your hammer blows should be and how often to change position of the backing tool. If you know a body and fender man, perhaps he could give you a few pointers. One advantage to this method of straightening is that it allows you to watch the progress of each dent as it comes back to shape. It also lets you observe the start of any cracking due to overstretching of the metal. Some brass caps have thick walls and harder blows are required to effect dent removal; however, thicker brass is usually more prone to cracking. If the dents are too deep to straighten or if cracking has occurred, fill welding might be considered as an alternative. Brass caps can be brazed, and there is a product on the market for simplified gas welding of aluminum.

Dent removal from the face of the cap is made easier by virtue of good access. I suggest the same method of placing the cap over a vise-held backing tool. Before getting carried away with face restoration, take a look inside for evidence of cotter-pin damage. Careless mechanics occasionally used too large a pin or improperly bent it over, allowing it to come in contact with the inside face. In this instance, considerable metal was removed making that area very thin; therefore, poking around with punches could pop out a large section of the face with loss of some letters in the name. It is best to leave this area alone or work very carefully. Small punches and rounded screwdrivers should be selected here to effectively remove a dent without distorting surrounding detail. With care, small punches can even reshape damaged letters, but if they are too far gone, you might need an engraver. A cap this far gone would not make a good display item, so why not experiment to see if you can handle the tedious work involved in letter restoration. You may find a hidden talent lurking at the tip of your fingers. Dents in the threaded area are relatively easy to remove, unless you have ideas about protecting the threads. Preserving threads should be a low priority since you will probably never use them on a car. However, if saving threads is a must, use soft wood as a backing while removing dents. Some hand thread chasing may be required as there are no taps this size. If you have a lathe, thread cleanup can be performed nicely. The lathe can also be handy for dressing some surfaces on the outside of the cap and for rotary sanding.

Much damage to caps was inflicted by their exowners. While most cars came equipped with a hubcap wrench, the car and wrench soon went their separate ways. Then the stage was set for the pipe wrench, channel locks, or the hammer to leave their permanent impressions. The hexagonal or octagonal faces of the cap which normally accept the wrench now have dents, teeth marks, and rounded corners. This area can be straightened by clamping a piece of three-quarter-inch *square* bar stock into a vise. Using the bar stock, anvil style, work dents out of each flat surface with the body hammer. Corners can be reshaped by using the edges of the bar stock. Sometimes a pointed punch has to be used to push the corners of the flats back into shape. Again I recommend putting the punch in the vise vertically and tapping on the cap from the outside, because a pointed tool can easily go through before you can catch it.

After the dent is removed, it is time to use the file. A fine or mill file is best. Using short strokes, smooth off any high spots created by punches and backing tools. Short strokes following the contours are most effective. When filing the wrench flats, sometimes a substantial amount of material must be removed to eliminate the deepest marks. Keep a file card or wire brush handy, and use it frequently when filing as aluminum has a tendency to pile up in the teeth of a file. (Brass is not nearly as bad.) This piled up metal can cause damage to the surface being filed by galling and inducing deep groves, making it necessary to file even more. Keep the square corners of your file away from any radius to prevent adding more unwanted grooves. If the inside radius needs filing, use a round or half-round file. If, after removing as much material as you dare, you find that some flaws remain, then additional straightening may be necessary or possibly welding.

The next step is sanding. With access to a lathe or one-inch belt sander, the task would be much easier. However, with a little patience, hand sanding can produce good results, too. Start with a

100 grit, the wet-or-dry type is best. This should remove the file marks. If you are power-belt sanding, be careful of the pressure applied or you could achieve the same piling effect that power wire brushing leaves. After the 100 grit repeat with 240 or 260 and finally with 400 or 600. You should now be ready for buffing. This must be done with power to be effective. You could use a quarter-inch drill motor clamped in a vise. This method is slow, because a small drill motor does not have sufficient power for buffing. The best method of home buffing is to use a drill press or a bench grinder with a buffing attachment. Use a six-inch cotton buff, but don't run over 4,000 R.P.M. in your drill press because you will get surface burn. (Bench grinders are fixed at 3,450 R.P.M.) If you don't have a drill press you can make an attachment for your standard one-third or one-half horsepower two-wheel bench grinder. Remove the right-hand nut and replace it with a half-inch Jacobs chuck. You now have a buffing wheel protruding four inches to the side of the grinder allowing sufficient access to buff small parts. A word of caution here: While buffing, always be aware of the grinding wheel that is also spinning four inches away from your knuckles; it can remove a hunk of skin rather quickly. A small margin of safety can be provided by wearing gloves. The gloves will also insulate you from the heat generated by buffing. If you have done an adequate job of sanding, buffing with a white compound will work fine, but if you short cut your sanding or you did not go past the 100 grit, you can use the black compound stick (emery). If you have a powerful (one-half horsepower or better) motor, you can do some heavy polishing with the coarser grit emery stick. Compound and metal tend to build up in the buff so clean occasionally by pressing an old screwdriver gently across the face of the wheel. Don't overload the wheel with compound, or it will build up on the surface and reduce the effectiveness of the buff. It is a good idea to wear safety glasses while using power equipment. When you have finished buffing, there will be some compound buildup around letters and depressed detail. This can be removed with soap, hot water, and a soft-bristled brush. You may have to use a toothpick in and around some letters.

After cleanup comes the final touch: background color application. During your initial cleanup take note of any paint traces around the letters that might indicate what the manufacturer used. It will be red or black in most cases. However, a few were color keyed to match the car by the factory, by the dealer, or even by the owner. Look at pictures of restored cars in books and magazines for clues to original colors. One method of applying this color is a draftman's ruling pen. Using gloss hobby enamel (Pactra or equivalent) thinned slightly, approximately ten parts paint to one part thinner, dip the ruling pen about a quarter of an inch into the paint, then touch it to the background while the cap sits flat. The paint will flow freely around the detail. The wider you adjust the gap of the pen, the faster the paint will flow. For the center of closed letters and numbers like A, B, O, P, Q, R, 6, and 8, use a tooth pick. If you accidently smear a little on top of the letters or detail, don't worry, just let it dry, then flake it off with a pocket knife.

A little automotive paste wax will protect your finished cap from rapid oxidation. But if displayed in an unheated building in a northern climate, no matter what you do you will have a constant maintenance job to prevent tarnish and oxidation. Sulfur or chlorine in the air attacks brass. Aluminum holds up a little better but is most affected by salt or calcium in the air.

When restoring brass caps you may choose to make an exception to the original. Many brass caps were nickel plated. If the cap and plating are in good condition, a light buffing is all you need, but if the plating is chipped off and straightening is required, it is best to visit a plater and strip off any old plating. Then proceed with the normal restoration process. When the brass cap is all finished you may choose to leave that beautiful gleaming brass exposed and perhaps paint a black background for contrast, but should you be a stickler for authenticity, return it to the plater for nickel plating. If you are pleased with your buffing job, insist that he plate only and not buff. Most plating shops are not meticulous with detail, and can easily ruin raised letters on your cap with the huge buffers used in their shops.

All this may sound like a lot of work, but a couple of hours on a Saturday or Sunday can produce some fine results for your den or even for your antique car. In fact, by the time you do four identical caps, you should be good enough to go back to number one and do it right!

Because of their relatively small size, approximately one hundred caps can be displayed in a 4 × 6 foot area. There are not too many novel ways to display caps, but a little imagination and a long hard look at the area available to you can produce some interesting ideas. As collections grow in size innovative ways fall by the wayside for the more general display format of nails in the wall or 4 × 8 foot sheets of plywood. Why not spruce up these conventional methods at a nominal cost? A 4 × 8 sheet of plywood can be cut into four 2 × 4 foot pieces, and when you have covered it with colored burlap and maybe even framed in nicely finished wood, you will have a wall hanging that might not be offensive to your wife. A little thought can provide an artistic arrangement of caps on these boards. If space is limited, rotate your boards once a month, storing away the excess. Or better yet, display only your favorites, keeping the balance handy to show other enthusiasts when they visit.

If you are fortunate enough to run across some candy display racks, they provide a quick-change, hanging wall display rack for caps. Department store glass-enclosed display cabinets are nice but consume a lot of space. The necessity for cleaning and dusting are greatly reduced by using an enclosed display case.

The most positive way to secure caps to a vertical display board is by sizing a wood block to fit snugly inside the threaded area of each cap. This must be done on a one-by-one basis, because the thread size varies so much. Fasten each block of wood to your board, and then press the cap firmly over it. Hooks and nails will support hanging caps but leave them vulnerable to damage if knocked off.

An interesting display is matching caps and wrenches side by side on a board, especially if the auto name appears on the wrench.

Even though hubcaps are not the standard fare for decorating most homes, displayed properly they can be both interesting and pleasant to look at. So take those caps out of hiding, and use a little ingenuity, creating a truly original wall hanging and keeping in mind the popular saying, "One man's 'junk' is another man's treasure."

CHAPTER 3

Spark Plugs

ORIGINALLY, internal combustion engines were not fired by an electrical sparking device such as a spark plug. Instead a much less efficient method called *flame ignition* was used. This crude method restricted R.P.M. and horsepower, resulting in slow vehicle speeds.

A true sparking device had been described in an 1860 patent application submitted by French engine designer Jean Lenoir. Lack of development of a good electrical power source prevented the widespread use of a sparking device until the late 1890s. With the industrial revolution in full swing, many new inventions emerged and existing ones were being improved upon. Availability of batteries and magnetos was making it practical to incorporate spark plugs into engine design. This single development greatly affected the future of gasoline powered vehicles. Engines previously capable of only 30 to 50 R.P.M. were now able to reach 600 to 800 R.P.M. due to the more precisely timed explosions in the cylinders.

The old cliche, "You don't get something for nothing," was soon evident as new problems of leakage, arcing, cracking, shorting, and fouling became evident. The search was on for the perfect insulator material. Mica from India was widely used in early plugs. Although mica is a fine insulator, it would eventually break down and absorb oil or moisture causing arc leakage to ground. Porcelain clay was imported from France to produce insulators, but it, too, left something to be desired. It was a long, slow process developing a material possessing all the properties needed for the perfect insulator. Consider what a spark plug encounters in its lifetime. It is subjected to temperatures ranging from –20° F to over 4,000° F, and this temperature rise can occur within two to three minutes. It is pounded with explosive pressures from 500 PSI in early low compression engines to over 3,000 PSI in the high-performance giants of the sixties. It is jolted with from 5,000 to 30,000 volts as many as 1,000,000 times in a single day. It is subject to spray from cold rain water. It is exposed to dirt, grease, and various chemical deposits. During all this torturous treatment, it is expected to fire properly each and every time and prevent gas leakage between the collar nut and base. Its expansion and contraction rate must closely match that of the surrounding metal so as not to crack. In addition, it has to be nonporous enough to repel saturation by oil or moisture.

After testing many different materials, a significant breakthrough came in 1915 from the Frenchtown Porcelain Co. Made of stoneware composition and capable of meeting all these physical requirements, it was dubbed formula 775. Many small companies using these insulators carried the 775 designation on their plugs. As time passed and more rigid requirements were put on insulators, newer and better materials were discovered. Frenchtown used a zircon-type ceramic in 1932, and Champion discovered sillimonite in 1933.

When one thinks of spark plugs today, almost inevitably, *AC*, *Champion*, or *Autolite* come to mind. You might call them the surviving big three to the spark plug world, just as GM, Ford, and Chrysler are to the auto makers.

According to the best estimates of the experts on the subject, the SPCOA (Spark Plug Collectors of America), there have probably been over 2,000 brand names applied to these sparking devices over an eighty-year existence. Many of these names were not manufacturers of plugs, but private branded labels sold by garages, auto-part houses, mail-order houses, stationary gas-engine manufacturers, auto and truck manufacturers, farm tractor companies, etc. Although the private branding of plugs is still done today, there aren't very many names left. Due to cost, only larger companies offer a plug bearing their own names.

Today there are fewer than a dozen manufacturers of plugs left. Like the many auto companies that failed, so too the small plug manufacturers fell victim to economics, inadequate advertising, poor sales, company mergers; and, of course, the Great Depression took its toll. Surely the founders of Champion and AC had no idea that someday they would be the big two in the industry. Champion got its start in 1907 in Detroit. Founded by the *Stranahan Bros.*, who were originally in the importing business, they hoped to produce a quality American plug to stem the tide of foreign imports. Their first major customer, John Willys, convinced them to move to Toledo and set up shop near the Overland plant. This was the beginning of their success story. In 1909 their design incorporated the use of copper gaskets between metal and porcelain parts, completely eliminating the leakage problem. There were many imitators, but their successful design, and ability to sell, made Champion number one in the marketplace. Almost every major auto producer, including Ford, became Champion users. With Ford as an exclusive user of Champion plugs, success was imminent. By 1919 Ford alone was using 3.5 million plugs a year.

About the same time that this great Champion success story was taking place, another Champion was emerging. This was Albert Champion (no relation to the Champion Spark Plug Co.), who started to produce spark plugs for Buick in Flint, Michigan. A friend of William C. Durant, founder of General Motors Co., he was persuaded to produce plugs for Buick and Oldsmobile. As the GM empire grew, the addition of Chevrolet, Oakland, Cadillac, and others provided for the continued success of AC.

The original company name was the Champion Ignition Co. (CICO), but obviously there must have been some conflict with the Champion Spark Plug Co. However, it wasn't until 1922 that the company name was changed to AC Spark Plug Co., after the founder Albert Champion. Both trademarks, CICO and AC along with *Titan* (a cheaper line of plugs), were used into the forties. But the AC was the most marketed name, and it has survived for over fifty years. In 1927 AC got a great boost when Charles Lindbergh used AC spark plugs for his historic transatlantic flight, and boasted of their flawless operation during the entire flight. In 1933 AC officially became a division of General Motors.

The depression meant hard times for everyone; spark plug companies were no exception. Many small companies went out of business. Trying to survive, larger companies bought up the assets of smaller companies, and did odd things like pasting their labels over the smaller companies' and putting new cores in old bases. A small printed paper label, pasted over the old name on the porcelain was a quick and inexpensive way to liquidate stock, i.e., *Road King*. The *Fox* spark plug used a new porcelain core inside a *Red Head* priming base. Examples like these are scarce, because once these small stocks were depleted, few were ever remade.

They don't make 'em like they used to

A look at today's miniaturized plugs for low-emission engines would lead one to think they were knocked out by a nut and bolt factory—not very eye appealing compared to the majestic look of the Rentz glass intensifier plug of 1920 with its visible spark window, nickel plating, and little wooden handles. Today a ten-dollar bill will buy a set of eight plugs. With average weekly salaries of $300.00, that is about one-thirtieth of your week's pay. The Rentz plug by contrast, is actually the most expensive plug ever sold. In 1920 this plug sold for $2.50. Eight plugs would cost $20.00, when weekly salaries were about $10.00. That amounts to two weeks' salary for spark plugs. If that same ratio were true today, a set of plugs would cost you $600.00. Think about that the next time you say, "They don't make them like they used to." Sometimes they are better and cheaper.

Problems with the low-grade gasoline of the early 1900s brought about a myriad of spark plug designs. There was no necessity nor technology to produce the multiple-step petroleum distillates we use today. Gasoline was made by a single distillation from crude oil, in a simple process called cracking. This gasoline was closer in consistency to kerosene, because there was a lot of oil still in suspension. Poor gasoline along with low-compression ratios and incomplete ignition caused many problems with spark plugs. Many plug manufacturers proclaimed a sootless or oil-proof feature. Although several unique and novel methods were used to combat the problem of oil and carbon deposits, it is interesting to note that the simplest of all designs was the one destined to survive. But thanks to all the gimmickry, we now have some rather interesting plugs to collect.

Intensifier Plugs

A very popular gimmick, this principle. If a primary gap is created, the spark will be more intense (have a higher voltage) when it jumps the secondary gap in the cylinder. Most people did not realize that the spark had already jumped a primary gap between the rotor and distributor or magneto cap. However, these were popular plugs since variations of this feature lasted for over thirty years, and some companies even produced add-on devices for this purpose. Some of these plugs had visible primary gaps; others were internal; and some had a double-gap intensifier arrangement at the electrode end. **Examples:** *Rentz, King Bee, Duro, Lloyd Omatic, Wonder, Aldor, Leonard, Twin Fire, Chain-o-Spark.*

Primer Plugs

Most early engines were aspirated by an updraft carburetor. On cold mornings it was tough cranking to get a vaporized mixture up to the plugs. To handle this problem, priming cups were perched atop each cylinder with small valve handles attached to drop raw gasoline into the cylinders. The spark plug manufacturers took this feature one step further by adding a priming cup to their plug base. The purpose for this was simple: By inducing fuel right at the point of spark, starting would be quicker. Some had cups on the side of the base, while others had a cup on top of the insulator and primed right through it. **Examples of side mount:** *All-in-One, Champion, E-Z Prime, Red Head, Vital, Mosler, Challenge.* **Examples of through the insulator:** *Heinze, Griffin, Star, Nabon.*

Self Cleaning

These were plugs with some device for cleaning the carbon deposits either manually or automatically. A most interesting manual clean plug was the Wellmans' *Turn Clean.* By loosening a knurled nut at the top of the porcelain, you could raise the anode up slightly, bringing a knife edge against the bottom of the porcelain. With a few rolls between your fingers and thumb, the carbon would be scraped away without dismantling the plug. The *Excelsior* could be rotated a quarter turn at the collar nut, exposing vent holes and letting suction and compression created by the piston purge any deposits. A most unusual method of automatic cleaning was featured by *Myers.* Several small porcelain balls were captive between the porcelain and base. Surging air from suction and compression would cause the balls to move up and down keeping deposits scrubbed free. *D & D Fouless* had a similar system with one ball in a cage to hammer away at carbon. A novel method of preventing deposits was devised by *Fan Flame.* A small six-blade fan was mounted on the end of the electrode. The rapid movement of air past the fan from suction and compression would spin it, slinging any oil deposits off it. There were six or eight points around the perimeter for the spark to jump, causing a ring of fire. Many plugs had an oil-proof feature designed into the tips, generally hook shaped, to cause oil to form in droplets away from the spark gap.

Breather Plugs

Still another solution to the soot and carbon problem was a small duct in the side of the base or through the porcelain, fitted with a spring-loaded ball check. This ingenious device would allow clean, cool air to be sucked in over the hot end of the porcelain. The rush of cold air would supply oxygen to assist in further burning away deposits. **Examples:** *LeVac Northwind, Challenger, Shurnuff, Blue Ribbon.*

Detachable Plugs

This was an attempt to sell easy serviceability without tools. These plugs had a handle extending to one side. A quarter turn would release the center of the plug from the base so that it could be removed and cleaned. The *Ever Clean* had a large wing nut for the same purpose. **Examples:** *Winestock, E.Z., Ever Clean, Blake, Bobra, Lengrad, Breech Block, BC.*

Double End

"Twice the plug for the price of one," was the claim made by the manufacturers. Some had a symmetrical porcelain with one threaded base attached, while others had two threaded bases. When one end wore out, you just turned it over and used the other end. **Examples:** *Twin, Hire Fire, Dubl Servis, Double Head.*

Series and Double Plugs

Similar in appearance, but different in application. A series plug was used in conjunction with another plug in the same cylinder under the theory that two sparks in different parts of the combustion chamber would provide more efficient burning of the fuel/air mixture. Each of two external connections went to an electrode. The spark jumped across the two electrodes rather than to ground. One connection went to the power source, while the other went to a second conventional plug in the same cylinder. A double plug is just what it implies, two plugs in one. Each of two external connections go to an electrode, which individually arcs to ground and can use two power sources firing simultaneously. **Examples:** *Bosch, Twin Tact, Edison, Sudig, Suton.*

Coil Plugs

Basically for marine application, this was a different type of ignition system using an individual coil housed in the spark plug assembly. This eliminates the need for high-tension wire connections to each plug. Instead, small (14 ga.) wire is routed from a battery switching device with the same timing sequence as a distributor or magneto. Each coil, when supplied with a primary voltage, induces a higher secondary voltage and automatically discharges across the spark tips. Manufacturers of this system claim it can be run under water, and it eliminates the chance of high voltage shock. **Examples:** *Perfex, Primary, Orswell, Connecticut Coil.*

Visible Spark

Although these plugs did nothing to improve performance they were interesting when viewed at night with the engine running. Constructed with glass insulators, or glass viewing port, the explosions in the cylinders could be readily seen. A quick visual check could pinpoint a fouled nonoperable cylinder. **Examples:** *Anderson, Viz Spark, Window.*

Exotic Metals

Ni-chrome steel was the usual for the electrode construction, but Mosler and Flash Light Plugs advertised the use of platinum tipped plugs. Platinum was an expensive metal ($50.00 per ounce) at that time. It is also by far one of the best electrical conductors known to man.

Perhaps taking a stab at the aristocratic market, Benford had one version of its Golden Giant, plated with 24-karat gold.

Kopper King dressed up its plug with copper plating, while many of the higher priced plugs were polished and nickel plated for appearance.

Miscellaneous

There was a multitude of electrode configurations, ring and disc arrangements, and even an auxiliary firing chamber in the Cleveland Plug. The advertisement claim was, "It shoots a flame into the cylinder."

The Moto Meter plug carried its own gap gauge under the wire nut.

Many versions of Ford Special, Henrys', Long Henry, For A Ford, 4 a Ford, etc., were directed at the huge after market brought about by the success of Ford's Model T.

Spark plug restoration

Enhance the appearance of your spark-plug collection. Consider partial or total restoration. Although total restoration is strictly a matter of personal taste, returning these little jewels to their original condition can be a rewarding experience.

Whether your restoration is to be partial or total, begin with the basics: First, disassemble the plug, however minor or major the project. Even an N.O.S. (New-Old Stock) plug with a little surface rust should first be disassembled to restore it properly. It stands to reason that if you separate the porcelain from the body of the plug, you lessen the chance of breaking it while working on the metal parts.

The easiest restoration is an N.O.S. plug that has been exposed to moisture over the years, creating a little surface rust. A simple rubbing with steel wool or a fine Scotchbrite pad will usually do the job of rust removal. Follow up with a light oiling using 3-in-1 oil or the equivalent.

Should you plan to tackle a complete restoration on a used plug, the first thing you must do is inspect the porcelain to determine if the name is paint, a decal, a silk screen transfer, or if it has been fired on. The majority of plugs have the name fired on, which means it is actually part of the smooth glazed surface and cannot be destroyed by any cleaning solvent.

A few early plugs had decals on the porcelain, the most fragile of all trademark applique. Wire brushing, steel wool, or any solvent will damage or destroy the decal. Careful dismantling and hand cleaning around the decal is necessary to preserve it. Some plugs known to have decals are *Benford, Hercules, Spitfire, Wards Leak Proof, Peerless, Keystone, Ovee, ·Helfi.*

In the forties and fifties the "Chicago" plug was quite popular. Chicago does not imply that all were built in Chicago, although the majority were. A plug of identical size and physical shape may be sold under as many as a dozen different names and in different parts of the country. This design was the last of the three piece repairable plug which eventually evolved into the one piece throwaway plug. These were highly competitive, private-brand plugs, and a few manufacturers, in order to keep production cost down, applied the brand name in rubber-stamp fashion with a silk screen process or painted it on. These, too, are very fragile, and care must be taken while cleaning the porcelain. Lacquer thinner, naphtha, and other solvents will·usually remove it immediately.

If you have determined that the name is fired on, you may proceed to dismantle the plug without fear of stripping off the name with accumulated dirt or rust in the collar nut (also called *packing* or *gland nut*). The best way to remove the collar nut is to first place the base of the plug in a vise. Use only a smooth-face vise or face covers, because a serrated or knurled face will leave unwanted marks in the hex flats of the plug. Secure the plug snugly, but don't be a Charles Atlas and overtighten your vise, causing undue tension on the collar nut and making removal difficult. Just to insure an easy exit, spray a little penetrating oil around the threads and a little between the nut and the porcelain. Avoid using adjustable or open-end wrenches. The collar nut has a thin wall and flexes easily. The best bet is a six-point deep socket or six-point box wrench. Most plugs will come apart with a minimum effort. Always hold your hand over the socket or box end of the wrench while trying to loosen, ensuring that it stays on the collar nut. The last thing you want is for it to slip off and break the porcelain. If you don't have a vise, set two box wrenches in scissors fashion, to give you good one-hand leverage. This leaves the other hand free to support and protect the porcelain from a slip of the wrench. You would be inviting disaster by placing the box wrenches ninety degrees apart holding one hand on each like a pair of hedge clippers. If a reasonable amount of pressure on the wrench produces nothing or if it feels like you are going to round off the corners, stop, soak it good with penetrating oil or kerosene, and leave it overnight. Nine out of ten times it will come loose with ease the following day. Let's say for the sake of it that you have a stubborn nut and nothing seems to work. Turn the plug upside down, clamp the collar nut in the vise with the top of the base flush with the top of the vise jaws. Get a box wrench the size of the base and a short piece of two-by-four. Heat the base evenly with a propane torch. Don't use an acetylene torch unless you are skilled with it, because a rapid rise and the intense heat produced by an acetylene torch could crack the porcelain. With the base heated up, quickly slip the box wrench on, and place the two-by-four horizontally over the plug. Exert a downward pressure on the plug with the two-by-four while turning the wrench. The board will serve to keep you from coming in contact with the hot plug, while the downward pressure keeps it from walking out of the vise. A high pitched squealing noise and feeling a chatter in the wrench lets you know the nut is coming loose. If this still doesn't work and you feel the vise crushing the nut or the corners rounding off, you have one more recourse. If the porcelain is a rare one, and you feel like making a new base, then use a band saw or hack saw to split the base vertically. This will free the nut. During any of the above procedures except heating, you can add a little margin of safety to the porcelain by wrapping it with duct tape.

Now that the hardest part of the job is done, the rest is sort of anticlimactic. Cleaning the porcelain is somewhat simple, as in most cases a little lacquer thinner, tulol, or naphtha will do the job. After removing the small brass wire nut from the porcelain insulator, you may want to clean the threads on the stud. The obvious is to run it across a rotary wire brush. This will certainly clean the threads, but you stand a chance of having the wheel snatch the porcelain out of your hand and smash it against the wall or floor. Furthermore, if you are not careful, the wire brush can permanently scuff the glazed surface, embedding metal particles in the minute surface pores. This condition can be cured with some skill in the art of lapidary and access to polishing equipment used for gemstones, but careful use of a Scotchbrite pad will also remove the silver-gray color. Use only the minimum amount of rubbing required to remove stain since the Scotchbrite will scratch and dull the glazed surface. However, if you are bent on using the wire wheel, then first wrap the porcelain with duct tape.

The other end of the porcelain is the business end that protrudes into the combustion chamber and will, of course, have carbon, oil, and other chemical deposits that solvents won't completely remove. The ideal way to return this end of the porcelain to its original soft-white appearance is to sandblast it with glass beads. Before blasting get the old duct tape out to protect the upper part of the porcelain so that the glass beads can't dull the glossy surface. Without access to sandblasting equipment, the next best thing to do is use solvent-dipped steel wool, or Scotchbrite pad to rub off the majority of deposits.

Now it is time to restore the base. A brass base is easy, because you don't have to contend with rust. Usually all that is required is a little dress up with a file on the flat surfaces and some buffing on a wheel.

If the base and collar nut are blued or nickel-plated steel, there is a little more involved in restoration. On nickel-plated parts you will find that some were just plated over the original rough textured surface and that some were smoothed and highly polished. If the plating is in good condition, just a little buffing will restore the original luster. If the plating is chipped or flaked away with rust showing through, then it is necessary to go to a plater and have the old nickel plating stripped off. This is the only proper way to do it. It is done chemically so that every trace of the old plating is removed, a task almost impossible to do with files and sandpaper. If the old plating is not chemically removed, the new plating will not look right when redone. Nickel-plated parts seldom show the deep rust you are likely to find on a blued-steel plug.

The most effective way to remove rust from a blued-steel base is by sandblasting with fine beach sand or preferably glass beads. This does a thorough job inside and out and gives the base a soft or frosty surface texture for new bluing to adhere to. Without access to sandblasting equipment, you will have to resort to the rotary wire brush for the exterior and some scraping, sanding, and rattail filing for the inside. Occasionally, rust pits will be rather deep. Careful filing with a single-cut mill file (fine tooth) will remove them from the flat areas, but the contours and round areas should be done on a lathe. Take your time when filing to prevent rounding corners or inducing chatter marks from the teeth of the file. File in alternating directions to avoid this. After filing, use a sanding block to smooth up file marks. It is best to draw the plug base across the sandpaper to avoid rounding corners. The hexagonal wrench flats on some plugs were originally formed by large grinding wheels or milling cutters. You will find this true on a plug that has some diameter larger than the hex. Most plugs were turned from hexagonal cold rolled bar stock. These plugs have a smooth textured surface on the hex. The moon-shaped traces left on the flats by grinding wheels can be duplicated merely by doing the same thing on your bench grinder. Hold the flats against the side of a one-hundred-grit wheel, but don't exert a lot of pressure, as these bench-type grinding wheels are not designed to be used on the sides.

A plug that has first been sandblasted and then filed and sandpapered will look odd when reblued. The repaired areas will be a shiny blue and the unretouched sandblasted areas will have a frosted look. It is then best to either reblast with glass beads before bluing for an overall frosted look or sand the entire surface for the more glossy appearance.

Commercial cold bluing is available in concentrate or dilute form at gun shops, sporting goods stores, and some hardware stores. Before applying the bluing make sure that the metal is free of oil or fingerprints by cleaning with lacquer thinner, naphtha, alcohol, or other solvent. Concentrate bluing can be applied with a cloth or cotton swab, as it works quickly, turning a dark blue.

Additional applications will make the metal even darker. When applying dilute bluing, it is best to use steel wool. Dilute bluing works slower, and it needs some assistance to start the etching action on the surface. Repeat the process until desired color tone is achieved.

Remember, older plugs (1900 to 1920) had a lighter shade of blue, sometimes referred to as *browning,* with an appearance like an antique gun. The later plugs of the thirties and forties had a dark bluing, almost black in appearance, the same as found on modern gun barrels. You may have to dilute your brand of bluing to achieve the lighter tones. Start with five parts water to one part bluing for an average. Experiment by increasing or decreasing the quantity of water to suit your own taste. After bluing, rinse with hot water to remove all traces of the bluing acid. If left it will form a powdery residue.

One final job before reassembly is to polish the little brass wire nut that fastens on top of the porcelain. Put the nut onto a small screw with the same thread size as the nut, snug it firmly to the head, and then grip the assembly with pliers while buffing. Don't try to buff it while it's still attached to the porcelain. The speed and gripping power of a buffing wheel has a tendency to quickly unscrew the nut and send it on a trip around the garage or basement, after which you can plan to spend five to fifteen minutes crawling around on your hands and knees looking for it.

In case you're wondering what to do with that nickel-plated plug that has been stripped and painstakingly restored, return it to the plater for a new nickel-plated finish. Be sure to tell him whether you want a high polish or a satin (frosty) finish.

Next is reassembly. Position the name on the porcelain to line up parallel to one of the flats enabling it to face straight forward on a display board. Some plugs have a name or patent date stamped on one of the flats. Of course, you want this to be the flat parallel with the name on the porcelain. A drop of oil on the packing nut threads will ease assembly and prevent future rust.

Those who are artistically talented or who have a steady hand can further improve the appearance of plugs with decals or silk-screen names. Any hobby shop will carry flat or gloss paints (Pactra, Testors, or equivalent) and 00 or 000 red-sable brushes necessary to reconstruct chipped decals or letters. Weak or chipped letters on Chicago-type plugs can be greatly improved in this manner.

Elusive names and patent dates stamped in plug bases can be brought into plain view by taking a small dab of paint and rubbing it over the depressed letters. After all the letters are filled, allow them to dry for a few minutes. Then with a cloth lightly soaked in thinner appropriate for the paint you're using and stretched over your finger, wipe off the excess paint left on surface. Don't rub too hard or you may draw paint out of the depressed areas, making it necessary to start over. Use white paint on blued plugs and black paint on brass or nickel plugs. Now the plugs can be viewed without holding them up to your nose.

After the plugs are restored, consider protecting them from rust and corrosion. Displaying or storing plugs in an unheated barn or garage, especially in a northern climate, is an open invitation to rust. Unless they are given constant attention, you will have problems. Clear lacquer has a tendency to yellow and gives the plug an unnatural appearance. Polyurethane coatings resist yellowing, and if a flat texture is used, it can hardly be detected. Do not put any coating on the porcelain because it will withstand anything that mother nature can dish out, at least while inside. When displaying plugs indoors at room temperature, any of the following would be adequate: a light coating with oil, a good automotive paste wax, or a rubdown with a gun cloth, which is a silicon-treated rag available at gun shops.

Some early aviation plugs will appear to have dull porcelain or nicked mica. This was caused by a sandblasting effect from the prop because early airfields were not paved. The mica can be sanded to smooth up the surface, and then it can be oiled or waxed. A good polyurethane coating over any decals will greatly help preserve them, too.

Displaying plugs

The ideal way to display anything is in glass cases. A glass case provides safety from sticky fingers and eliminates the task of dusting. It can also be lighted to better show off your little gems. However, most collectors choose the conventional display-board method. Covered with colored burlap, a two-by-four-foot piece of Masonite with some one-by-one-and-one-half wood framing will hold about eighty plugs without looking too crowded. The plugs can be anchored to the board with small pieces of wire, one at the threaded end and another at the wire-nut end.

Occasionally, you can find some auto store spark-plug display cabinets, which make attractive show pieces, but they do not house many plugs.

Trying to display alphabetically is not practical unless you want to spend a lot of time reshuffling your collection for new additions.

A more practical way is to display by topic RE: Brass and Mica Plugs, Primer Plugs, Chicago Plugs, 10mm Plugs, Tractor Plugs, etc. Perhaps you specialize in one brand, AC or Champion.

Be original. Make artistic displays. Put all the different Rajah connectors and accessories around a set of Rajah Plugs.

With the multitude of electrode designs available, pick out ten or so of your favorites, and mount them in a thin board so that the threads are snug enough to prevent them from falling out. Then when you want to show these to someone, just turn the board over for easier viewing.

Bill Bond has a unique way to mount his plugs. He uses a heavy wire lug (for number ten or twelve ga. wire with a three-sixteenths hole) fastened to a piece of burlap-covered pegboard with a sheet-metal screw. The wire lug protrudes out from the board so that each eyelet can accept the threaded end of a porcelain. Plugs hang out away from the board in 3-D fashion and make for a very neat display. This method also provides easy shuffling of specimens.

Unplugging the names

From their humble beginnings in small garages, factories, and job shops in the late 1800s, spark plugs have shared a similar history to the automobile.

Many new ideas and designs were tried in the early years. Competition was stiff as many small companies were getting into the business, and, of course, each of these companies had to have a name for its product. Like the automobile, spark plugs were named after many things: cities and towns, designers or manufacturers, gimmicks, the end user, and non-auto-related products. Apparently, some companies regarded the spark plug as a good advertising medium. WNAX was a Yankton, South Dakota, radio station as well as the hometown of Lawrence Welk. *Bond Bread* was exactly that, *Dr. Coyles Wonder* was a medicine, *Watkins* was the familiar line of home products, *Cloud* was a Chicago newsstand drugstore. Because the spark plug was a small, seemingly insignificant part of the auto, more often than not its name was the attention getter. Oftentimes a gimmick name was used. One such approach was using names that would suggest faultless quality: *Best, Ever Best, Genuine Reliable, Ideal, Perfect, Precision, Protecto,* and more cleverly, *Inde-Structo* and *Dur-A-Ball.* A direct attack on the paramount problems of early gasoline engines, oil fouling and carbon deposits, provided still another approach. Armed with a dictionary full of adjectives and a seemingly never-ending play on words, plug makers produced names like: *Oil Proof, Nonoyle, Sootless, Sootproof, Fouless, Kant Foul, Kant Miss, Non Foul, Never Miss, Never Skip,* or *No Skip.* The cleanliness ploy was not overlooked with names like *Burn Clean, Ever Clean, Eze Kleen, Keeps Kleen, Prime Kleen,* and *Cleanez.* A spark plug's ability to possess tip-top performance was well covered in the name game with *Full Spark, Hot Spark, More Spark, Sharp Spark, Shur Spark, Shur Fire, Shur Hit, Sure Thing, True Fire,* and *Quickfyr.* Mechanics who had to contend daily with these old plugs could have coined a few names of their own: "*Never Hit, Miss Fire, Ever Foul, Dud-O-Matic, Nofyr, Kanthit,*" and a few more descriptive but unprintable names. Who knows the reasoning behind the naming of the *Billy Hell* plug? But it surely must have raised a few chuckles.

Just as *Traffic* seemed to be the ultimate name for an automobile, so must *Spark Plug* have been most appropriate for a spark plug. Perhaps this company was ahead of the times by using generic names.

With the much appreciated assistance of the S.P.C.O.A.* (Spark

*The S.P.C.O.A. was founded in 1976 by William H. Bond of Ann Arbor, Michigan. The club was formed for the mutual benefit of all spark-plug collectors, with present membership at 250. For further information write S.P.C.O.A., P.O. Box 2229, Ann Arbor, MI 48106.

Plug Collectors of America), this fine composite list was put together for the convenient reference of all collectors. Only through the combined efforts of club members can this wealth of information be brought forth in a single format. At the time of publication, the list is as complete as possible, but as time passes new plugs will surface, adding new names to any future list.

In most cases minor differences have been omitted. Some duplication may occur due to collectors arranging their lists differently. Example: *Bougie Mercedes* will also be found under *Herz*.

AA
AAA
AB
ABC Toledo
Abbott
AC
AC Aircraft
AC Allis Chalmers
AC Carbon Proof
AC Cico
AC Coralox
AC CP *carbon proof*
AC Ford
AC Harley-Davidson
AC IHC
AC Marine
AC Midget
AC Oleo
AC Packard
AC Radio
AC Sphinx
AC Star
AC Titan
AC Tractor
Accel
Acco "Super Flash"
Ace
ACF *French*
ACK
Acme
Adams
Adonis
Aero
Aero Klein
Aetna
AFC Affinity
AFP
AG
Agway
Ahico
Aim Auburn
Aim Auburn Long Henry
Aim Blazer
Aim Junior
Aim Long Henry
Air Friction
Air Kool
Air Ministry
Air-O-Fire
Air Valve Ign. Co.
Ajax
A-K
Akko
Aladdin H.W. Co.

Albright
Aldor
Aldor Automatic
Aldor Thermo-Resistor
Al Jo
All American
All Car
Allen Grade
Allied
All-In-One
Allis Chalmers
All Service
Allstate
Allstate *rubber cover*
All Weather
Almquist
Alpha
Aluninite
Alvo
AM
AMA
Amesco
American
American Ace
American Bakeries
American Bosch
American Eagle
American Machine
American Parts
Americo
Ameron
AM-I-CO
Amoco
Anchor
Anchor Giant
Anderson
Andrae
Andree
Animated Air Valve
Another United Product
Answer
Apco Ford Special
Apollo
Apple
AQ
Arclite
Arc-O-Fire
Arco Ribbon Fire
Arc Toledo
Aris *French*
Aristo
Arlan's
Armee
Armor

Arrow Reflex
A&S
A-Scho
Asco
Asco Red Devil
Asko
Aster
Astley's Giant
Astley's Hi Power
Astley's Quality
ATA
Atco Quality
Atlantic
Atlas
ATO
A to Z
Auburn
Auburn Long Henry
Auburn NYM & M Co.
Auburn Blazer
AUC
Aurora
Auto Fire
Auto Gas
Auto Graph
Auto King
Autolite
Autolite Cosmoline
   Sealed
Autolite Marine
Autolite Power Tip
Autolite Racine
Autolite Resistor
Autolite Transport
Automa
Auto Marine
Automark
Automat Self Cleaning
Automatic
Auto Queen
Atomic
AV
AV Magnito
Avalanche
AVC
Avia
Axwell
AYC
Azet

B
Baby
Baby Reflex

Badger Eye
Baird
Baird Self Cleaning
Baker
Balco
Bald Head
Baldwin
Ball Arc
Ball Bearing
Ball Belvidere
Ball Multi
Ball-O-Fire
Ball Point
Ball Spark
Bal Lite
Balso
Banner
Barclay
Barney Google
Barnsdall
Barnsdall Oil Proof
Bates
Bathurst
Bathurst Air Cooled
Baysdorfer Affinity
Bay State
BB
B&B
B&B Air Cooled
B-Brand
BBSC
BBSCO
Becco
BCO
Beacon
Beacon Lite
Bear Cat
Beat-M-All
Beck
Beckly Ralston
Bee Brand
Beeco
Belmark
Belvidere
Bendix
Bendix Aviation
Bendix Turbine X
Benetz
Benford
Benford Blue Giant
Benford Golden Giant
Benford Golden
   Giant *24k gold plated*
Benford Golden Wonder

Benford Monarch
Benford Primer
Benford Reliable
Benford Overland
Benford Peerless
Benford White Cap
Bengal
Benoist *French*
Benton
Bergie National
Bergine
Berkshire
Berry
Beru
Beru IMC
B E S *Australia*
Bessemer
Best
Bethlehem
Bethlehem Aviation
Bethlehem Five Point
Bethlehem Fordson
  Tractor
Bethlehem IHC
Bethlehem Long Life
Bethlehem Motorcycle
Bethlehem One Point
Bethlehem Packard
Bethlehem Stutz
Better
B&F
B F Goodrich
BG *Brewster Goldsmith*
BG Self Cleaning
BG Non Shortable
B-Hi Compression
B High Comp
Bicknell
Biederman
Biehl
Big Brute
Big Chief
Big Drive
Big 4
Big Streak
Billancort
Billy Hell
Biltmore
Biltrite
Bingham
Bingo
Biplug
Bitter Root
Bittle Serirco
BJ
Black
Black Eagle
Black Hawk
Blake
Blanchard's
Blaze
Blazer
Blazer Aim
Blazer Stone
Blazer Vim
Blick
Blitz
Blitzen

Blitzen Giant
Blitzen Janitor
Bloom
Blue Bird
Blue Blaze
Blue Crown
Blue Crown 500 Indy
  Winner
Blue Crown Husky
Blue Crown Motor
  Master
Blue Devil
Blue Flame
Blue Head
Blue Jacket
Blue Ribbon
Blue Streak
Blu-Fyr
B L U M I
B-M-C *Bosch*
Bobar
Bodin
Bodin No Carbon
Bodin No Chamber
Boe
B Oil Proof
Bond Bread
B 1 Plug
Borg Warner
Bosch
Bosch D R P
Bosch German
Bosch Honoid
Bosch Magneto
Bosco
Boshe *French*
Bougie Eyquem
Bougie Mercedes *Herz*
Bowers
Bowes Seal Fast
Bowes Seal Fast Special
Bowman
Boyd
BP
Bradley
Brassco
Breech Block
Brevette
Bricknell
Brighton
B-Rite
Brite Way Master Craft
Bro-Gar
Brown
Browne
Browning
Brunswick
BRW
Buckeye
Buffalo Carb Co.
Buffy
Bugatti *Italian*
Buhl
Buick Special Service
Bull Dog
Bull Frog
Bullock
Bull's Eye

Bumex *Mexico*
Bummells
Burlington Route
Burn Clean
Burnham
Burns
Burrel Bros.
Buscoba
BZ

Cadillac
Camp
Campbell
Capital
Carbo Gas
Carbon No
Carey Circle Fire
Cartridge
CAS
Cat
Catalytic
CAV
Cavco Boering
Cayuga
CB
C&D Porcelain
Center Fire
Central Lumber
Central Tractor
Century
Ceruco
Certified
CGS
Chain-O-Spark
Challenge
Challenger
Champion
Champion Aero
Champion Ford *script*
Champion Ford A
Champion Double
  Ignition
Champion Franklin
Champion Gas Eng.
  Special
Champion Harley-
  Davidson
Champion Hudson
Champion IHC
Champion Maytag
Champion Midget
Champion Needle Primer
Champion Overland
Champion Packard
Champion Reliance
Champion Toledo
Champion Tractor Special
Champion X
Champion Yellow
Champion Primer
Champion Wankle
  Experimental
Chaplin
Charland
Charter
C H *Claudel Hobson*
Check
Chesapeake & Ohio RY

Chicago
Chrysler
Chryco *Chrysler of Canada*
CI-AC-CO *AC*
Cincinnati
Circle Fire
Circ-O-Fire
Cities Service
CL
Clark Anchor
Clark Equipment
Cleanez
Clean-E-Z-Prime
Clearcut
Cleveland
Cleveland Shoots-A-
  Flame
Clifton
Climax
Climax Magneto
Cloud 75
CMC *Chandler Motors*
CMS
Coast To Coast
Co-B
Cock Shur
Colin
Col-Mac
Colmer Hot Spot
Columbia
Combination
Come
Comèt
Competition
Common Sense
Community Service
Confidence
Congress Special
Conical Reflex
Conical Standard
Conill *French*
Conn Toe
Connecticut T&E
Constant
Continental
Co-Op
Co-Op Jet Flame
Co-Op Tri Fire
Copper Head
Copper King
Corning
Corsair
Cox Edick
C P M C *Constant*
CR
Cresent
Crest
Crist
Cromwell
Cromwell Atlas
Cross Country
Cross Country Rubber
  Top
Crown
Crown Point
Crum's Bullseye
Crusader
Cushman

CT
Culp Plan
Cumming
Cupples
Cupples Rhinos
Cupples SC
Curran
Curtis
Cushman
CVT
Czar

D.A.P. *French*
Dandy Heavy Duty
Dandy Improved
Dandy Primer
Dandy Pyro Action
Dandy 999
Dalco
Dale
Daly
Dansereau
Day
DB
D&D Co.
Deck
Decker
De Dion Bouton
Deering
Deeton
Defender
Defiance
Delmark
Delta
Delta Primer
Delux
Deluxe
De Masco
De Mun
Denso
Derf
Derf Hi Speed
Dering
Desco Quartz
Detroit
Diablo
Diamond
Diamond A Jr.
Diamond M
Diamond Reflex
Diamond Z
Dickson
Dico
Diktator
Dinger Oil Less
Disbrow
Disco
Diskomatic
Dixie
Dixon
DK
DL&W
DM
DNXLD
Doddwill
Doering
Dollar
Dome Top

Doran
Double A
Double Action
Double C
Double Check
Double E
Double End
Double Head
Double L
Dow
Dragon
Dr. Coyle's Wonder
Dreadnaught
Dr. Ferrell 606
Dr. Jerrell 606 Jr.
Dr. Ferrell Special for
    Ford
DRGN
Drips Klean
Dual Duty Air Spark
Dubl Servis
Duffy
Dunlop
Dunlop Gas Saver
Dunlop Gold Cup
Dunmore
Duo Sport
Duplex
Dur-A-Ball
Durabilt
Dure
Durf
Duro
Duryea *coil plug*
Dutchess
Duval
Duval Auto
DX
Dykes
Dyna Fire
Dynam
Dynamic Leggetts
Dyno Diesel
Dyres

Eagel *Ireland*
Eastern States
ЭЭ *Russian*
Eccentric
Echo
Ecle *French*
Eclipse
Economy
Ed Co
Edge
Edison
Edison Albinite
Edison IHC
Edison Indian
Edison Splitdorf Albanite
Edmond
EG
EH
EIC
Eisner
EJ
Eklips
Eklips Giant

EKO
Elbridge
Electra
Electric
Electric Disc XL
Electro Spark
Elgin
Elite
Elk
Elkhorn
Ellenness
Emco
Emerge
Empire
Endurance
Energex
Ensign
Entente
Eole *French*
Erie Railroad
Ersuler
Ertgo
Esco
Esso
Esteco
Esteed
Etna
Ever Best
Ever Clean
Everfire
Everite
Ever Ready
Excel
Excelsior
Exventric
Exploder
Exploder *coil plug*
Express
Express *Frenchtown
    porcelain*
Express Oil Type
Express Oil Special
Express Type One
Express Type Three
Express Type Seven
Eyquem Paris *French*
EZ
Eze Kleen

Fan Flame
Fasta
Favorite
FEC
Fedco
Federal
Ferlor Paltine Pur *French*
Fert
FH
F&H Air Cool
Fidelity
Fireball
Fire Brand
Fire Crown
Fire Fly
Fire Injector
Fire Injection
Fire Right
First American

Firestone
Firestone Polonium
F I R O L
Fisher
Fisk
Fitz. Co.
Fitzgerald
Flapper
Flash
Flash Ball
Flash Glass Fry
Fleetwing Air Spark
Flint
Flint Aero
Floquiet
Flynn
FM
FMC
Fole
Fool Proof
For-A-Ford
For 4 One
Ford
For-Do
Foremost
Forster
Forward
Fouless
Four Star
Fox
FP
Franklin
Franks Pride
Franks Window
Fred Meyer
Frigo *French*
Fromar
Fry
FRSE
FT
Fuel Igniter
Full Spark
Funke
Furber
FWD
Fyrac
Fyresm

Gamblers
Gambles Deluxe
Gambles Tractor
Gardner
GE
Geer's
Gem
General
Gentleman
Genuine Reliable
Genuine Soot
    Proof *Mezger*
Gets
Gets Clay Core
Gets Priming
Gets 999
Geysco
GH
Gibraltar
Gibson

Twenty-three restored screw-on hubcaps are proof positive that a display of these can be very colorful.

"The Great License Plate Piggyback." Those who originally conceived license plates probably never dreamed that so many things would be added to or hung on the unused mounting holes. Shown here are a few of the hundreds of items bolted onto or near the plate. Motor club badges, insurance company emblems, political ads, safety slogans, patriotic signs, city vehicle tags, state validation tabs, gross weight tabs, oil and tire company logos, world fair badges, etc. Also shown are six miniature metal license plates from breakfast cereal boxes. These are part of a 1953 set accurate in every detail as to proportionate size, physical shape, validation tabs, and even the raised rib around the perimeter of the plate. General Mills offered these in regional sets by mail order first in 1953 and 1954, then on and off until today. The latest is the 1979 set. If space is limited this is a good way to collect many plates.

A contrast of today and yesteryear. The 1914 Michigan plate is typical of the much sought after porcelain-coated cast iron type used up until the late teens. Small seal can be seen as a permanent part of the porcelain coating. The Michigan plate is surrounded by miniatures from the 1979 General Mills set. The ones shown are the bicentennial designs that carried through as five-year plates, and the new pictorial-type plates that some states are adopting. The current miniature set, although a good likeness of plate design, is not as authentic as the 1953 set. They have rolled an exaggerated bead around the edge unlike its real counterpart.

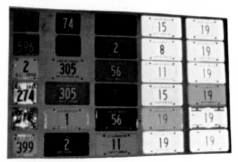

1

3

2

4

5

6

1 & 2. An impressive collection of low-number Illinois license plates from 1910 to 1977.

3. Special holder for license plate, city vehicle tax tag, and club badge, 1927 Illinois.

4. A complete low-number run of Illinois motorcycle plates, from 1911 to 1974. The 1928–1931 plates, with tag number four, measure only two inches square.

5. A complete collection of City of Chicago vehicle licenses from 1903 to 1931. From 1932 to present, paper windshield stickers were used.

6. A display of club badges.

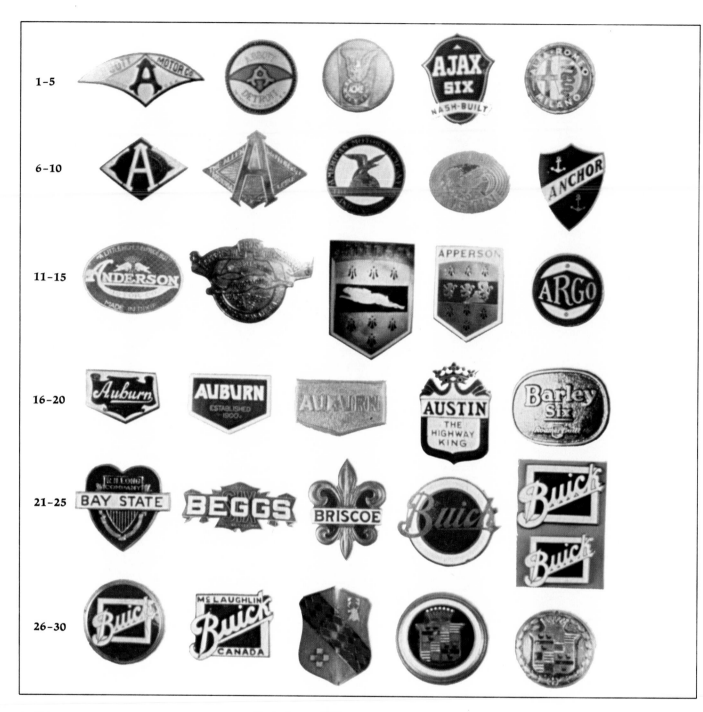

1–5

6–10

11–15

16–20

21–25

26–30

1. Abbott	11. Anderson 1921	21. Bay State 1922
2. Abbott	12. Apperson Jack Rabbit	22. Beggs
3. Acme	13. Apperson Jack Rabbit	23. Briscoe 1915
4. Ajax 1926	14. Apperson	24. Buick 1912
5. Alfa-Romeo 1925	15. Argo	25. Buick 1920s
6. Allen	16. Auburn 1916–1919	26. Buick 1933
7. Allen	17. Auburn 1925	27. Buick (McLaughlin) 1925
8. American (underslung) 1912	18. Auburn 1930	28. Buick 1940
9. American Austin 1932	19. Austin 1913	29. Cadillac 1925–1926
10. Anchor	20. Barley 1923	30. Cadillac 1928

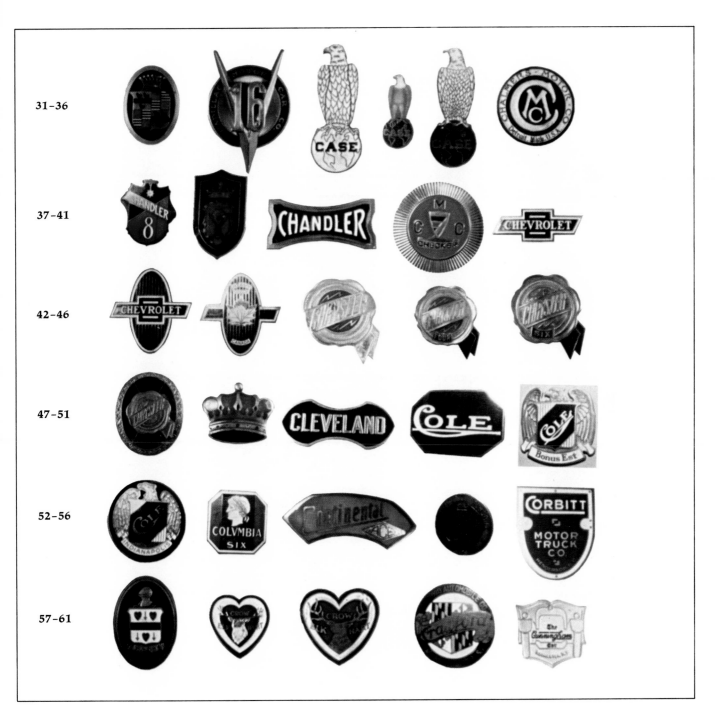

31-36

37-41

42-46

47-51

52-56

57-61

31. Cadillac
32. Cadillac V-16, 1930
33. Case 1924
34. Case
35. Case
36. Chalmers 1917
37. Chandler 1927
38. Chandler 1928
39. Chandler 1925
40. Checker 1955
41. Chevrolet 1927

42. Chevrolet 1929-1930
43. Chevrolet 1929-1930
44. Chrysler 1925
45. Chrysler 1926
46. Chrysler 1926
47. Chrysler
48. Chrysler Imperial 1953, V8-hubcap Emblem
49. Cleveland 1925
50. Cole
51. Cole

52. Cole
53. Columbia 1920
54. Continental 1933
55. Continental 1934
56. Corbitt 1912
57. Cord 1936-37
58. Crow Elkhart 1919
59. Crow Elkhart 1920
60. Crawford 1922
61. Cunningham 1921

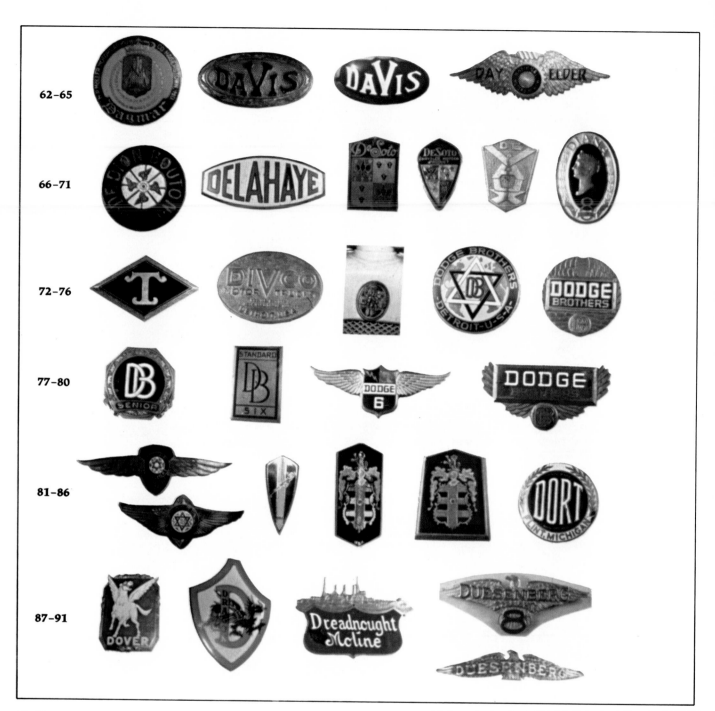

62. Dagmar 1923	72. Diamond T 1925	82. Dodge
63. Davis 1924	73. Divco	83. Dodge 1937
64. Davis 1924	74. Dixi	84. Dodge 1947–1948 (front)
65. Day Elder	75. Dodge 1914–1928	85. Dodge 1947–1948 (rear)
66. De Dion Bouton	76. Dodge	86. Dort 1920
67. DeLahaye	77. Dodge	87. Dover
68. DeSoto 1929–1930	78. Dodge	88. Dragon
69. DeSoto 1931	79. Dodge 1930	89. Dreadnought 1913
70. De Vaux 1931	80. Dodge	90. Duesenberg 1921–1926, Model A
71. Diana 1926	81. Dodge	91. Duesenberg 1929

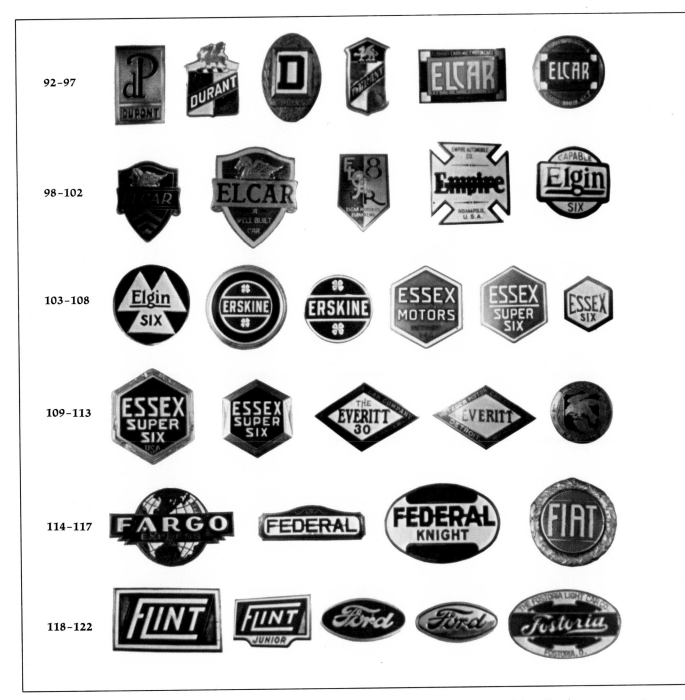

92-97

98-102

103-108

109-113

114-117

118-122

92. Du Pont 1928

93. Durant 1926–1927

94. Durant 1928–1929

95. Durant 1930

96. Elcar

97. Elcar 1919–1920

98. Elcar 1925–1926

99. Elcar 1926

100. Elcar 1927–1928

101. Empire 1917

102. Elgin

103. Elgin 1920

104. Erskine

105. Erskine 1929

106. Essex 1919

107. Essex

108. Essex

109. Essex 1928

110. Essex 1929

111. Everitt

112. Everitt

113. Falcon Knight 1927

114. Fargo

115. Federal (12″ long)

116. Federal Knight

117. Fiat 1960s

118. Flint

119. Flint Junior

120. Ford 1928–1930

121. Ford 1931

122. Fostoria 1916

123–127

128–132

133–137

138–142

143–147

148–152

123. Fox 1923	133. G.M.C.	143. Halladay 1917
124. F.R.P. 1917 (Finley Robertson Porter)	134. Gramm	144. Hamlin Holmes
125. Franklin 1923–1924	135. Graham Bros.	145. Haynes
126. Franklin	136. Graham Bros.	146. Haynes 1921
127. Franklin	137. Graham Paige 1929	147. H C S 1919–1920
128. Frazier 1947–1948	138. Graham Paige 1930	148. H C S 1921
129. Gardner 1919–1920	139. Grant	149. Henry
130. Gardner 1928	140. Gray	150. Henry
131. Garford	141. Gray	151. Herff-Brooks 1915
132. G.M.C.	142. Gray Dort 1921	152. Hudson

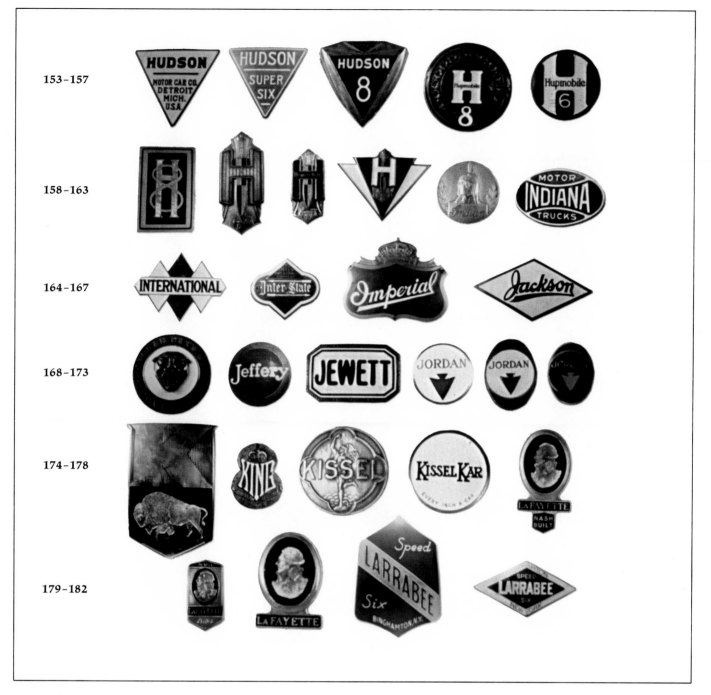

153–157

158–163

164–167

168–173

174–178

179–182

153. Hudson 1917
154. Hudson
155. Hudson 1930
156. Hupmobile
157. Hupmobile
158. Hupmobile 1929
159. Hupmobile
160. Hupmobile
161. Hupmobile 1931
162. Indian

163. Indiana
164. International 1932–1934
165. Inter-State
166. Imperial 1913
167. Jackson
168. Jaguar
169. Jeffery 1916
170. Jewett
171. Jordan 1927
172. Jordan

173. Jordan
174. Kaiser 1947–1948
175. King 1916
176. Kissel 1926
177. Kissel-Kar 1916
178. LaFayette
179. LaFayette—400
180. LaFayette
181. Larrabee
182. Larrabee

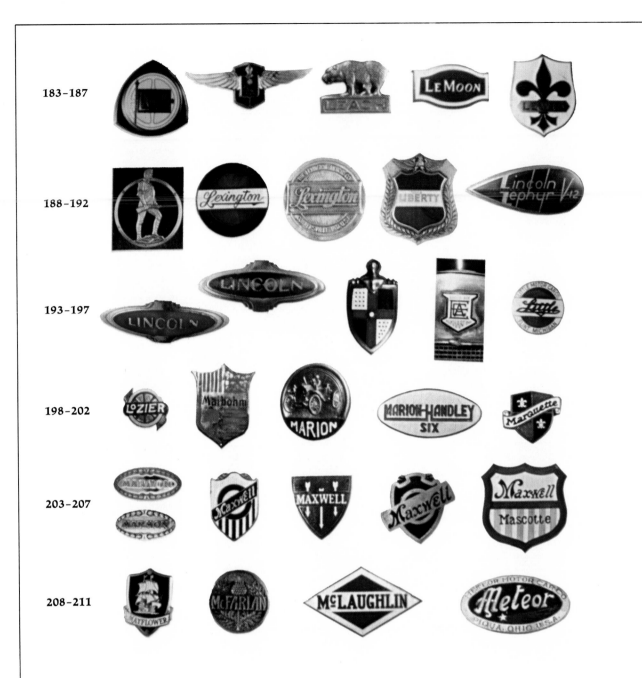

183–187

188–192

193–197

198–202

203–207

208–211

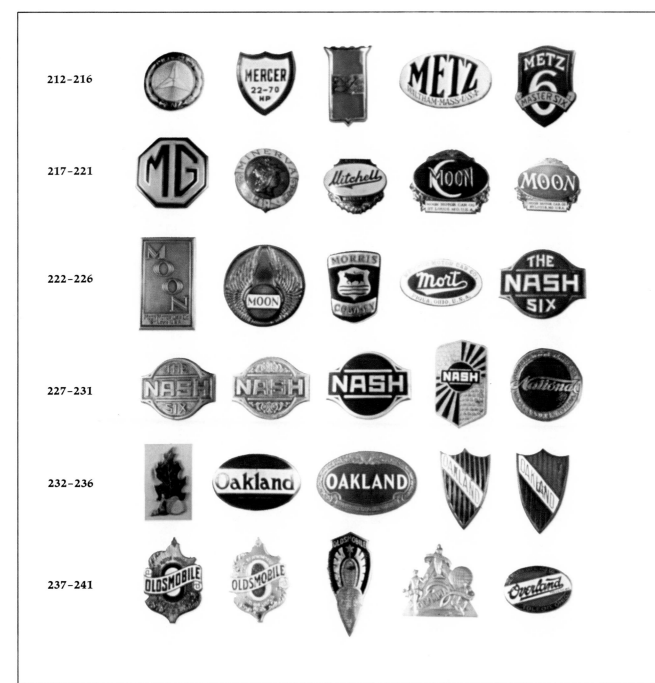

212-216

217-221

222-226

227-231

232-236

237-241

212. Mercedes 1960s
213. Mercer 1917
214. Mercury Park Lane 1964 (fender)
215. Metz 1914
216. Metz
217. MG 1960s
218. Minerva
219. Mitchell 1922
220. Moon 1916
221. Moon 1923

222. Moon 1926
223. Moon 1928 (Model 880)
224. Morris Cowley
225. Mort 1920
226. Nash 1921
227. Nash 1926
228. Nash 1926
229. Nash 1928
230. Nash 1929
231. National

232. Oakland 1920s
233. Oakland 1927
234. Oakland 1928
235. Oakland 1929
236. Oakland 1930
237. Oldsmobile 1921
238. Oldsmobile 1925
239. Oldsmobile 1937
240. Olympian 1920
241. Overland 1916-1924

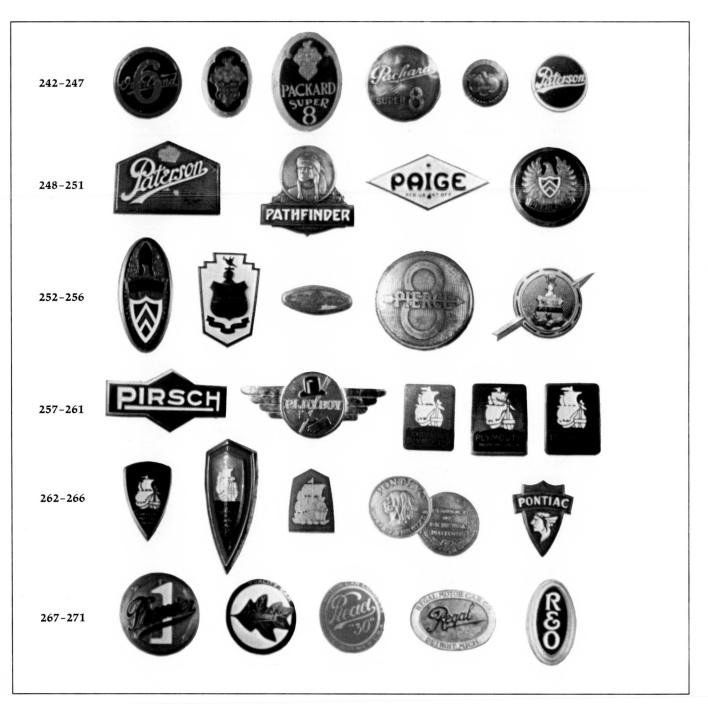

242–247

248–251

252–256

257–261

262–266

267–271

242. Overland

243. Packard Trunk 1936

244. Packard Crank Hole Cover 1936

245. Packard 1939–1940 (hood)

246. Pan American 1919

247. Paterson

248. Paterson

249. Pathfinder 1917

250. Paige 1922

251. Peerless 1922

252. Peerless 1930–1931

253. Pierce Arrow 1928

254. Pierce Arrow Trunk Rack 1935–1936

255. Pierce Arrow Trunk Rack 1937–1938

256. Pierce Arrow 1932–1938

257. Pirsch (fire engine)

258. Playboy 1948

259. Plymouth

260. Plymouth

261. Plymouth

262. Plymouth

263. Plymouth

264. Plymouth

265. Pontiac 1926

266. Pontiac 1932

267. Premier 1920

268. Premier

269. Read 1914

270. Regal 1916

271. REO

272–275

276–280

281–285

286–291

292–296

297–301

272. REO
273. REO
274. REO 1928
275. REO Speedwagon
276. REO Speedwagon 1927
277. REO
278. Revere
279. Revere—Hubcap disc
280. Rickenbacker 1922–1923
281. Rickenbacker 1924–1926

282. Rickenbacker 1924–1926
283. Rollin 1922
284. Roosevelt 1929
285. Roosevelt 1930
286. Ruggles
287. Rockne 1933
288. Rugby 1930 (Durant for export)
289. Rugby
290. Ruxton 1930
291. R & V Knight 1921

292. Scripps Booth 1915
293. Sampson-Tractor
294. Sanford
295. Saxon 1917
296. Saxon
297. Schacht (pronounced "shot")
298. Seagrave (fire engine)
299. Sheridan 1920
300. South Bend 1919
301. Speedwell 1913

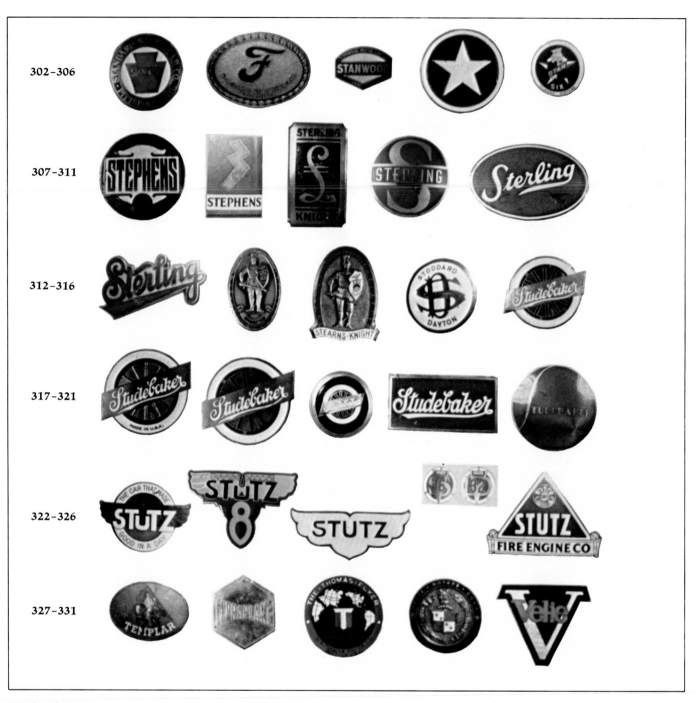

302–306

307–311

312–316

317–321

322–326

327–331

302. Standard 1920

303. Standard Truck

304. Stanwood 1920

305. Star 1925

306. Star 1929

307. Stephens 1921

308. Stephens 1923

309. Sterling Knight 1925

310. Sterling

311. Sterling

312. Sterling

313. Sterns

314. Sterns Knight

315. Stoddard Dayton

316. Studebaker 1920s

317. Studebaker 1920s

318. Studebaker 1920s

319. Studebaker

320. Studebaker

321. Studebaker 1937

322. Stutz 1915–1920

323. Stutz 1926

324. Stutz

325. Stutz V16-V32 (valve count, not cylinders)

326. Stutz Fire Engine

327. Templar

328. Terraplane

329. Thomas Flyer 1914

330. Velie

331. Velie 1922

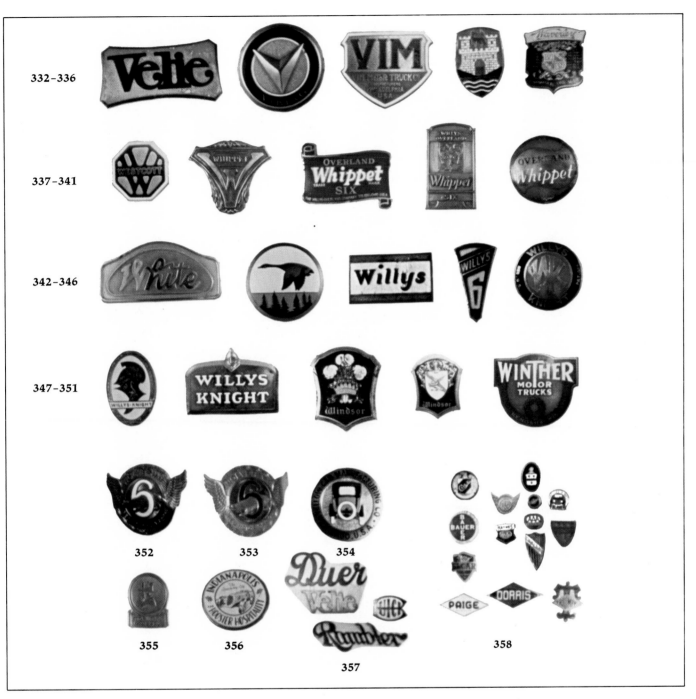

332. Velie 1917	341. Whippet 1928	350. Windsor
333. Viking 1929	342. White	351. Winther
334. Vim	343. Wills St. Claire 1925	352. Wolverine 1927
335. Volkswagen	344. Willys	353. Wolverine 1928
336. Waverly 1912	345. Willys 1930	354. Yellow 1925
337. Westcott 1921	346. Willys Knight 1926	355. Murray Body Plate
338. Whippet	347. Willys Knight	356. Souvenir Speedway Badge (circa 1920s)
339. Whippet	348. Willys Knight	357. Four brass radiator scripts
340. Whippet	349. Windsor	358. An assortment of miniature emblems

1. Very colorful can of "WHIZ" roadside hand cleaner. Car and clothing atire date this can around 1910. The can is remarkably preserved considering the decal label. Can construction is crimped, but must be earliest attempt at crimping as all seams are also heavily soldered. Early advertising claims are fascinating, each one usually claiming several uses for their product. This one is no exception, it says, "No water is required," but, "Where water is available it may be used as a high grade antiseptic liquid toilet soap." It goes on to say, "As a shampoo compound it is unexcelled." It sounds as though the manufacturers are suggesting that you take a bath on the roadside after adjusting your carburetor!

2. Gas pump globes are very colorful as can be seen in this 1940s Road Supreme. Birds, Indians, and many other things were pictured on these lighted globes.

3. In the 1950s and 1960s, oil companies gave tin bank miniature versions of their full size counterpart cans to promote their product. The practice was given up due to cost.

4. Auto products of all kinds came in tins. Because of their fragile nature, tins usually rust away if exposed to damp weather. Oil cans, of course, are filled with a natural preservative, and many have survived. Most auto manufacturers packaged lubricants under their own name to provide total service, and grab a larger share of the aftermarket profits. The Nash can is for central lube systems. The emblem

of the face of this can dates this product between 1929 and 1934. A major oil company has introduced graphite as an oil additive, but the idea is not new as evidenced by the 1940s vintage Centennial can in right center. The face price on the can is thirty-five cents.

Gilardoni
Gilbert
Gill
Gilt Edge
Gladiator
Glass Core
Glenmore
Globe
Globe Full Spark
Gloria
GM Co.
Gnat
Go-Far
Goldblatt Bond
Gold Bond
Gold Comet
Goldcrest
Golden Eagle
Gold Label
Gold Metal
Gold Metal Kar Life
Goliath
Goodrich
Goodyear
Goose Neck
Gordon
Gotham
Grand Superfire
Grant Anchor
Grants
Grammes
Green Core
Green Crown
Green Dragon
Green Jacket
Green Halgh Garage
Green Seal
Greyhound
Griffin Renewable Bar
GT&R Co.
Guaranteed American
Gun Fire
Gun Powder
Gun Shot
Gyro
GVT
GWR

Haco
Hades Jr.
Hagstrom
Hall
Halox
Hampshire
Harriman
Harris
Hartford Arc Light
Harvard
Hasteel
Hastings
Hawley Junior
Haynes
HC
Heath
Heather
Heavy Duty Deluxe
Heco
Heinze

Helfi
Hel-Fi Co.
Hemmeter
He-Mo-Jo
Henley ZN
Henry's Special
Hercules
Hercules Jr.
Herz
H-Fire
HHH
Hickory
Hi-Fre-Co
Higginson
High Comp
High Duty
Highway
Hildebrand
Hill
Hi Power
Hire Fire
Hirsch
Hi Speed
Hi Speed Homes Twin
Hitachi
Hi Way
HM
HMS
HMS Bulldog
Hobson
Holley
Holms Twin Shot
Holsten
Hooper Agalite
Horn
Hornet
Horseshoe
Hot Point
Hot Shot
Hot Spark
Hot Stone
Howard
HP
HT Aviation
Hub City
Hullman
Hunt
Hunt Porcelain
Hurleman
HWI
Hyatt Hi Power
Hy Power

Ideal
Igna
Ignito
IIPL
Illinois Central RY
IMC *Ceru*
IMP
Imperial
Improved Long Distance
In-Da-Co
Indestructible
Inde-Streucto
Indian
Infer
Inferno

Infinite Spark
Ingle
Inland
Inner Fire
Inpaco
Insulator
Invader
Invincible
Irco
Irvings
Isotta

James
Janesville
Janesville Tractor
Janney Steinmetz & Co.
JA Red Giant
Jarvis
Jaugey
JBC Co.
JBM
JC Brand
JD Conical
JD Conical Henry Special
JD Conical Platinum
JD Petticoat Type
JEF
Jet Fire
Jet Ignition
Jet Igniter
Jewel
J H Westinghouse
Jipe
JM
JM Mezger
JMS
Johns-Manville
Johnson
Johnson Bros.
Johnson Giant
Jol
Joly *French*
Jolly
Jordan
JPG
J&R
J&R Standard
JS & Co.
JSH & Co.
Jubilee
Jumbo Giant
Jumbo Molite
Junior
Jupiter
Just
J&W Waterproof

K&A
Kacym Ford
Kahm Mfg. Co.
Kansas Special
Kant Break
Kant Foul
Kant Miss
Kant Short
Kar Kare
KB Jr.
KC

Kem
Keo
Keystone
Kid Reflex
King
King Bee
Kings
Kingston
Kinsley
Klean
KLC
KLG *German*
K Mart
Knicks
Knicks Mend Rite
KO
Kohler
Koil
Kopf *German*
Kopper King
Kosmak
Kottler
Krafve
Kuco
KW

L'As *French*
La Giant
Lapel
Lansing
Larco
Lasalle
Lasco
Latch
Lava Lite
Lawrence Kennedy
Leader
Lectra
Lectra Fuel Igniter
Lectra Spark
Lec-Tro
Leda *French*
Lee
Lee of Conshohocken
Legnard
Lehman
Leisure
Lemke
Lenax
Lenox
Leonard Air Cooled
Leonard Atomic Flash
Leonard Beck Motorcycle
Leonard Harley-Davidson
Leonard High
  Compression
Leonard Oilfiring
Leonard Vented
Lepel
Lepco
Lesota
Le Vac Air-O-Matic
Lewis
Liberty
Liberty Spitfire
Life Long
Life Time
Lightning

Lightning Reflex
Lincoln
Lininger
Lion
Lissen
Little Gem
Little Giant
Little Jeff
Little Pep
Livewire
Lloyd
LM
Lock-Em-All
Lodge *British*
Lodge *blue porcelain*
Long
Long Bros.
Long Distance
Long Henry
Long Life
Lore
Lorraine
LPM *Lift Parts Mfrs.*
L&S
Luckey
Luthy
Luthy Aero
Lux
LXV
Lydon Lynamite
Lynx
Lyons

Mac
Mac-Kay
Mac-Kay Blitz
Maco
Maco Super
Macquaire
Macys
Magic
Magnetic
Magnetic Marelli
Magneto
Magnex
Maher
Mail Flyer
Majestic
Major
Mallory
Manhattan
Man-O-War
Many Miles
Mapco
Marathon
Marbo
Marchal Corindin
Marchat
Marchot
Marchilli Magneto
Marco
Maro
Mars
Marvel
Masco
Maserati
Mason Hi Duyty
Massa

Master
Mastercraft
Matador
Matz
Maxin
Maxon
Mayo
Mazda
MBM *Venezuela*
Mc Cord
Mc Cormic
MCD
Mc Geihan N.O.
Mc Nutt
MCS
Mea
Meaker
Meissner
Menominee
Mercedes
Mercury
Merit
Mesco
Meteor
Meteor Eveready
Meter
Metor
Metropolitan
Mezger Soot Proof
MF *Massy Fergison*
MFG
M&G
MG Byran Ohio
Miami
Mica
Mica Ford Vesuvius
Mica Insulator
Mica Lain
Mica Por
Mica Sealed
Mica Special
Micro
Midland
Midwest
Mighty
Milbro Pep
Mill
Miller
Mills
Milo
Milwaukee
Minogue
Misco
Mitchell
M&M
M Mallory
MM Co.
Mobilite
Mock
Modco
Modern
Mogul
Molla
Monamobile
Monarch
Monarch Giant
Monroe
Mopar

More Fire
More Spark
Morgan
Mor-Power
Morris
Mors Magneto AV
Mosel
Mosler
Mosler Conical Type
Mosler Junior
Mosler Spitfire *many*
Mosler Superior
Mosler Vesuvius
Moto King
Moto Master
Moto Meter
Motor Car Supply
Motor Craft
Motor King
Motor Master
Motor Meter
Motor Pace
Motor Pep
Motorite
Motorola
MP
MPCO Ford
MSC
MTY
Mulkey
Multi Gap
Multiplex
Multi Point
Munroe
Murray
Mutual
Myer's Self Cleaning
Myles Standish
Myres

Nabon
Naco
Napa
NAT-I-ONAL
National
Nationalease
National Giant
National Tractor
Natoli Ney Ohio
Naylor
ND
Nebuco
Neff-T
Neiuport
Neustad
Neutronic Fuse
Never Miss
Never Skip More Spark
New Departure
Ne-We
New Way
NGK *Japan*
Nitro
Nixill
Nixite
NKW
Non Foul
Nonoyle

Nonstop
Norleigh Dismond *Japan*
North American
Northern King
Northern Primer
Northern Pacific
Northwest
Northwind
Norwest
No Flame
No-Skip
No-Ta
Not-Nac-Ford
NPA Co.
Nuport
Nu Point
Nu Star
Nu Static
Nu Way
Nurwalk
Nwee

Oda
O-Gee
Ohi-Gee
Ohio
Oil Proof
Ojus Ring Fire
OK
O Kay
O Keh
Old Dutch
Oleo *French*
Oleo Avation
Oleo Magneto
O.L.M. *Italian*
Olson
Olympic
Omatic
One For Four
100%
One Point
Only
OO
Opto
Our Own
Orswell
Ovee
Overland
Over Seas
Owl
Oxy
Ozark

Pace Setter
Pacific
Packard
Pacy
PAF
PAF Non Foul
Pal
Panhard
Panther Buick
Panther Delux Giant
Panther Ford
Panther Overland
Par
Paramount

Parkin Cleveland
Parkin Phila.
Parlo
Pasco
Pasha *Rajah*
Patten
Paulin
PDQ
Peco
Peerless
Peliter Primer
Penn
Penn Power
Pep
Perfect
Perfection
Perfex Coil Type
Perflex
Perma-Loc
Perron Oil Proof
Petticoat Standard
PF
P&H
Pharis
Philco
Philectric
Phillips 66
Phixt It
Phoenix
Pickwick
Pilot
Pioneer
Pittsburgh Visible
Pittsfield
Plain
Plain Primer
Pognon *French*
Pognon Constructeur
Pognon Hobson
Pognon Renault
Poindex
Pointless
Poky
Pola *French*
Ponsot *French*
Porter Keepskleen
Portland
Poulan
Power
Power Chief
Power Flash
Power Flyte
Power Plug
Powers
Powemower
P&P
Precision
Precision Bilt
Precision Bilt Automatic
Premier
Presto
Presto Kleen
Prest-O-Lite
Prime
Prime Kleen
Prime-Or-Kleen
Prismatic
Pro-Mo-Tor

Pronto
Pronto Omaha
Prosper
Prosper Champion
Protecto
Protek Plug
Proven
PRS
PRSCO
Purolator
Purotan
Pyro Action
Pyro Tex

Quad
Qualified
Quality
Quick Action
Quick Fire
Quick Fire XIV Ford
Quickfyr
Quick Start

Raccoon
Race
Radd
Radia
Radio
Radium
Raflex
Rainbow
Rajah
Rajah Cadillac
Rajah Giant
Rajah M Ford
Rajah Pasha
Rajah Primer
Rajah Rajite
Ra-Loy
Rambler
Ramseys Oil Proof
Randa
Randall
Ranger
Rapid Fire
Ray-O
Rays Special
RE
REA
Record
Red
Red Chief
Red Cross
Red Devil
Red Giant
Red Head
Red Head Big Boy
Red Mag Plug
Red Head Priming
Red Hot
Red Line
Red Marvel
Red Seal
Red Shield
Reed Hot Tube
Reeve
Reflex
Reflex Arrow

Reflex Conical
Reflex Diamond
Reflex Ford Special
Reflex Giant
Reflex Heavy Duty
Reflex Kid & Baby
Reflex Lightning
Reflex Marvel
Reflex Primer
Reflex Ranger
Reflex Torpedo
Reflex Tractor
Rejax
Reliable
Reliable Mutual
Reliance
Reliance Magneto
Reliance Spark in Water
Relishoe
Remax
Remax Rossing
Renault *French*
Renault Feres
Rentz
Rentz Buick
Rentz Deluxe
Rentz Nash
Rentz Glass Top
    Intensifier
Rentz Packard
Rentz Regular
Rentz Vita Stone Big Boy
Renu
Republic
R.eV. *French*
Reversible
Rev-O-Noc
Rex
Rex-A-One
Rex Lion
Rhelco
Rhodes Mor Fire
Rich
Rich Spark
Richfield
Riker
Rite
Rite Line
Riter
Rival
Riverside
Riverside Giant
RK
R&L Visible
RM
RMC
RMP
Road King
Robert Inst. Co.
Roche
Rocket Ign. Unit
Roda
Rogers
Roman
Romey
Rosa
Rosco
Royal

Rudex *French*
Ruillet *French*
Ruli DRP
Rulisons Red Devil
Rummells Aero
Rummells Super
RWB
Ryan

Safety
SA Fire Injection
SA Fire Igniter
Sando
Sandow
Samson
Saver Elsen
SC
Scavenger Pointless
SCDC
Schenectady
Schlecht
Schlee
Schucht
Schug
Scientific
Seagrave
Seal Pak
Sears
Seaver
Segic
Seiberling
Sentry Deluxe
Serb *French*
Service
Service Giant
Service Special for Buick
Service Special for Ford
Service Stone
Servis
SEV
SH *German*
Shainn
Shains Air Gap
Shamrock Jr.
Shark
Sharp
Sharp Spark
Shawnut
Shell
Sherman
Shield
Short
Shorty
Shur Fire
Shur Hit
Shurnuff
Shur Spark
Siberling
Sid
Siebert
Siemans
Sierre
Signal
Silt Edge
Silver Gun Shot
Silver Shield
Silver Sparker
Silver Streak

Silvex Co.
Simfrad
Simms
Simmons E. B.
Simmons E. C.
Simplex
Simplicity
Sioux Service
Skelko
Skelly
Sligo
Small Engine
SM Co. Detroit
SM Co. Jackson
Smith.
SMS Buick
Smyth Giant
Snappon
Snyder AG
Solar
Soo Line
Sootless *Dow & Oaks*
Sootproof
Southern
Southern RY
Southland
SP
Sparker
Sparko
Spark-O-Matic
Spark King
Spark Plug
Spark Rite
Special for Ford
Special Reflex for Ford
Special Service
Sped
Speed
Speedway
Spinx
Spiro
Spiro Anderson Ind.
Splitdorf
Splitdorf *blue hex.*
Splitdorf *green hex.*
Split Edge
Split Fire
Spoon Point
Sportman
Square Deal
SR
Standard
Standard Conical
Standard Power
Standard Ventilated
Standardware
Sta-Rite
Sta-Rite Detroit
Sta-Rite Gotham
Sta-Rite Venus
Sta-Rite Vulcan
Star
Star K
Star Priming
Star Spark
Starter
Start Rite
States

Static
Steel King
Sterling
Stevens
Stewart
Stewart-V-Ray
Stitt
Stitt Junior
Stitt Senior
Stitt Gasengin HD
St. Louis Aero
Stonebridge
Stone Core
Stonite
Stroms Special
Stromberg
Sturdy
Su-Dig
Sunbeam
Sun Power
Sunset
Super
Super Fire
Super Leader
Super Life
Super Macy
Super Patco
Super Power
Super Riverside
Super Trojan
Super Ward
Super Ware
Super X
Superior
Supreme
Sure Fire
Sure Pop
Sure Spark
Sure Thing ·
Surety JBC Co.
Survivor
Su Ton
SV
SVP *special parts*
Syracuse

Tabasco
Tad
Tago
Target
Tasco
Tayco
Tecumseh
Tekonsha
Tell Tale
Tetlows Aero
Texaco
Texas
That Stang
The Ball
The Edco
The M M M M
The Oil Proof
The P D
The Pel Co.
The V-Ray
The Point
The Soot Proof

The Starter
The Window
Ther Best
Thermos
Thoma Plug
Thomas
Thomas HC
Thor
Tig
Toger
Timesco
Tipco
Tiptop
Titan
TNT
Toffler
Torbensen
Toronado
Torpedo
Torpedo Reflex
Torrent
Towmotor
Town & Country
TPX
Tractor
Tramp
Trample Non Foul
Tri Lux
Triple
Triple A
Triple Diamond
Triple Fire
Triple L
Triumph
Triumph Cvitite
Trojan
Trojan Multi Fire
Trova
Troy
Tru Fire
True Test
True Value
Trump
Tungsten
Tungsten *blue porcelain*
Tungsten Heavy Duty
Tungsten Ford Special
Tungsten Primer
Turbo Fire
20th Century
Twin
Twin Fire
Twin Tact
Two-In-One
Two Spark
Two Spot
Two XL

UDS
UKO Model A
Uncle Sam
Unico
Unique
United
United Chicago
United Delco
United Delux
Universal

Universal Parts Inc.
UNO
UNXLD
U.S.
U-See-It
U.S. Rubber
Utility
Utility Trailers
Utopia

VA Car
Vacuum
Vacuum Fire
Valco Giant
Valcon
Valley Forge
Vanguard
Vanness
Vans OK
Varcon
Varcon Delux
Varcon Dual Fire
Varcon Premium Quality
VB
VD
Velox
Venus
Vibro
Vic-Mac
Victor
Victory
Viking
Viking Canada
Vim
Vim Blazer
Viso
Vital
Vital Bigsby
Vital Motorcycle
Viz Spark
Volcano
Volta
V-Ray
Vulcan
VW

Wachmans Sure Fire
Wade
Wagner
Wagner Lockheed
Walden
Walter
Wards Commander
Wards Riverside
Wards Standard Quality
Wards Supreme Quality
Wards Twin Electrode
Warnock
Warrior
Wasco
Washington
Wasp
Watkins
Watkins Tractor
Watters All Spark
Wayde Intensifier
Wayne
W-B-Hand-E

WC	Westric	Wisner	XL G-M-E Co.
Wearever	Wezlman	Witherbee	X Ray
Wearwell	Whitaco	Wizarc	XS Power
Web	Whitaker	Wizard	XXX
Wellman Breather	White Ace	Wizard Standard	
Wellman Howe Push Clean	White Cap	Wizard Supreme	Yale
Wellman Turn Clean	White Deamon	Wizard Thermo Disc	Yankee
Well Motor	White Flame	Wizard Twin Fire	York Giant
Wermes Leakproof	White Magic 50	WK	Yortox
Wes	Whites Delux	WNAX	
Wes Plug	Whites Supreme	Wollo	Zenith
West Plug Ford	Whyte	Wonder *Dr. Coyles*	Zenith Imperial
Wes Plug Giant	Wico	Woodworth	Zephyr
Wes Plug Junior	WIK Bonded	Workall	Zig-Zag
Wes Plug Special	Wiley	World	Zip
Westchester	Willard	Worth More	Zit Zit
Western Auto	Williams E.Q.	Worth More Supreme	ZWP
Western Electric	Window Spark	Wright	
Western Electric Pittsfield	Windsor	Wright Automatic Cleaner	
Western Giant	Winestock *detachable*		
Western Weld	Wing Foot	XLCR	
	Wipac		

This mini list may help those who intend to collect only car names on plugs. The following were for the cars whose names appear on the plugs.

Allstate *car and plug, both sold by Sears*	Franklin	Packard
Bugatti	FWD *truck*	Panhard *possible*
Buick	G.M.C. *truck and farm*	Rambler
Cadillac	Haynes	Renault
Chalmers	Hudson	Sea Graves *truck*
Chandler	I.H.C. *truck and farm*	Studebaker
Chrysler	Isotta	Stutz
De Dion Buton	La Salle	Subaru
Ford	Nash	
	Overland	

This list of familiar car names are only coincidental, and were not for those particular cars.

Acme	Columbia	Lincoln	Peerless
Ajax	Gardner	Mercedes	Star
Auburn	Imperial	Mercury	Thomas
Cleveland	Jordan	Mitchell	Viking

Following are a few ads out of old automotive magazines of the early teens showing how plug manufacturers vied for the highly competitive market.

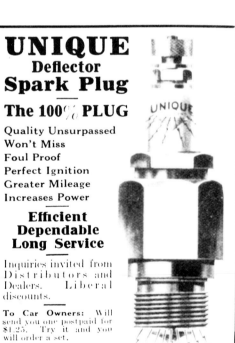

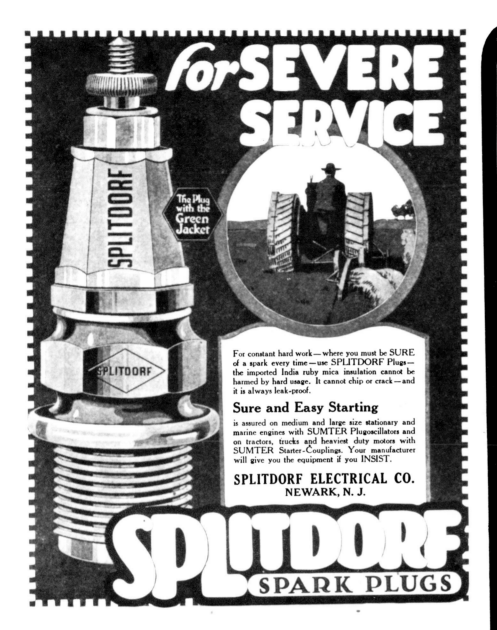

The pictures on the following pages represent the multitude of electrode arrangements and design variations patented during the first thirty years of manufacture.

All spark plugs have a center electrode, or anode, which is insulated from the outer body. Every spark plug has one or more grounding electrodes or cathodes connected to the spark-plug body. The fixed or adjustable gap between these two electrodes is where the spark occurs.

Spark plugs can be categorized by counting the number of points between which the spark jumps. The first group are two-point electrode arrangements, similar to today's popular surviving design.

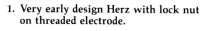

1. Very early design Herz with lock nut on threaded electrode.

2. Common two point similar to today's design.

3 & 4. Two variations of the hooked grounding electrode. Hook is intended to carry oil drips away from gap area. Example shown: Curtis.

5. End-to-end gap with exaggerated drip hook. Example shown: Janesville Tractor.

6. Another end-to-end design with fluted center electrode. Example shown: The Oil Proof.

7. This end-to-end has a little mini-chamber in the center of the electrode. Example shown: Radd.

8. An arc shoot or channel to blow out oil deposits when ignited. Example shown: Express.

9. A flattened flush center electrode when loosened from top can be turned for cleaning. Example shown: Nabon.

10. Large center electrode, milk-bottle shape, is an attempt at carrying more heat away from gap. Example shown: Champion Aircraft.

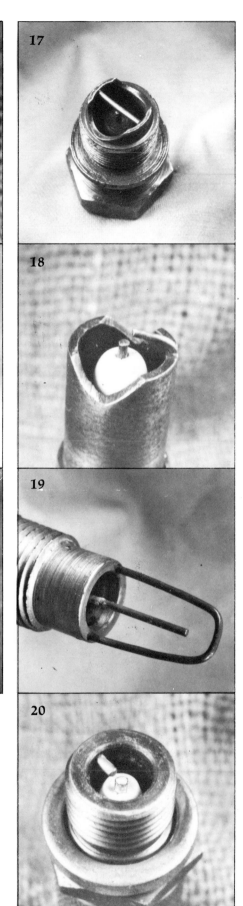

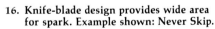

11. Bullet-shaped electrode serves same heat dissipating function. Example shown: Rhodes More Fire.

12. Built-in soot chamber creates smaller initial combustion area to blow out potential deposits. Example shown: Dr. Coyles Wonder.

13. Almost totally enclosed soot chamber creates a venturi-like blowout action. Example shown: BG Self Cleaning.

14. A rather complicated way to do a simple job. Example shown: Moto Metor.

15. Crossbar with double oil-drip points. Example shown: Benford.

16. Knife-blade design provides wide area for spark. Example shown: Never Skip.

17. Crossbar with relief cuts in skirt for better airflow. Example shown: Heinze.

18. Another version with relief cuts in skirt. Example: Never Miss.

19. This deep dip positions spark more accurately in the center of the combustion chamber. Try to oil foul this one! Example shown: Rajah.

20. Flush or recessed design is typical of aircraft plugs. Example shown: Champion Aero.

21

25

28

22

26

29

23

27

30

24

21. The fancy step arrangement was probably for greater heat convection or soot traps. Example shown: Perkin.

22. Another recessed design with vent holes. Example shown: Gyro.

23. Flush crossbar. Example shown: Bethlehem Aviation.

24. No apparent advantage to this loop design. Example shown: Anderson.

25. Very deeply recessed; must have fouled easily. Example shown: Griffen Renewable.

The next group is called three point, having one center elec-

trode and two grounding electrodes, creating two places for the spark to jump. The thinking behind this design must have been that two gaps are better than one.

26. Simple three point. Example shown: Rev-O-Noc.

27. Oil drip version of gas engine special used in Maytag Multi motors. Example shown: Champion.

28. Nicely designed version by Bosch.

29. French chisel design by Joly.

30. Violin shape by Herz.

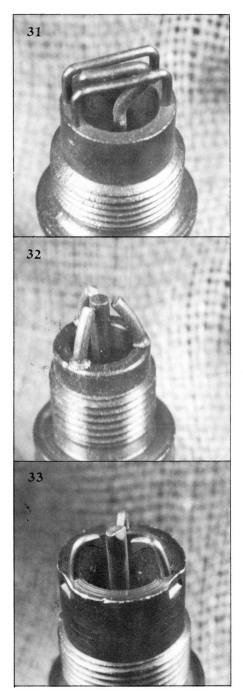

31

32

33

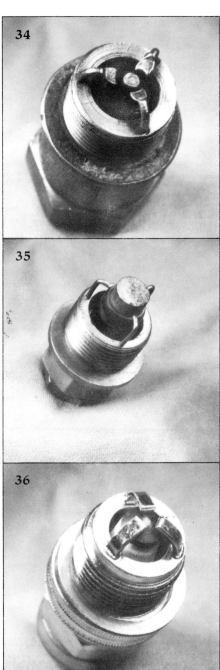

34

35

36

37

38

39

31. Parallel-bar design, large arcing area. Example shown: Fyrac, National.

This group represents the four-point electrode design, which includes three grounding electrodes and a single center electrode. Three separate gaps are created for the spark to jump.

32. A very sturdy design. Example shown: AC #14.

33. Crimping attaches grounding points to Red Head Big Boy.

34. Flattened points create more surface area for spark. Example shown: Bosch.

35. A very showy design by Dow.

36. Another showy, well-constructed design. Example shown: Stitt.

One more step in the multi-point design is the five point. Two basic variations of this type exist. One uses four individual points for grounding electrodes, while the other has a continuous circle surrounding the center electrode, slit crossways to create four separate surfaces for arcing. The slits were most likely for better ventilation and heat dissipation.

37. This Bethlehem design called five point showed a five-point star on the porcelain.

38. Aircraft plugs utilized the five-point design as seen in this Champion.

39. This cloverleaf cover created a soot chamber effect. Example shown: Herz.

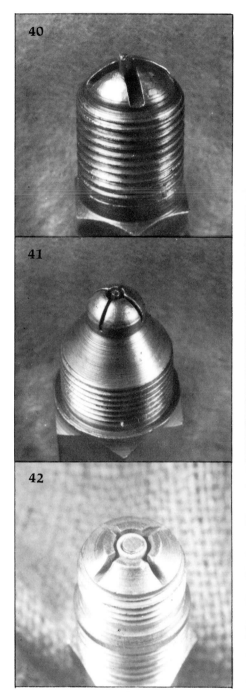

40

41

42

43

44

45

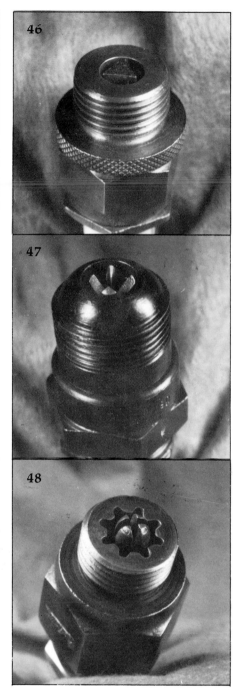

46

47

48

40. Early attempt at slotted design. Example shown: Never Miss #8.

41. Clean-appearing four slot by Sharpspark.

42. A more recent entry by Lectra.

43. The four slots in this cage affair had a blowout effect like a soot chamber. Example shown: Lectro.

Multi-point center electrodes.

44. Two-point center is a more recent Bitter Root design.

45. Interesting two-point center is a nice display piece. Example shown: Pittsfield.

46. A three-point center is formed by a triangle. Example shown: Tri-Lux.

47. This Poky split-end electrode forms four points.

Single-point plugs are actually two point, with the absence of a grounding electrode. The base completely surrounds the center electrode forming a soot chamber. The gap on these plugs is basically fixed.

48. Similar to Poky this early Packard script, has a four-point electrode arcing to eight points around perimeter.

49

50

51

52

53

54

55

56

57

58

49. A twelve-point center arcs to outer circle. Example shown: Albright.

50. A four-point center electrode arcs to two semicircle ground electrodes.

51. Belmark & Delmark.

52. Flash.

53. Mosler.

54. Splitdorf.

55. Breech Block.

56. Auburn.

57. American Eagle.

58. Hill L&M.

59

60

61

62

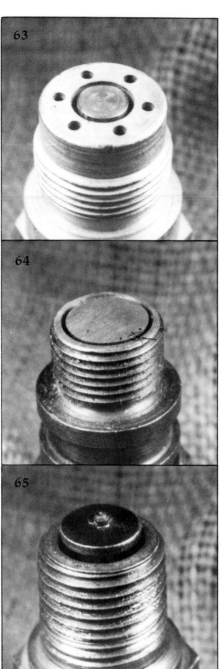

63

64

65

66

67

68

59. Standard.
60. Mosler.
61. Wraparound saddle unscrews for cleaning.
62. This single point is adjustable.

Full-disc electrodes have a full 360° surface to accept the spark. Some are adjustable, and others are not.

63. Double E.
64. Bethlehem Life Time.
65. Unique (Adj.)
66. Pep.
67. Dr. Ferrels (Adj.)
68. Winestock (Adj.)

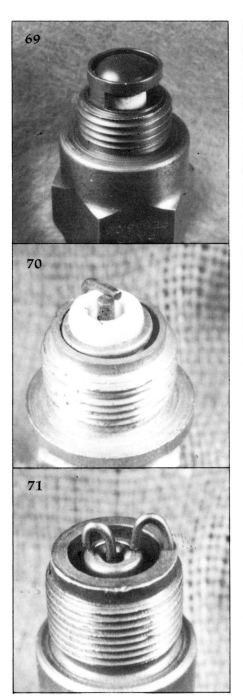

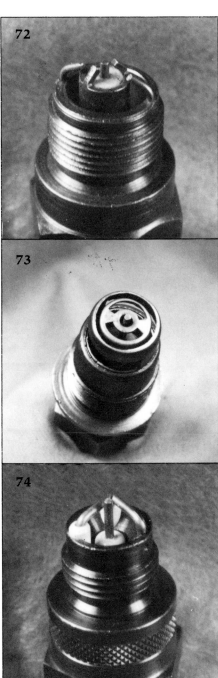

69. **Best (Adj.)**

Double-gap electrodes are actually intensifiers located at the business end of the plug. A distinct advantage here is that the two sparks occur simultaneously in the combustion chamber.

70. Ojus-Ring of Fire.

71. Twin Fire.

72. Two Spark Double Plug.

73. Chain-O-Spark.

74. Holms—Twin Shot.

Few plugs have moving parts, but those that do make interesting pieces.

75 & 76. Two styles of the Fan Flame, one with eight notches, and one with ten. Another version, not shown, has no notches. Moving air causes the fan to spin, slinging any oil deposits away.

77. This spur, or fan arrangement, is much the same as the Fan Flame. Example shown: Multi-Point.

78. A captive ball gets pushed around during combustion and cleans carbon away. Example shown: Dur-A-Ball.

79

80

81

As with any collection there is much associated material. Spark-plug collecting is no exception.

79. Spark-plug wrenches supplied in auto manufacturers' tool kits or sold in auto stores make interesting displays.

80. Small wrenches were given away as advertisements, included in tool kits, or with replacement magnetos. They were intended for plug gaping, magneto adjustment, or top wire nut removal.

81. A collection of accessories including wire terminals, intensifiers, splash shields used on motorcycles and wash machines, static supressors, and (on far right) a spark tester. A tube of gas (probably neon) inside this tester is sensitive to high voltage, and the little window glows when metal end is held against plug wire.

82

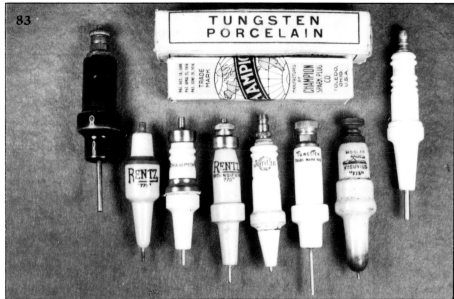

83

TUNGSTEN PORCELAIN

84

That's the Plug!

Champion
DEPENDABLE SPARK PLUGS

CHAMPION SPARK PLUG CO. TOLEDO. OHIO. U.S.A

85

ARROW

REFLEX

SPARK PLUGS
EVERY PLUG FULLY GUARANTEED

82. Cutaway display plug for dealers shows construction of typical Chicago-type plug.

83. Replacement cores. New porcelain cores were sold to be inserted into old plug bodies.

84. Tin sign circa 1920. 12 × 18 inches.

85. Reflex storage case.

86. Auto Lite counter display case with round glass front makes nice enclosure for collection but holds only a few plugs.

87. Electrified counter display lets customer see spark jump across gap when button is pushed. Note add-on brass ring with alligator clip. An easy conversion, so you can observe any plug.

88. When acquiring new old-stock plugs, don't throw the boxes away, as they, too, make a nice colorful display.

89. Some plugs used to come in metal lithographed cans. Quickway is a small socket set made by the Bethlehem spark plug company.

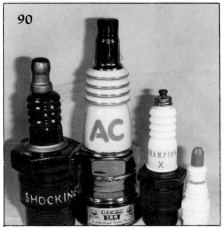

90

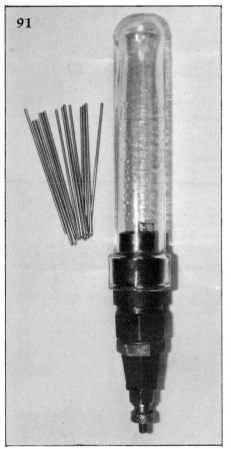

91

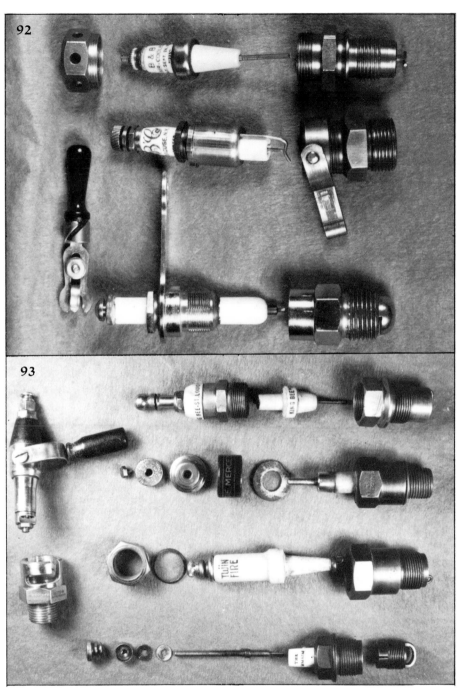

92

93

90. Beam whisky bottle and rubber
    Champion bottle used as advertising
    display and small Champion Avon
    aftershave. Shocking is unknown
    ceramic bottle.

91. Early method of plug cleaning was this
    glass tube affair. Pour in a little
    kerosene, and snug the plug in a
    rubber grommet. Hold tight and shake.
    The pointed pins inside would chip
    carbon away.

92. Quick-detachable plugs top to bottom:
    B & B Air Cooled, BC, Breeck Block.

93. Winestock Q.D. at top, left to right.
    The MMMM with removable center
    and grounding electrode while

porcelain stays crimped into base. Twin
Fire is representative of the majority of
replaceable core plugs. Herz has an
insulator as an integral part of the
base, and a decorative porcelain
overshield to brandish the name. King
Bee has two porcelains; the internal
one acts as an intensifier.

94

95

96

97

94. Bill Bonds' fabulous working display of intensifiers. Tied into a Model T coil and a rotary-type switch, each porcelain and intensifier combination can be observed arcing to a common center disc.

95. Miniature spark and glow plugs used in model airplane engines. Penny shown for size comparison.

96. 10 MM plugs were used for a short period of time in the late thirties and forties by Chevrolet and Packard.

97. Early Champion plugs.

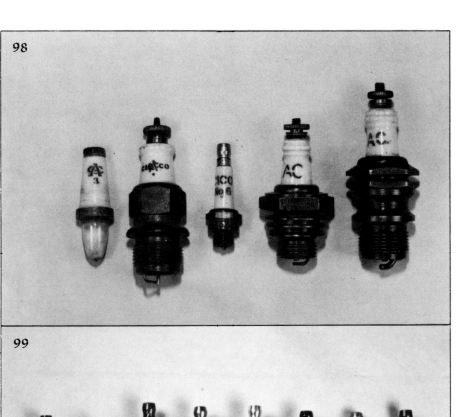

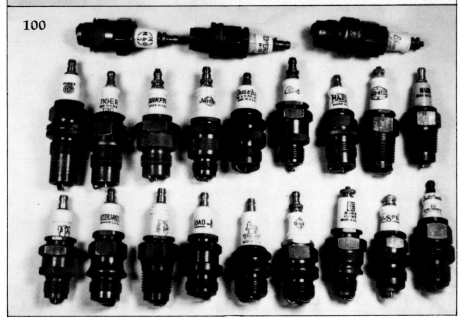

98. Early AC plugs. Notice logo changes.

99. 14 MM plugs 1940s to present are not very desirable to collect. Some have interesting porcelain-like Fisk tires with child and tire, Coast-to-Coast and Allstate with U.S. map. Very few had packing nut with replaceable porcelain. For the name collector, some names appeared only on 14 MM size plugs.

100. Common Chicago-type plugs, too numerous to picture all.

101

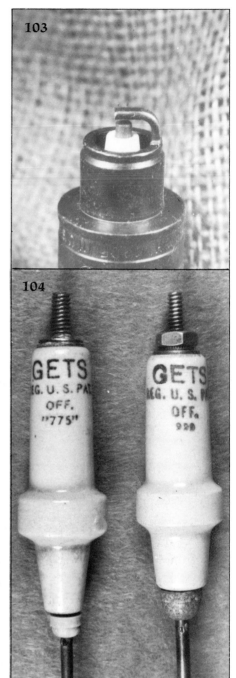

103

102

104

101. Throw away ⅞ plugs of most recent production were one-piece construction with no possibility of replacing the porcelain.

102. Some popular names in private labeling.

103. Like the off-center coin or the upside-down airplane on a stamp, every hobby has its freaks. This threadless spark plug must have slipped past quality control.

104. "999" spark plugs with light-blue porcelain were an ill-fated attempt at one-upmanship over the popular 775 porcelain.

105

106

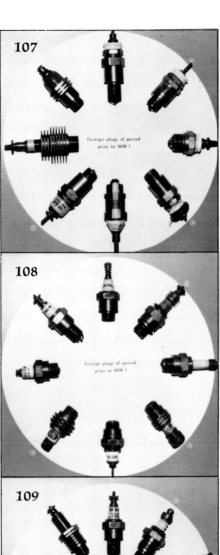

107

108

109

110

111

105 & 106. Aircraft engines were shipped with protection plugs in place of spark plugs. They were filled with silica gel to absorb moisture.

107 & 108. The Air Force Museum in Dayton, Ohio, has a nice display of early aircraft plugs. Shown here are a few examples of foreign plugs prior to World War I.

109. Another Air Force Museum group of plugs developed between World War I and 1930. Notice in all three pictures the heavy use of cooling fins.

110 & 111. Ponsot & Pognon are two similar-sounding French aircraft plugs.

112

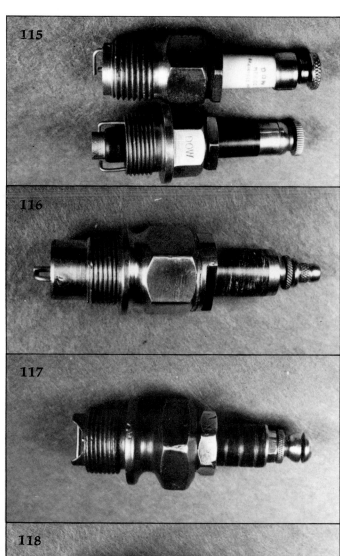

115

116

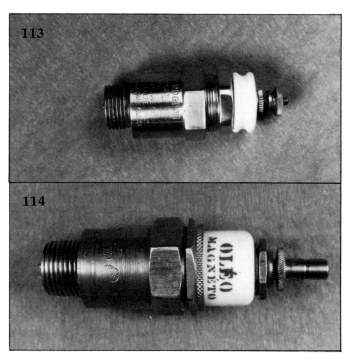

113

114

117

118

112. Early aircraft plugs
Left to right, top row (all mica): B.G., Frigo, Champion, Splitdorf (brass), Bethlehem Life Time with phenolic plastic cover removed.
Bottom row: Kopf (German), Leda (French), Champion Aero, Bethlehem, Lodge, Bosch.

113. A very showy Pognon 18 MM aircraft plug.

Shown next are a group of mica insulated plugs, not for aircraft use.

114. Oleo, another popular French aircraft plug.

115. Dow mica top on right has all brass base and is shown next to its porcelain counterpart. A comparison of the two popular thread sizes can also be seen with the ½-inch pipe thread on left used primarily in Fords! The right-hand plug is the popular ⅞-inch thread, used on most all other makes.

116. Sootles with all-brass body.

117. Heinze has steel body and brass packing nut.

118. Wright, notice script name stamped on nickel-plated base.

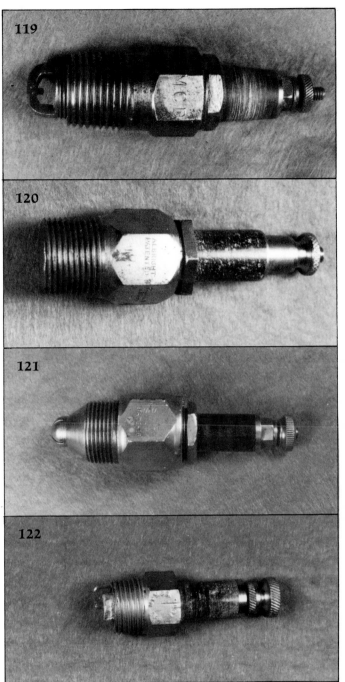

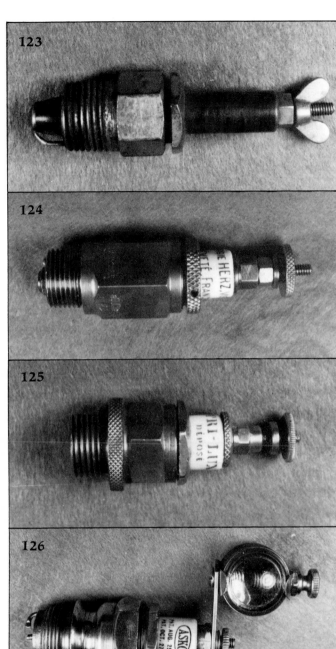

119. MCD, notice removable saddle-type grounding electrode arrangement similar to the MMMM shown earlier in chapter.

120. Albright has nice, clean look.

121. Sharp Spark carries a 1908 patent date.

122. Some mica plugs had no name showing; however, this one has a November 1901 patent date.

123. Another example with no markings at all.

All brass plugs are much sought after by collectors.

124. This very early example of a brass Herz is the imported plug before they were manufactured in the U.S.

125. Tri-Lux early French brass.

126. Asko with aftermarket intensifier attached, 1921 patent date.

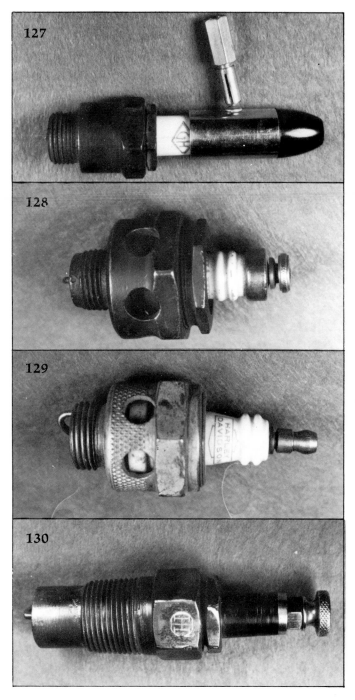

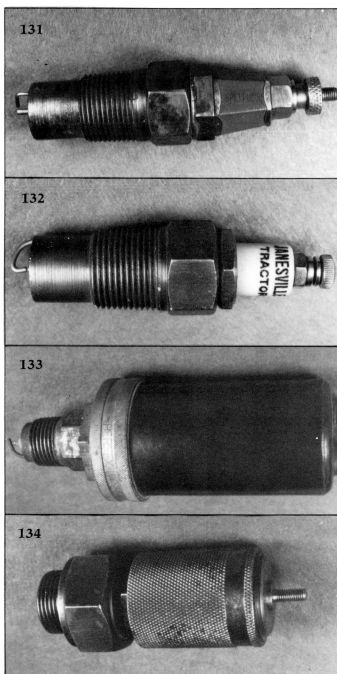

Motorcycle plugs had an 18 MM thread like aircraft plugs, and were usually fitted with some cooling device.

127. GH, a Belgian motorcycle plug with a spring-loaded top. A slight push against the Bakelite tip moved the outer sleeve down to contact the base, grounding out the plug to stop the engine.

128. Champion.

129. Champion, made for Harley-Davidson.

Tractors and stationary engines used the largest plugs, some as long as six inches with a ¾-inch pipe thread.

130. This IHC plug was made by Bethlehem.

131. Splitdorf has hexagonal green porcelain over shield. Actual insulating material is mica.

132. Janesville Tractor.

The next three examples are coil plugs, which were used primarily in boats.

133. Perfex.

134. Bosch.

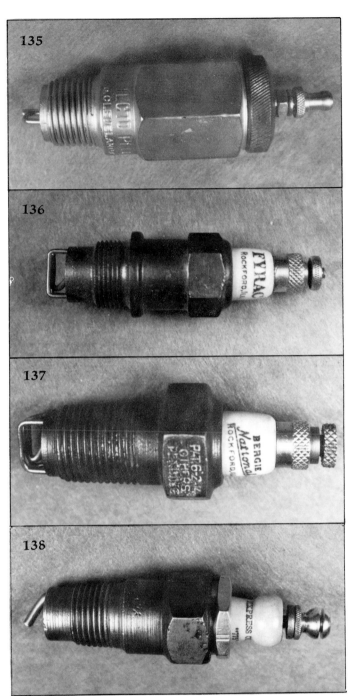

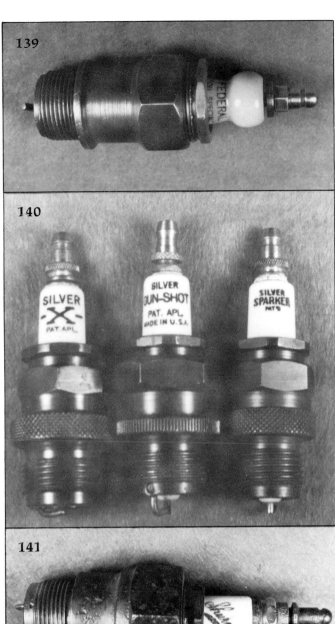

135. Protecto.

Look-alike plugs are very similar in appearance and construction but carry different names. Some companies had a premium line and an economy line of merchandise. Others used the same design for their own brand as well as the private branding they may have supplied to others.

136. Fyrac.

137. National carries June 1914 patent date.

138. Express Oil Type.

139. Federal Oil Special.

140. Silver X, Silver Gun Shot, Silver Sparker, all sold by same company.

The next four examples are air-breather plugs.

141. Shurnuff, small breather mechanism missing from this plug normally sticks up over top of base hex.

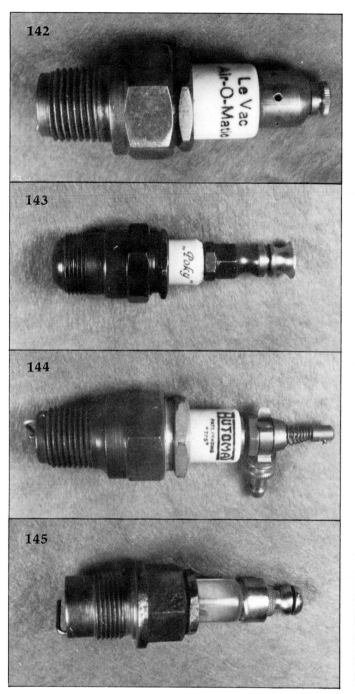

142. Levac Air-O-Matic.

143. Poky, breathes through porcelain.

144. Automat, has an external spring-loaded check valve.

145. Beacon Lite.

146. Prismatic.

147. Anderson.

148. The Window.

149. Viz Spark, has magnifying lens on top of the porcelain and carries a November 1917 patent date.

Here are five visible spark glass insulator plugs. These plugs allowed you to observe the explosion in the cylinder. Imagine an eight- or twelve-cylinder engine running at night with these. It must have been like having a built-in theater marquee.

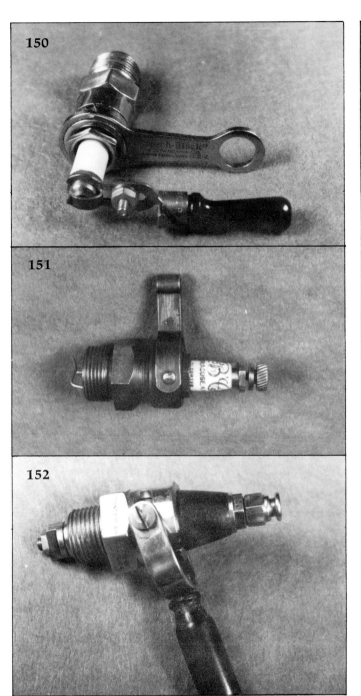

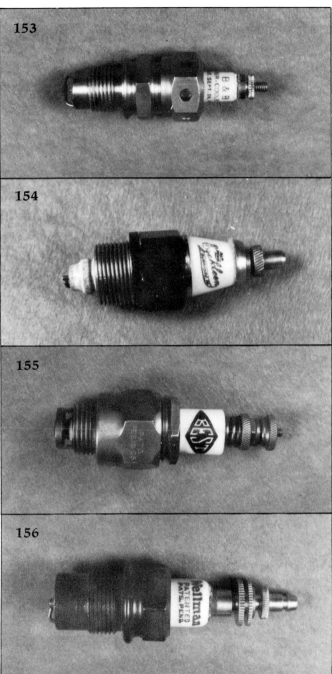

Quick-detachable plugs are probably the most desirable among collectors. They are very interesting to say the least.

150. Breech Block also has quick-detachable wire terminal.

151. BC.

152. Winestock.

153. B & B Air Cooled had no handle but was only supposed to be finger tight. Dated 1922.

154. Ezekleen, not a true detachable because it required a wrench, but still easier than total plug removal.

The do-it-yourself quick-cleaning game goes on with two more approaches.

155. Best. Depress a strong spring to upset a compression seal while engine is running and force cold air in and out to purge carbon deposits. Dated February 1906.

156. Wellman. Loosen large knurled nut; raise center electrode; and turn against bottom of porcelain.

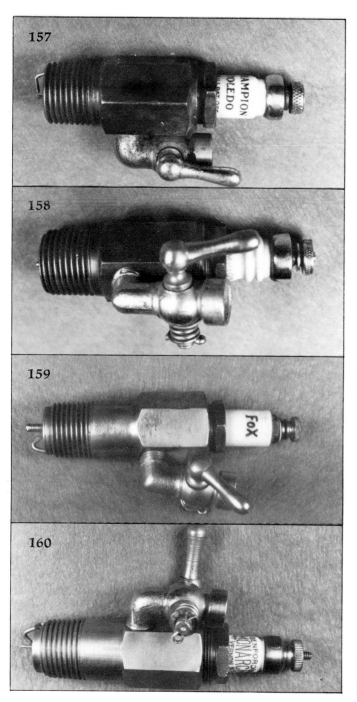

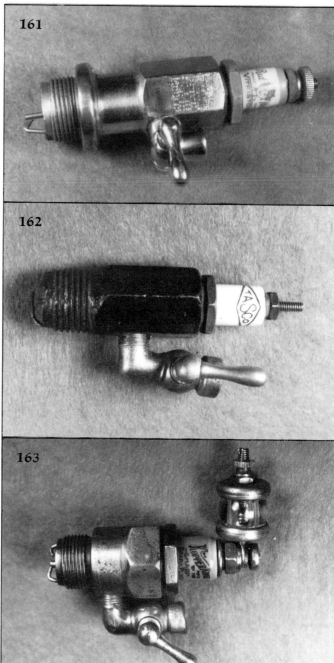

Primer plugs are also sought
after by collectors, and many
varieties exist.

157. Early Champion.

158. Later Champion.

159. Fox using Red Head base.

160. Benford's Monarch.

161. Red Head.

162. Tasco.

163. This cup was apparently added on by
owner.

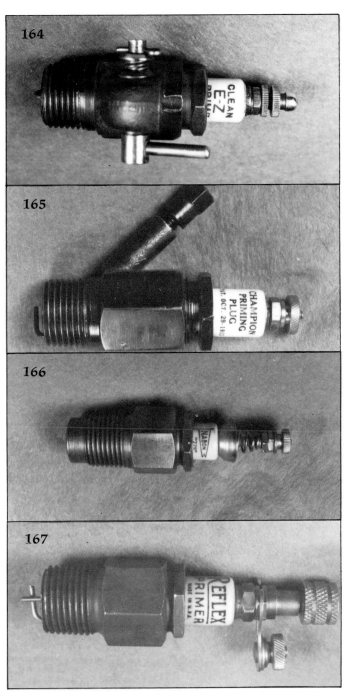

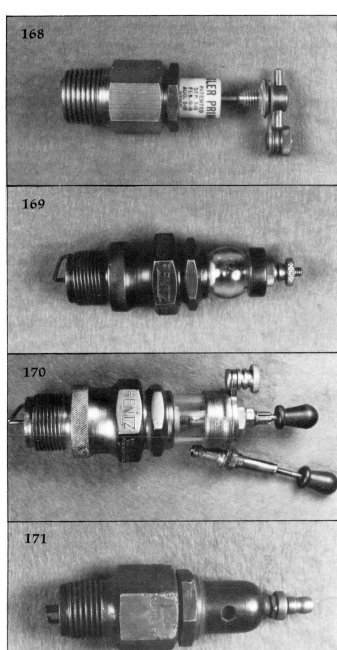

164. E-Z Clean Prime. This version has a priming cup cast on as an integral part of the base.

165. Champion needle point primer.

166. Nabon, spring-loaded release valve through porcelain.

167. Reflex. Turn-lock device primes through porcelain.

168. Mosler. Very impractical; wire had to be removed. Center electrode unscrewed and reassembled, a rather time consuming exercise. 1915.

Several styles of built-in intensifiers have emerged through the years.

169. Early Rentz version never got off the ground.

170. More popular Rentz with rare grounding lug. For some reason these lugs were cut off most plugs. Possibly the small retaining pin broke under vibration, causing the handle to fall and shorting out the plug, thereby creating a nuisance for their owners. This plug was the most expensive plug ever sold, containing over twenty-five different parts and weighing ½ pound.

171. Certified has external spark window in fiberoid-type insulator cover. Brass base.

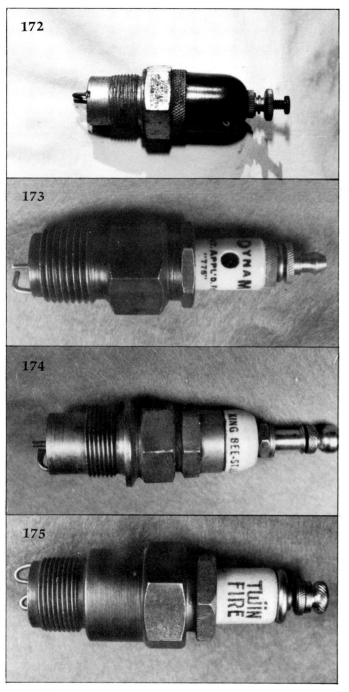

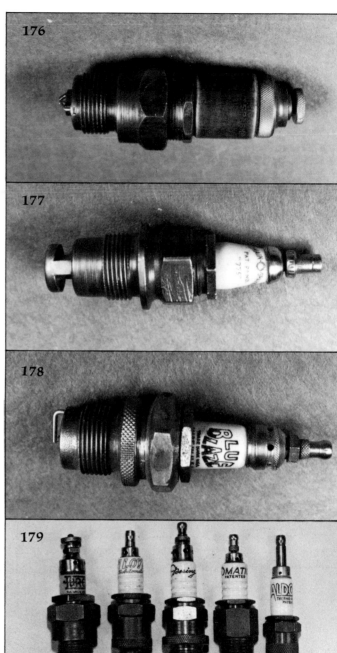

172. Cumming, similar to Certified.

173. Dynam, viewing hole in porcelain.

174. King Bee, built-in intensifier not visible.

175. Twin Fire early type of combustion chamber intensifier.

176. Two Spark Double Plug, same type as above, dated 1920.

177. Chain-O-Spark, another in "cylinder" double gap.

178. Blue Blaze, with top-mounted intensifier.

179. A group of more recent top-mounted intensifiers. Left to right: Duro, Lloyd, Dering, Omatic, Aldor.

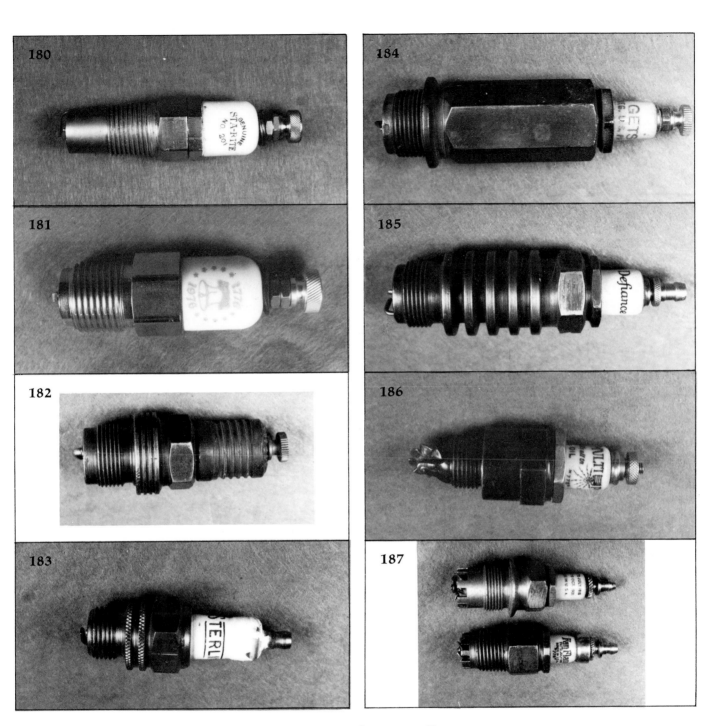

Miscellaneous oddities abound in spark plug design; here are but a few.

180. 1907 Sta-Rite.

181. 1976 reproduction of Sta-Rite by AC; only one hundred made.

182. Cross Country, rubber top over porcelain.

183. Sterling, white paint and rubber-stamp-type name crudely put over Blue Crown was probably due to a shortage of cores to supply production needs.

184 & 185. Gets & Defiance, very tall, undoubtedly an attempt at cooling, these plugs measure four inches tall.

186. Multi Point, has spinning spur. "It's all in the wheel."

187. Fan Flame, with spinning fan, dated 1918.

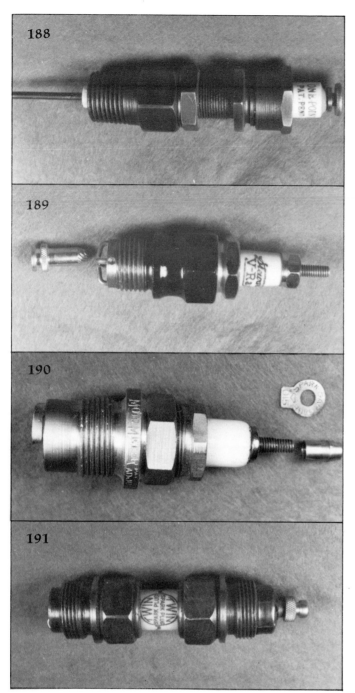

188. One Point, was intended to fire off the top of the piston. These must have been tricky to adjust.

189. Stewart V-Ray. When wire nut is removed it can be used to clean electrodes.

190. Moto Meter. Each plug supplied with a .015 gap gauge under the wire nut.

191. Twin, a reversible end plug. When one wore out you just turned it over.

192. Twin-Double Service.

193. Series and double plugs from left to right: Sudig, Peco, and Superior.

194. Diesel glow plugs.

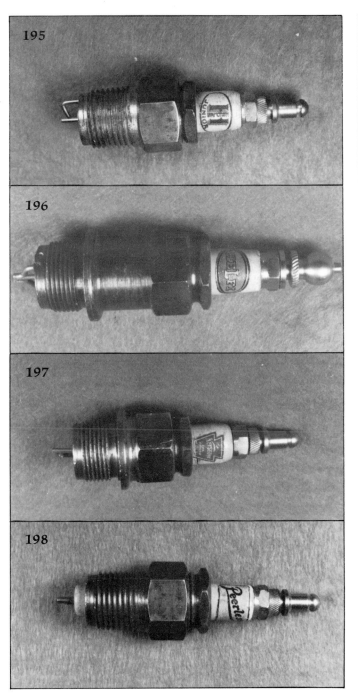

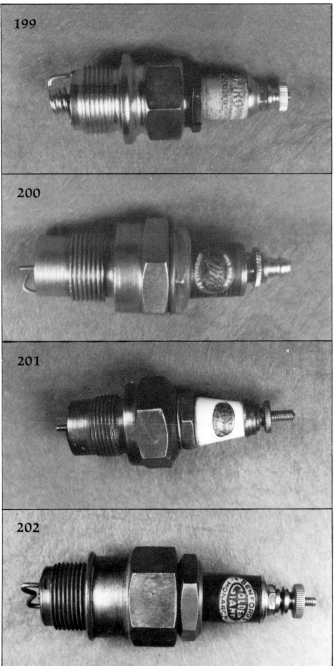

Decals were used primarily on clay-core plugs. Hunt porcelain of Kokomo, Indiana, produced this nonglossy insulator. Names were unable to be fired on this type of insulator.

195. Hercules.

196. Helfi.

197. Keystone.

198. Peerless.

199. Spiro. This clay core had name depressed in surface.

200. Ovee, decal on mica top.

201. Wards Soot Proof uses decal on porcelain "over shield."

202. Benfords Golden Giant has decal on one piece porcelain.

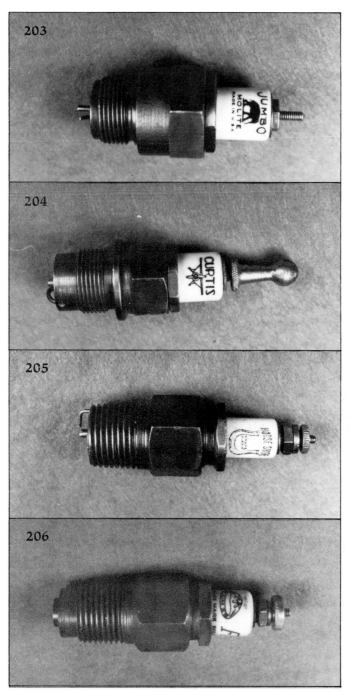

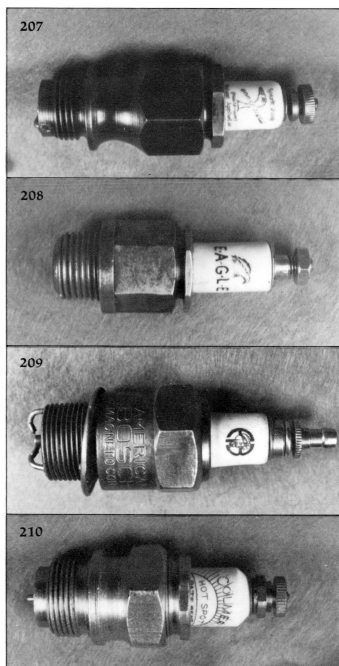

A small group of plugs make interesting display material, because of eye-catching art work on the porcelain.

203. Jumbo has elephant.

204. Curtis with 1930s-style monoplane.

205. Horse Shoe.

206. Flash shows 14k ring.

207. Goose Neck.

208. Eagle is an Irish plug.

209. American Bosch shows race driver's face with goggles.

210. Colmer Hot Spot has an aurora look.

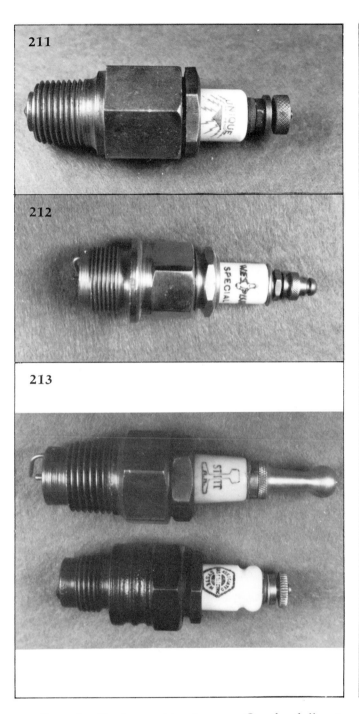

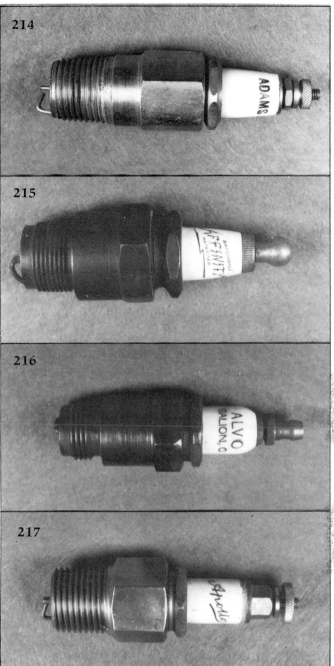

211. Unique has blue letters with red lightning radiating.

212. Wesplug has miniature plug but poor quality printing.

213. Stitt & Associated Gas & Electric depict a railroad iron and a chain-link hex nut. Both of these plugs were attempts by their users to prevent theft.

On the following pages is an alphabetical presentation of typical collectible plugs, most of which are standard plugs with no special features.

214. Adams.

215. Affinity.

216. Alvo—Rare.

217. Apollo—brass base.

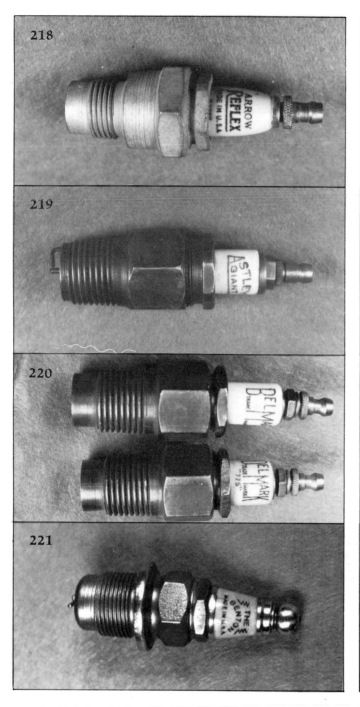

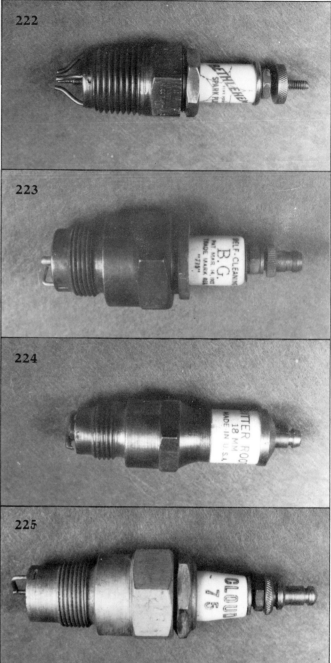

218. Arrow.

219. Astley.

220. Belmark—Delmark, a spelling error on a private brand created two variations when a second order was placed.

221. Benton blue porcelain.

222. Bethlehem—Five Point, dated October 1898.

223. B.G. Self-Cleaning, dated March 1922.

224. Bitter Root, a 1950s plug.

225. Cloud 75, a Chicago newsstand drugstore.

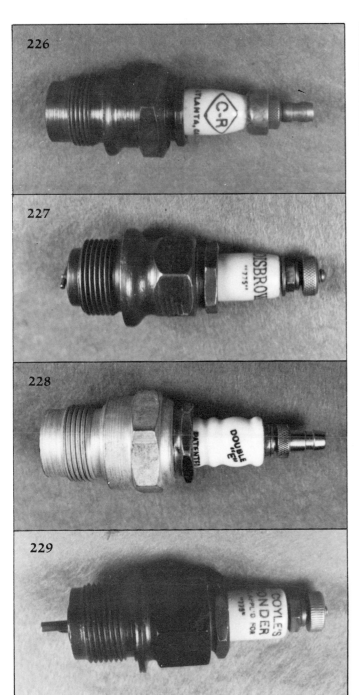

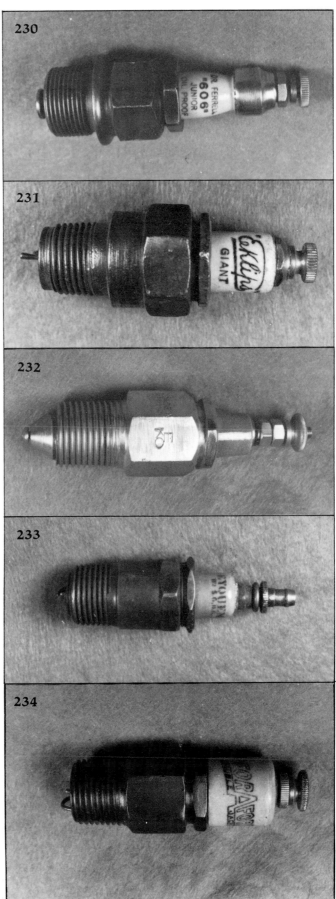

226. CR stands for Charles Rentz.

227. Disbrow.

228. Double E.

229. Dr. Coyles Wonder, actually a medicine.

230. Dr. Ferrell 606 JR.

231. Eklips Giant.

232. Eko, blue porcelain, German.

233. Eyquem, French brass plug with orange porcelain.

234. For a Ford, orange porcelain.

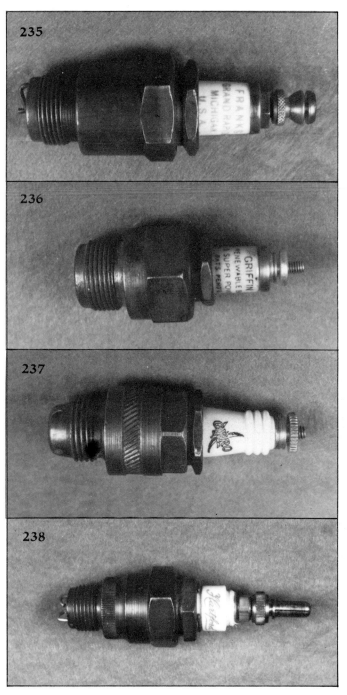

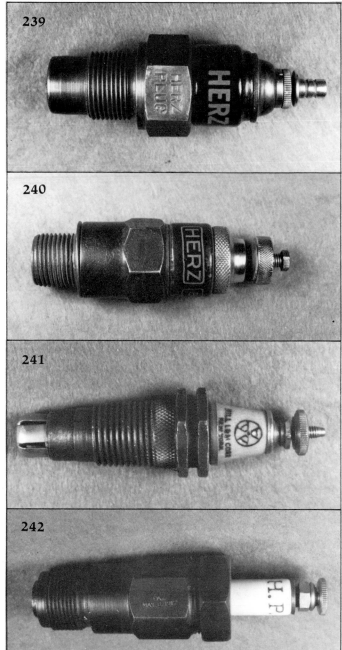

235. Franks, a rather plain, but rare plug.

236. Griffin, Renewable Bar.

237. Gyro.

238. Hartford.

239. Herz.

240. Herz.

241. Hill L & M. This one is also called AAA.

242. H.P., dated May 1917.

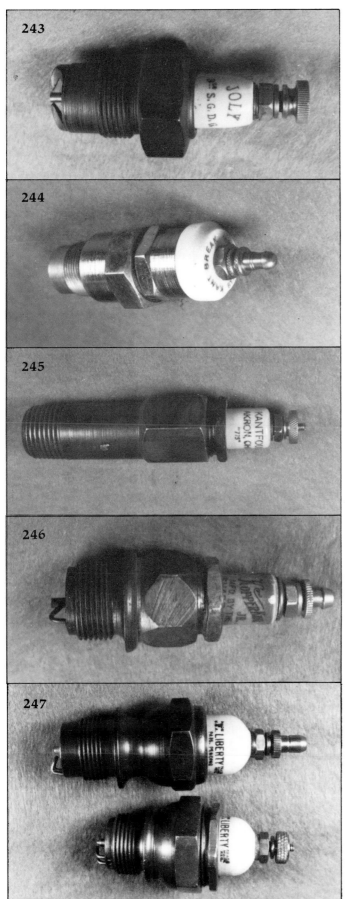

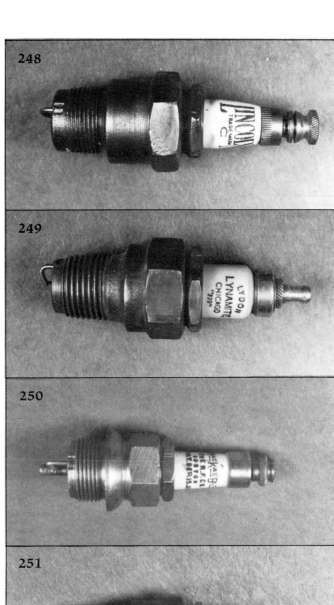

243. Joly.

244. Kant Break.

245. Kantfoul.

246. Kopper King Jr.

247. Liberty. Shorter plug is brass.

248. Lincoln (not the car).

249. Lydon Lynamite.

250. Mackaeblitz, dated September 1903.

251. Macquaire, blue porcelain with white area for name.

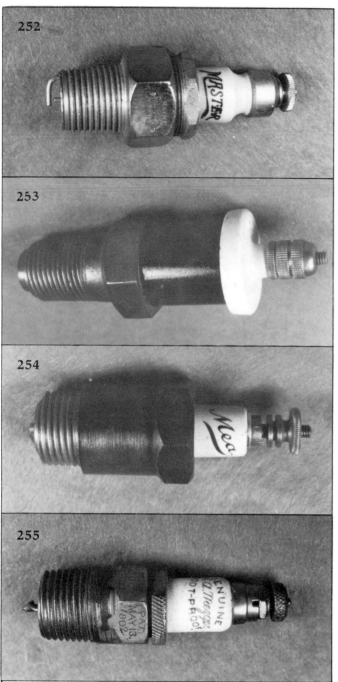

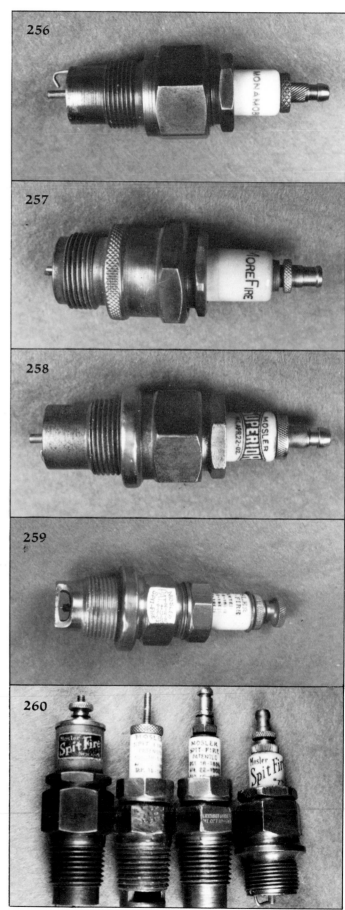

252. Master, dated October 1898.

253. McCormick.

254. Mea.

255. Mezger, May 1902.

256. Monamobile.

257. More Fire.

258. Mosler.

259. Mosler, very nice displayable plug with date on porcelain and stamp in base.

260. Mosler, one of the earliest U.S. manufacturers of plugs, made a wide variety of designs. Some had a fiber sleeve over the porcelain with a decal affixed.

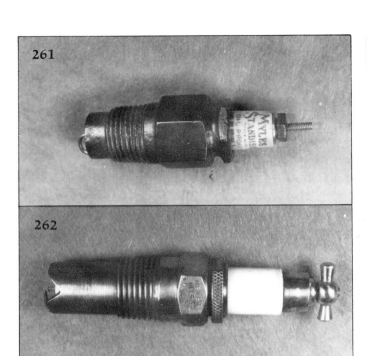

261

265

262

266

263

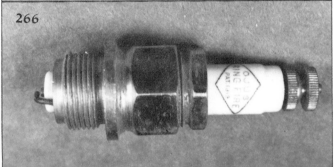

267

264

268

261. Myles Standish.

262. Never Miss.

263. Never Miss.

264. Never Skip.

265. Nonoyle. This plug carried patent number rather than date.

266. Ojus—Ring Fire.

267. Packard, May 1897 and October 1898.

268. PAF Non Foul.

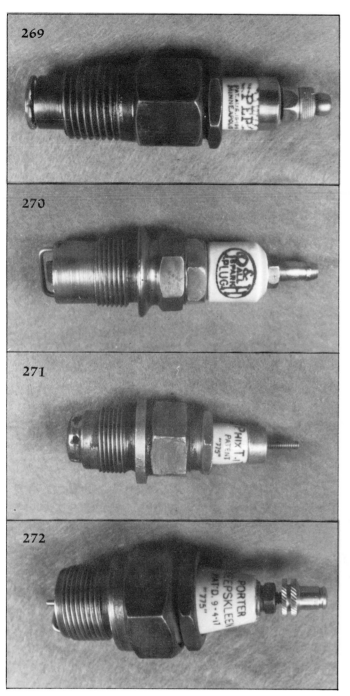

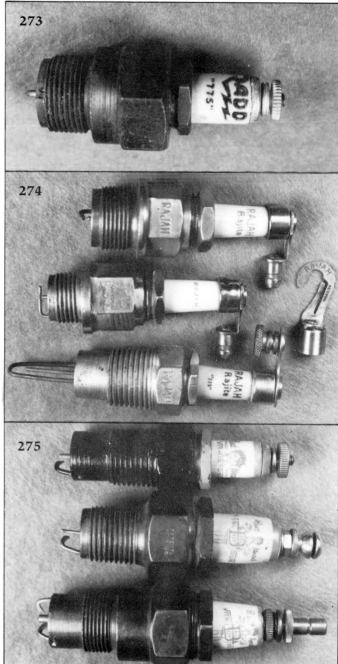

269. Pep, August 1914.

270. P & H All Spark.

271. Phixt-It.

272. Porter Keepskleen, September 1917.

273. Radd.

274. Rajah. They also made their own connectors.

275. Redhead. Plug on top has black painted body, and red painted packing nut. This usually indicated a rebuilt plug.

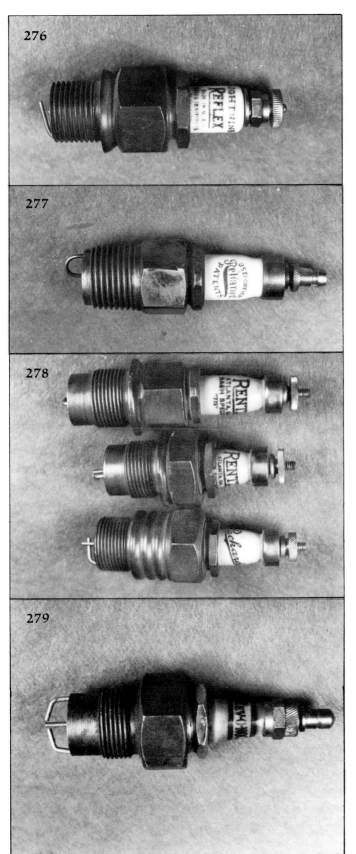

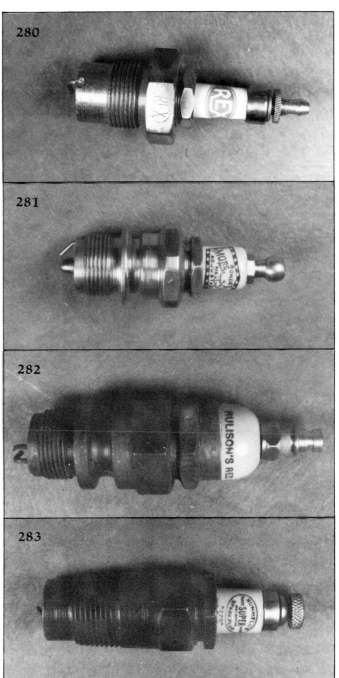

276. Reflex, could also be called Lightning.

277. Reliance.

278. Rentz, made plugs for Nash, Buick, and Packard.

279. Rev-O-Noc, brown porcelain.

280. Rex.

281. Rhodes-More Fire.

282. Rulison's Red Devil, looks like King Bee.

283. Rummell's.

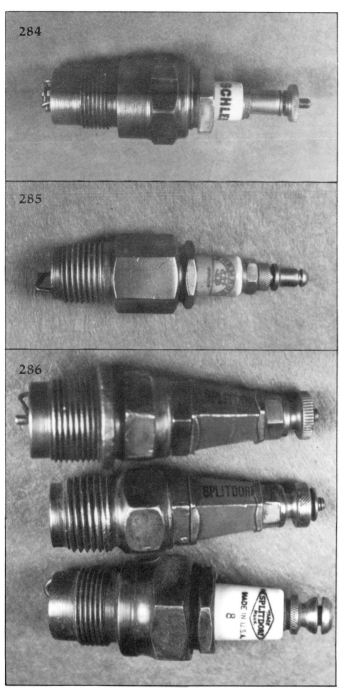

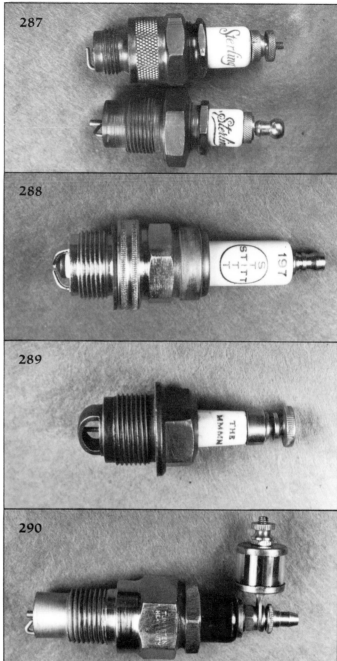

284. Schlee.

285. Shamrock, brown porcelain.

286. Splitdorf, two on top have green porcelain.

287. Sterling.

288. Stitt.

289. The MMMM.

290. Tungsten, with aftermarket intensifier attached.

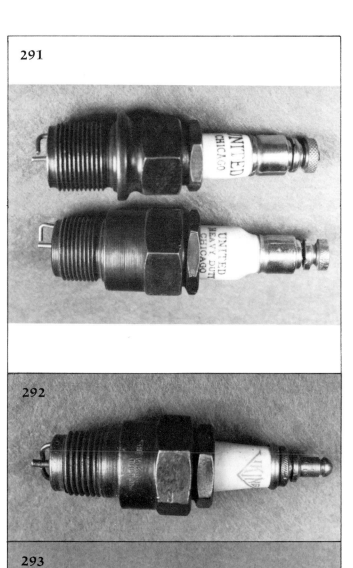

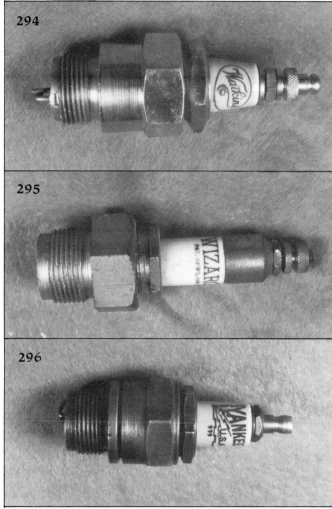

291. United.

292. Viking, light blue porcelain.

293. Wade.

294. Watkins.

295. Wizard.

296. Yankee.

CHAPTER 4

License Plates

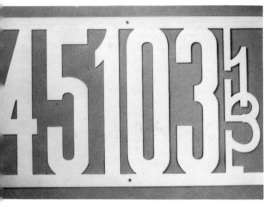

AUTOMOBILE licensing has been around for approximately eighty years. Recognized by government officials as a new means of taxation, a few states had started some form of vehicle registration as early as 1901. At first, licensing did not provide much revenue, with most states having less than one thousand cars, and fees ranging from twenty-five cents to six dollars, with the average at two dollars. Iowa, for example, registered one hundred and fifty-five vehicles in the first year, 1904, at one dollar each. That probably covered the cost of the tags and paperwork.

Most early registrations were handled at the municipal level. Because most autos never went beyond a twenty-mile radius, local registration was convenient. Small aluminum discs called tags were issued and were required to be affixed to the dashboard. Some even required the number to be painted on the body of the car. As vehicle design improved, people were driving farther, and in some states in order to comply with licensing laws, they were required to have a tag for each municipality they passed through. For example, if you lived in a suburb but worked in Chicago, you either bought a Chicago tag or parked outside the city limits and took the streetcar (trolley car) to your destination. Motor vehicles operated in other states required a plate for each state. Laws were getting out of hand, and this fact was brought to light in a 1906 automobile accident, involving a pedestrian and a hit-and-run vehicle in Chicago. A witness gave three or four different license-plate numbers, which confused the matter. This pointed out the need for uniform licensing laws and reciprocity clauses.

The first true plates as we know them were called *pre-state*. These were license plates required by state law, but not issued by state agencies. Requirements for these plates were set forth by state legislatures, and vehicle owners were required to have the plates made, usually by a harness maker. Most were required to be made of leather or fiber board and affixed with aluminum numbers. Some had no date or state identification, which made them hard to identify. Requirements were also set for the location of plates on the vehicle.

As auto registrations increased the need for a more uniform procedure was evident. Therefore, states started producing their own plates with state identification and dating.

Plate size varied all across the board. Smaller numbers meant smaller plates and vice-versa. The smallest plates were four inches high and from four to fourteen inches long. The largest plate was a toss-up between the 1914–1915 Illinois at 7½ × 14½ inches, and

South Carolina, 1926, at 5 × 16¾ inches. Finally, in 1956 all states agreed on a uniform size of 6 × 12 inches.

Plates have been made of many different materials: porcelain-coated cast iron, lithographed steel, embossed steel, hand-lettered steel, zinc, aluminum, cardboard, fiberglass, copper, brass, and even soybeans. Metal shortages during the war years caused new nonmetalic materials to be used. Louisiana found that cardboard did not hold up; Arizona found fiberglass to be too brittle; and Illinois found soybean-based materials to be durable, but farm animals found them tasty. Many a set was eaten right off the car. Over the years, aluminum (first used in Connecticut in 1937) has been found to be the most durable when coated with clear plastic.

The greatest development came in 1947 when the Connecticut legislature enacted a law requiring plates to be reflectorized. Millions of glass beads in suspension of a clear coating cause intense reflection of light from any angle. Nighttime rear-end collisions were greatly reduced, and soon many states adopted the procedure.

Many states are going to a five-year plate to reduce costs. This will ease the amount of specimens required to fill a collection.

Almost every state issues a vanity or personalized plate at some premium fee. Many interesting things can be seen on these plates. Whenever you are in a large city, especially near the financial district or the "Beverly Hills" part of town, you can always find those special plates. "ROLLS" on a Rolls-Royce, "JOE 1," Ernest Borgnine's plate, "BORG 9," or Lawrence Welk's "A1-A2-A3." Other clever combinations would be "4-U-2," "U-AS-4-IT," or the car lovers' plates, "VETTE," "T-BIRD," CHEV-2," "31-A" (on a 1931 Model A Ford), "HOT ROD," and "JAG." The possibilities are endless, but for the collector they are tough to acquire, as most owners prefer not to part with them.

The majority of plate collectors either collect one plate from each state or every plate from one state. Trying to collect them all is almost impossible. It would be very costly, and the space required to properly display them would be tremendous.

Hartungs' License Plate and Auto Museum in Glenview, Illinois, houses a complete United States and Canadian license plate collection, the only one in the country, and this fully displayed collection all but fills the 40- × 300-foot building.

Most states have sample plates available. At one time they were free for the asking, but the popularity of license-plate collecting induced all states to place a fee on these plates. The fee ranges from two to ten dollars.

Throughout the fifty states there are many categories plates are issued for. Some categories are described differently in some states. Antique car plates are also called Historical Vehicle plates, Horseless Carriage plates, Classic, Special Interest, Old-Timer, and Collector plates.

There are also many special one-of-a-kind or very limited-issue plates. Georgia has a plate for the Commander of Jewish War Veterans. Plates have been issued for participants in professional golf tournaments. Indiana issued two hundred official pace-car plates in 1978.

The following list represents the more popular topics seen on license plates from coast to coast. Next time you take a vacation, even if you don't collect plates, it might be fun to note how many different topics you can spot.

Agricultural
Air National Guard
Amateur Radio
Ambulance
Antique
Apportioned Trailer
Apportioned Truck

Bicentennial
Bus
Business

Camper
Citizen Band
City Owned
Civil Air Patrol
Classic
Collector
Commercial Vehicle
Common Carrier
Congressman
Consular Corp.
Contract Carrier

Dealer—Farm Tractor
Dealer—Highway
   Building Equipment
Dealer—New Car
Dealer—Used Car
Demonstration
Disabled Veteran
Distributor
Drive Away
Driver Training
Dual Purpose Vehicle

Emergency Vehicle
Exhibit

Farm
Finance Company
Fire Department
Foreign Consul
Forest Products
Forest Service
For Hire
Former Governor

Governor

Handicapped
Ham Radio
Hearse
Highway Maintenance
Highway Patrol
Historical Vehicle
Hobby
Horseless Carriage
House Car
House of Representatives

In Transit

Legislature—State
Legislature—U.S.
Lieutenant Governor
Limousine
Livery
Loaner

Manufacturer
Medal of Honor
Moped
Motorcycle
Motor Home
Municipal

National Guard
National Park Service
News Photographer

Official—(many)
Old-Timer
Omnibus

Passenger—(regular car,
   also called private,
   plate)
Permanent
Personalized
Police
Prestige
Prisoner of War
Prorate
Public Service

Rental

School Bus
Senator—State
Senator—U.S.
Special Interest
Special Mobile Equipment
State—Auditor
State—Owned
State—Patrol
State—Treasurer
State—University
Street Rod

Taxi
Tax Only
Temporary
Thirty Day
Tow Car
Tow Truck
Tractor
Trailer—Boat
Trailer—Dealer
Trailer—Private
Trailer—Rental
Trailer—Semi
Trailer—Travel
Trailer—Utility
Transporter
Truck—(many)

U-Drive-It
United States House
United States Senate

Vanity
Volunteer
VIP

Wrecker

Many plate collectors partake in the numbers game, accumulating plates with low or repetitive numbers.

1–3. Almost an impossible task, assembling a 1-to-100 number run for any given state, especially with today's right-to-privacy laws. Lee Hartung has put this complete Illinois run together.

4. Poker players would delight in owning this plate number. Connecticut plates, 1911–1916, from Hartung's Auto and License Museum.

5. Some plate collectors prefer to save pairs; this pair also has a catchy number.

6. Interesting combination of matching state tag and city tag numbers.

7. Prior to 1956, when license plates were standardized by all states, plates with short numbers were shorter in length. Size comparison can be seen here with this progressive set of one through seven digits.

8. Early autos had no bumpers, so plates were usually hung from a radiator-mounted bracket.

9. Due to plate size and location, Illinois decided to perforate the front plate in 1912 to allow air to pass through to the radiator. The rear plate was solid.

10. In 1913 Illinois went one step further and blanked out the background, while leaving the rear plate solid.

11. From 1914–1918, small slots were used between the digits in order to return sturdiness to the plate.

Some collectors chose to collect only one plate from each state. To make the collection interesting, some states had special slogans, or silhouettes, or pictures. Some for one or two years, and some for many. Here are a few examples.

12. In 1958 only, Colorado displayed a skier.

13. Wyoming's "Bucking Bronco" has been around since 1936, and in 1980 a corral fence was added to the plate. (Coincidental four aces again!)

14. Louisiana used a pelican from 1932–1963 with the exception of 1940 and 1941 when a state map appeared. The pelican changed its appearance six times, and in 1950 it was two color.

15. Idaho had a skier in 1947 only, and in 1948 a potato appeared. The same plate was used again in 1949 with a tag.

16. Tennessee shaped their plate like the state for twenty years, from 1936–1956.

17. Georgia had a small peach in 1940 and a large one in 1941.

18. Kansas had two small sunflowers in 1942 only.

19. The 1949 Iowa plate had a small checkerboard pattern embossed in the surface.

20. Many states issue sample plates, usually displaying all zeros, dashes, or the letters SAM-PLE. At one time they were free for the asking, but due to the popularity of collecting, all states charge some fee now.

21. Illinois issued a collector edition of its 1976 bicentennial plate. The design was selected from entries submitted by the public.

22. Almost all states have vanity or personalized plates but are expensive and hard to come by unless you can talk the owners out of one of the pair. This plate could have belonged to a cute girl or a guy boasting of his hobby.

23. Probably the most interesting license plate to come along for some time is this Northwest Territories bear.

24. The Yukon plate has a gold-panner.

Many special issue plates were struck for various reasons.

25. In the early years some states issued visitor plates. This rare 1917 New Hampshire plate had its corners cut to indicate visitor.

26. 1916 Colorado Visitor, both from Hartung's collection.

27

30

28

31

27. Even cities issued visitor plates and windshield decals.

28. Rare Civilian Conservation Corps. circa 1934.

29. Most states issue auto manufacturer plates, but these are unique because they belonged to the Tucker Car Company. The small 14 is the set number, indicating that there were at least 14 sets made. Hartung's Museum.

30. Two examples of special-event plates.

31. A variety of official, governor, and political plates.

States issuing only one plate left a vacant mounting space on the front bumper. American ingenuity soon found many things to fill that space.

32. F.D.R. campaign plates circa 1930s.

33. The move to repeal prohibition was flaunted in license-plate form. Early 1930s.

34. Bicentennial plate.

35. With the passing of Elvis, this was bound to become a popular plate.

Miscellaneous

36. In the 1950s hot-rod and car clubs were abundant. Most had cast-aluminum club placques, with their name and city. These are seldom seen today.

37. Very early brass Hawaii Territory dated 1913, from Hartung's Museum.

38. This 1905 two-inch brass dashboard tag is typical of the type most states used in the early years.

39. A complete collection of California plates is what a typical collection may look like.

40. Chauffeur badges are a form of licensing and make an interesting display. Shown here are State of Illinois and City of Chicago plus auto-plant employee badges from Ford Rouge Works, Chrysler, and Fisher Body.

41. The Disabled American Veterans issued these miniature key chain tags from about 1940–1976. In 1976 the right-to-privacy laws prohibited them from securing registrations. Early tags were printed on cardboard, laminated, and enclosed in metal frames with a separate metal back. In the 1950s the same cardboard tag was enclosed in plastic. Later in the 1950s a plastic one-piece tag was hot stamped, but the design was dropped, and a return to the metal tag followed. The late 1960s saw the introduction of the aluminum-enclosed cardboard. Random filling of these, created left- and right-hand versions. Each tag was sent in pairs, which are hard to locate now. Tags with license numbers were discontinued in 1975. V.I.P. tags were sent in 1975 and 1976. Just one more bit of Americana relegated to the history books.

State license-plate historical facts

The following is an alphabetical listing of each state and a brief history of its automobile-licensing procedures since the license plate's debut in the early 1900s. This information is designed to be helpful to collectors seeking the unusual, rather than the complete historical background. For simplification's sake, I have used the following abbreviations:

fy First year of state-issued plates.
pp Porcelain plates and the date(s) of use.
if Interesting facts.
sl Slogans as they appear on different years will be listed chronologically.
ps Pictures or silhouettes as they may appear on some plates will be described and dated here.

Alabama

fy 1912.
pp 1912–1915.
if Date not shown until 1917. Passenger plates marked "Private," 1922–1926. "Front" spelled out, 1937. Windshield sticker, 1943. Reflectorized, 1969–present.
sl "Heart of Dixie," 1955–present.
ps Large heart, 1955. Small heart, 1956–present. Prior to 1912, porcelain plates were issued by cities and bore the name of that city: Montgomery, Mobile, and Birmingham.

Alaska

fy 1922.
pp None.
if Plates were very small through 1931. Metal tab, 1944. 1945–1947 appear to be made of same fiberboard material as in Illinois war years. Reflectorized, 1966, 1967, and 1975.
sl "North to the Future," 1966, 1967, 1970–1974. "The Great Land," 1968 and 1969.
ps Flag, 1948–1965 and 1969–1974. Totem pole, 1966 and 1967.

Arizona

fy 1913.
pp None.
if No date or state shown on 1913, only city name, i.e., Tucson. Copper used 1932–1934 but proved to be too soft. Rounded corners, 1941–1955. Fiberglass used, 1943, 1944, and 1946. County name displayed, 1936–1939. Reflectorized, 1955 and 1966–present.
sl "Grand Canyon State," 1940–present.
ps None.

Arkansas

fy 1911.
pp 1911–1913.
if Same plate used, 1914 and 1915. Front and rear plate market, 1928–1931. Windshield sticker, 1943. Reflectorized, 1966–present.
sl "Centennial Celebration," 1936. "Opportunity Land," 1941, 1948, and 1949.
ps Map of state, 1924, 1925, and 1938.

California

fy 1914.

pp 1914-1919.
if No date shown, 1915-1919.
Metal "V" for Victory tab, 1943.
Windshield sticker, 1944..
Metal tabs, 1946, 1948-1950, 1952-1955.
Rounded corners, 1940-1955.
Alternate use of black and yellow, 1929-1969, except 1939, 1945, and 1946.
sl "World's Fair," 1939.
ps Bear, 1916.
Poppy, 1917.
Bell, 1918.
Star, 1919.

Colorado

fy 1913.
pp 1913-1915.
if Sticker added to 1919 plate for 1920.
Metal tab, 1944.
Reflectorized, 1971-present.
sl "Colorful," 1950-1955, 1958, 1959, 1973, and 1974.
ps Skier, 1958.
Mountains, 1960-1972, and 1974.
Bicentennial design, 1976.

Connecticut

fy 1905.
pp 1905-1916.
if No date or state identification shown, only large "C," 1905-1913.
Painted numbers on flat plate, 1917-1919.
First state to use aluminum, 1937.
White on blue used, 1957-present.
sl None.
ps None.
Although the unpainted aluminum background from 1937-1956 provided a certain amount of light reflection, Connecticut was still the first to adopt a reflectorized design. In 1948 a coating was added to the aluminum plate which carried through to 1956. When the new federal standards for plate size were adopted, Connecticut lawmakers felt that reflectorization had outlived its usefulness. Cars now had more chrome and better lighting, so the reflective coating was eliminated from new plates.

Delaware

fy 1907.
pp 1907-1915.
if Reflectorized numbers were riveted to a flat background from 1951-1969. (White on black through 1958.) A blue reflectorized background was used from 1959 on.
sl "The First State," 1963-present.
ps Small diamond, 1929-1935.

Florida

fy 1918.
pp 1918.
if From 1912 to 1917 porcelain plates about half regular size were issued by counties. 1918 was the first full size state issued plate.
Reflectorized numbers, 1955, 1966-1971.
Reflectorized background, 1972-present.
sl "Sunshine State," 1949, 1950, 1952-1963, and 1965-1978.
"Keep Florida Green," 1951.
"400th Anniversary," 1965.
ps State map, 1923-1926.

Georgia

fy 1910.
pp None.
if No date until 1914.
Metal tab, 1943.
Short plate, 1944.
Reflectorized, 1971-present.
County spelled out, 1971-present.
sl "Peach State," 1940, 1941, and 1947-1970.
ps Small peach, 1940.
Large peach, 1941.

Hawaii

fy 1922.
pp None.
if Windshield sticker, 1943-1945.
Reflectorized, 1957-present.
No date on 1957-1968.
When statehood was passed, dated windshield stickers were used, 1959-1968.
Date reappeared, on 1969 plate.
sl "Aloha State," 1957-present.

ps None.

Idaho

fy 1913.
pp None.
if Windshield sticker, 1943 and 1944.
Reflectorized, 1968-present.
sl "50 Years Statehood 1890-1940."
"Scenic," 1941-1946.
"Vacation Wonderland," 1947.
"World Famous Potatoes," 1948, 1949, 1953, 1956.
"Famous Potatoes," 1957-present.
ps Huge potato, size of plate, 1928.
Skier, 1947.
Colored potato, 1948 and 1949.

Illinois

fy 1911.
pp None.
if No date on 1911.
Perforated front, 1912.
Background blanked out front, 1913.
Slots in front, 1914-1918.
Large size, 1912-1915—7½ inches high and up to 14½ inches long.
Soybean-base fiberboard plates, 1942-1948.

sl "Land of Lincoln,"
1954–present.
"18" . . . "18" on each end of
1968 plate stood for 150th
year of statehood..
ps State map, 1927.
Bicentennial design, 1976.

Indiana

fy 1911.
pp 1913.
if In 1943 a small metal tab
was added to the rear 1942
plate. The front 1942 plate
had to be turned in to be
processed in making a
smaller 1944 plate.
Long metal tag, 1952–1954.
The 1954 tab was high
reflective red.
Reflectorized numbers only,
1964 and 1965.
Reflectorized background,
1966–present.
sl "150th Year," 1966.
"Drive Safely," 1956–1958.
"Safety Pays," 1960–1963.
"George Rogers Clark,"
1979.
ps Minuteman, 1976.
State map, 1977.
Race car, 1978.
Fort, 1979.

Iowa

fy 1913.
pp None.
if One plate issued for
1916–1918 with no date.
Paper windshield tag, 1943
and 1944.
Metal tabs, 1948, 1951, 1954
1955, and 1957.
Reflectorized, 1967–present.
sl "Corn State," 1954 and 1955
ps None.

Kansas

fy 1913.
pp None.
if No date shown until 1921.
Metal tab, 1943.
Small plate, 1944.
sl "The Wheat State,"
1948–1959.

"Centennial," 1960 and 1961.
"Midway USA," 1965–1970.
"Wheat Centennial," 1975.
ps Upper right corner cut out
like shape of state,
1951–1955.
Silhouette of state,
1956–present.

Kentucky

fy 1910.
pp 1910.
if One plate, 1910–1914.
County name appeared from
1927–present.
Front and rear identified,
1929.
Windshield sticker, 1943,
1945, and 1952.
Blue and white alternate,
1953–present.
sl "Tour Kentucky,"
1954–1957.
"For Progress," 1930.
ps None.

Louisiana

fy 1912.
pp 1912–1914.
if Front and rear plates different color, 1922–1932.
Paper windshield tag, 1943.
Cardboard plate, 1944.
Reflectorized, 1968–present.
Aluminum not used until
1974.
sl "Yams," 1954.
"Sportsman's Paradise," 1958
and 1959, 1961–1973.
"LSU Centennial," 1960.
"Bayou State," 1974–present.
ps Pelican, 1932–1939,
1942–1963.
State map, 1940 and 1941.

Maine

fy 1905.
pp 1905–1915.
if Same plate used 1905–1910.
No date appeared until 1914.
Windshield sticker, 1943 and
1947.
sl "Vacationland," 1937–present.
ps None.

Maryland

fy 1910.
pp 1911–1914.
if 1910 was hand lettered.
Metal tabs, 1943, 1944, 1946,
1947, 1949, 1950, 1951,
and 1953.
sl "Tercentenary," 1934.
"Drive Carefully,"
1942–1947.
ps None.

Massachusetts

fy 1908.
pp 1908–1915.
if 1916–1919 were not embossed.
Windshield sticker, 1943 and
1944.
Windshield sticker again in
1950, 1952, 1954, 1956,
1958, and 1960.
Some 1942 plates had green
background after maroon
was used up.
Reflectorized, 1966–present.
sl None.
ps Small fish, 1928.

Michigan

fy 1910.
pp 1910–1914.
if State seal, 1910–1919.
Metal tab, 1943, 1960–1964.
Reflectorized numbers only,
1969–present.
sl "Water Wonderland,"
1954–1964.
"Water Winter Wonderland,"
1965–1967.
"Great Lake State,"
1968–1975.
ps Bicentennial design, 1976.

Minnesota

fy 1909.
pp 1911?
if From 1912–1920 plates were
issued for a three-year period and carried all three
dates.
Metal tab, 1943.
Reflectorized, 1956–present.
sl "Centennial 1849 . . . 1949."
"10,000 Lakes," 1950–present.

ps None.

Mississippi

fy 1912.
pp None.
if 1912 had date; no date again
until 1919.
New plate each year during
the war.
County name, 1941–present.
Reflectorized, 1972–present.
sl None.
ps None.

Missouri

fy 1911.
pp None.
if Reflectorized, 1973–present.
sl "Show Me State," 1980.
ps Validation sticker shaped like
state, 1953–1955.

Montana

fy 1914.
pp None.
if Metal tab, 1943.
Soybean type (like Illinois),
1944.
Windshield sticker, 1947 and
1952.
Reflectorized, 1968–present.
sl "Treasure State," 1950–1956
and 1963–1966.
"Big Sky Country,"
1967–present.
ps State map outline,
1933–1943, 1945–1956,
and 1968–present.
Bicentennial design,
1976–present.

Nebraska

fy 1915.
pp None.
if Metal tabs, 1943, 1944, 1947,
1953, and 1959.
Reflectorized, 1966–present.
sl "The Beef State,"
1956–1965.
"Centennial," 1966–1968.
"Cornhusker State,"
1969–1974.
ps Capitol building, 1940 and
1941.

Nevada

fy 1916.
pp None.
if Painted plate, 1917–1922.
Metal tab, 1943.
Reflectorized, 1967–present.
sl None.
ps None.

New Hampshire

fy 1912.
pp 1913–1921.
if No date on 1905–1911 pre-
state.
The colors green and white
have been alternated for
the entire history of the
plates.
Metal tab, 1943.
No reflector plate.
sl "Scenic," 1957–1962,
1964–1970.
"Photoscenic," 1963.
"Live Free or Die,"
1971–present.
ps Face of "Old Man in Mountain," 1926.

New Jersey

fy 1908.
pp 1908–1915.
if Metal seal riveted on
1908–1915.
Metal tab, 1943.
Reflectorized, 1959–present.
sl "Garden State," 1959–present.
ps None.

New Mexico

fy 1912.
pp 1920–1923.
if The same porcelain plate was
used for four years with a
new-shaped tab to show
current validation,
1920–1923.
Windshield sticker, 1943.
Reflectorized, 1961–present.
sl "1540–1940 Coronado
Cuarto Centennial."
"The Land of Enchantment,"
1941–1951.
"Land of Enchantment,"
1952–present.

ps Sunburst appeared in four
different configurations,
1927–present.
Year shown in center of sun,
1927–1951, except 1932
and 1940
Red diamond, 1921.
Silver Hexagon, 1922.
Yellow six-point star, 1923.

New York

fy 1911.
pp 1912.
if No date until 1913.
Yellow and black alternating,
1927–1965.
Metal tab, 1943, 1949, 1952,
1954, 1956, 1959, 1961,
and 1963.
Reflectorized, 1973–present.
sl "New York World's Fair,"
1938–1940, 1963, and
1964.
"Empire State," 1951–1963.
ps None.

North Carolina

fy 1913.
pp 1913–1916.
if Metal tab, 1943.
Reflectorized, 1967–present.
sl "Drive Safely," 1954,
1956–1963.
"First in Freedom,"
1975–present.
ps None.

North Dakota

fy 1911.
pp None.
if Plate issued each year during
the war with additional
windshield sticker, 1943.
Reflectorized, 1960–present.
sl "Peace Garden State,"
1956–present.
ps None.

Ohio

fy 1908.
pp 1908–1911.
if Painted numbers on flat
plate, 1912–1917.
Windshield sticker, 1943 and
1952.

Reflectorized, 1974–present.
sl "150th Anniversary N.W. Terr.," 1938.
"1803 . . . 1953," (for 150 years of statehood).
"Seat Belts Fastened?" 1973–1975.
ps Ox-drawn Connestoga wagon, 1938.

Oklahoma

fy 1914.
pp 1914.
if Windshield sticker, 1943.
Metal tab, 1947.
Reflectorized, 1967–present.
sl "Visit Oklahoma," 1955–1962.
ps None.

Oregon

fy 1911.
pp None.
if A single plate was issued 1905 undated and used until 1910.
Windshield sticker, 1930, 1943–1945.
Yellow on blue, 1956–1976.
Reflectorized, 1977–present.
sl "Pacific Wonderland," 1961–1964.
ps None.

Pennsylvania

fy 1906.
pp 1906–1915.
if Wood grain background, 1912.
Reflectorized, 1977–present.
Metal tab, 1943.
sl "Bicentennial State," 1971–1976.
ps Keystone symbol, 1910–1919.
State map, 1937–1970.
Liberty Bell, 1971–1976.
Keystone, 1977–present.

Rhode Island

fy 1904.
pp 1904–1917.
if No date appeared until 1918.
Alternate use of black and white for entire history

except 1946 and 1947.
Windshield sticker, 1943.
Two different plates in 1946, white on black, and black on silver.
sl "Discover," 1967–present.
ps None.

South Carolina

fy 1917.
pp None.
if Longest plate ever made, 16¾ inches, 1926.
Long metal tab, 1944.
Reflectorized, 1976.
sl "Iodine," 1930.
"Iodine State," 1931.
"The Iodine State," 1932.
"The Iodine Products State," 1933.
(Apparently they gave up trying to convince everybody in 1934, or they just ran out of room for a longer slogan.)
"1670–1970, 300 Years."
ps Palmetto tree, 1926, 1927, 1976.
Bicentennial design, 1976.

South Dakota

fy 1912.
pp None.
if Same plate for 1912 and 1913.
No date appeared until 1916.
Metal tab, 1943.
Windshield sticker, 1944.
Reflectorized, 1957–present.
sl "Rushmore Memorial," 1939.
ps Four heads appear from 1952–present.
Three red stripes on Bicentennial design, 1976.

Tennessee

fy 1914.
pp None.
if Front and rear plate identified, 1926–1928.
Metal tab, 1943.
Reflectorized, 1976–present.
sl "Volunteer State," 1976–present.
ps Plate sides cut like shape of

state, 1936–1956.
Large state outline on standard rectangle, 1957.
Small state outline around "Tenn," 1958–1975.

Texas

fy 1917.
pp None. (Some pre-state plates were porcelain).
if Texas started off by issuing one plate for the life of the vehicle with a yearly radiator seal. Stocks ran out and the identical plate was reissued in 1922. An entirely new plate was issued in 1924, still with no date showing, but with *Texas* spelled out in lieu of *Tex.* In 1924 another radiator seal was issued. From 1925 on a new plate was issued each year with a date. Front and rear plates were distinguished from 1927–1930.
Metal tab, 1943 and 1944.
Reflectorized, 1969–present.
sl "Centennial," 1936.
"Hemisfair," 1968.
ps Round radiator seal with star, 1917–1919.
Rectangular radiator seal, 1920–1922, 1924.

Utah

fy 1914.
pp None.
if Letter U only, 1915–1922.
Windshield sticker, 1943.
Small plate, 1944.
Reflectorized letters only, 1963–1972.
Reflectorized background, 1973–present.
sl "Center of Scenic America," 1942–1946.
"This is the Place" (famous quote from Brigham Young), 1947.
"The Friendly State," 1948.
ps None.

Vermont

fy 1905.

pp 1905–1915.
if One plate from 1905–1908.
Metal tab, 1943.
Reflectorized, 1967–present.
sl "Green Mountains,"
1948–1950.
"See Vermont," 1957–1966,
1970–present.
ps None.

Virginia

fy 1906.
pp 1906–1913.
if First plate used 1906–1910.
Metal tab, 1943.
Combinations of black and
white, 1932–1977, except
1936, 1944, 1953.
sl None.
ps None.

Washington

fy 1916.
pp Validation tab only, 1920.
if 1920 plate used a tab over
1919.
Windshield decals, 1943,
1944, 1946, 1948, and
1952.
Metal tab, 1953, 1955, and
1956.
Reflectorized, 1964–present.
sl "Golden Jubilee 1889–1939."
ps None.

West Virginia

fy 1905.
pp 1905–1917.
if The word *licensed* appeared
1905–1917.
First dated plate, 1909.
Metal tab, 1943.
Windshield sticker, 1944.
Reflectorized, 1961–present.
sl "Centennial 1863–1963,"
1963 and 1964.
"Mountain State,"
1965–1975.
"Wild Wonderful,"
1976–present.
ps State map, 1976–present.

Wisconsin

fy 1911.
pp None.

if Numbers riveted to flat
plate, 1911–1913.
Round corners, 1942–1949.
Metal tabs, 1943–1945,
1947–1952, 1954, 1956,
1958, and 1960.
Reflectorized, 1968–present.
Windshield sticker also used
1943, front plate ordered
removed.
Two styles of 1940 plates,
one with state and date
across the top, the other
with same vertically in
center.
sl "America's Dairyland,"
1940–present.
ps None.

Wyoming

fy 1913.
pp 1915 and 1916.
if State seal on 1913–1917, also
no date shown.
Two different plates in 1921,
one with large metal tab,
the other embossed with
1921.
One of the few states to
issue a new plate each of
the war years.
Reflectorized numbers,
1957–1971, background
1972–present.
sl None.
ps Bucking horse, 1936–present.

CHAPTER 5

Emblems and Script

EMBLEMS are the means by which an auto maker identifies his wares, boasts about his products, and displays his coat of arms. Since the beginning of the automobile there has been some form of manufacturer's identification. In the late 1800s, sill plates, decals, and dashboard-mounted tags identified the maker. Soon this evolved into large brass scripts sprawled across the front of the radiator. Some of these scripts were quite large, as they ranged in size from six inches to over two feet. The Pierce Great Arrow had a spear in its script, large enough to do battle with. The first American car to brandish a script was the 1905 Packard. By 1907 most cars were using script.

Telling an original script apart from a reproduction is difficult, even for an expert. Anyone who has collected script or emblems for a few years most likely recognizes the name Harry Pulfer. Harry was a noted expert on the subject and made many exact reproductions for car restorers and collectors. He also repaired and restored emblems. He used a simple method of reproduction on scripts called a rub. Placing a piece of paper over an original, he would rub lightly with a pencil lead to leave an exact-size image on the paper. This method was much better than tracing, as the pencil point width would cause the new piece to be slightly larger. Reproduction of these scripts is very time consuming, though. It requires much hand sawing with a jeweler's saw, filing, sanding, and buffing. This rubbing method can also be used in correspondence with other collectors in place of more expensive photographs. It works well on emblems, hubcap faces, body plates, embossed badges, and tools.

Scripts with tabs attached are prior to 1910, and those names preceded by *THE* are prior to 1912. Some have a trademark stamped on the reverse side.

Shortly after 1910, most car makers began using smaller emblems mounted to the upper radiator tank. These colorful emblems are the most desired by collectors. Constructed of die-stamped copper, they were inlaid with vitreous (ground up) colored glass called *enamel* or *cloisonne*. Production emblems were heated red hot, and molten glass was flowed in between the die-stamped barriers. The piece was then buffed and plated.

The early emblems were soldered onto the radiator tank, but as car makers began to cover the radiators with shells, the emblems were then bolted on or pressed in.

Emblems started out with a single location on the radiator, but by the early thirties, they had found their way into many locations. The same emblem would appear in various sizes on bumpers, headlight bars, headlight rims, taillight brackets, trunk racks, trunk lids, hood side panels, dashboards, glove-compartment doors, hub-cap faces, and crank-hole covers. The smaller size emblems found on glove compartments or headlight rims were highly prized even by those with no intention of collecting. These miniaturized versions of the radiator adornment made attractive tie tacs, cuff links, or charms. Many emblems have been reproduced in this small size. The large size for radiator mounting has also been reproduced from time to time but often in small quantities that were soon bought up. Following is a list of the more popular companies that manufactured these little gems. The first two are the most common.

D. L. Auld—Columbus Ohio
Gustav Fox—Cincinnati, Ohio
L. F. Grammes—Allentown, Pennsylvania
Ross Ad Seal—Indianapolis, Indiana
Bastian Bros.—Rochester, New York
Robbins Co.—Attleboro, Massachusetts
Greenduck—Chicago, Illinois

These companies also manufactured emblems for refrigerators, stoves, aircraft engines, marine products, and beer tap knobs. You will find their names on the reverse side of most emblems.

Car makers also put information on these emblems other than their name. Some displayed horsepower like, *Stoddard, Dayton, Regal,* and *Everitt,* while others boasted the number of cylinders from 4 to V16. Many put the city of manufacture or the submodel name. A few chose to be aloof using only initials like *H.C.S.* (Harry C. Stutz) and *R.E.O.* (Ransom E. Olds). Then there were combinations of other companies like *E.M.F.* (*Everitt, Metzger,* and *Flanders*).

Eagles and bird wings were plentiful in emblem design, as they were in mascot design for Duesenberg, Dodge, Reo, Rickenbacker, Stutz, Wolverine, La Salle, Moon, Pierce Arrow, and Peerless. Several used a knight in armor as part of their coat of arms: Cord, Packard, Lincoln, Willys Knight, and Crosley. The word *Knight* appears on many emblems. This stands for Charles Knight, designer of the sleeve-valve engine. He dictated that any manufacturer using his engine would so carry his name on the emblem: Willys Knight, Sterns Knight, Falcon Knight, R. V. Knight, Federal Knight, and Sterling Knight.

Some auto makers occasionally used a two-piece emblem, which proved to be more decorative: Graham Paige, Packard, Haynes, Erskine, Cadillac, and Cord. The 1925 Alfa Romeo used two identical emblems, one on either side of a V-shaped radiator. By 1934 radiators were well hidden by grilles, and most were V shaped. Hence, the demise of the emblem was in sight. The use of copper for producing these emblems was slowly phased out in lieu of pot metal.

The emblems got smaller and became V shaped. Some used painted backgrounds and eventually the names no longer appeared on the emblem. Script was now slowly creeping back into car design. By 1941 most use of cloisonne had ceased. After the war only a few used it in any form. Lincoln and Dodge had nice postwar enameled emblems. Where color was needed, plastic was now being used.

The new use of script continued to grow, and in the mid-fifties some were again quite large, up to eighteen inches long. Since then, they have been reduced in size to an average of four to six inches, and presently some are of cheap plastic construction—so cheap that after a few car washings the silver color wears off exposing the black plastic underneath.

An interesting sideline to collecting modern scripts is the die-cast dealer names that were affixed to the trunk lids in the forties and fifties. Some had not only the dealer's name but also the brand of the car he sold, for example, *"Smith Ford,"* These are more desirable than one that might say, *"Smith Motors."* These items too have evolved into decals, pressure sensitive transfers, and molded plastic.

What you collect pertaining to emblems or script is entirely up to you, as there are thousands of possibilities to choose from.

1. One of the most interesting ways to display emblems is using old radiators or shells. This one is a 1911 Stevens Duryea.

2. An array of modern emblems, quite easy to come by for younger collectors.

3. Scripts from cars that have since passed into history.

4. Mostly larger scripts from the fifties and the sixties.

5. Newer and smaller scripts from the seventies.

6. Dealer name tags. The three on left are die cast, top right is plastic, lower right and bottom are pressure sensitive transfers.

Color emblems

There is nothing currently in print that exhibits the beauty in full color of yesteryear's cloisonne emblems. The emblems shown in the color insert, which follows page 80, range from common to extremely rare. Most were mounted on boards, and some were hanging in sealed glass cases in museums. This made the task of photographing difficult, to say the least. Lighting was a serious problem and created some reflections. But in an effort to show as many as possible, exceptions were made.

They are arranged in alphabetical order and dated where possible. The single date may not be the only date the particular emblem appeared on the car, but has been seen on a car of that year, in a dated advertisement, or verified by another collector. Those not dated are unknown.

Advertising

AUTOMOBILE advertising comes in many forms. From billboards to matchbook covers, from showroom ads to television ads, every possible medium has been used to promote the wares of the auto makers. This leaves many possibilities for collections. In most cases where space is limited, a person should specialize. Sign collectors have to be quite selective as most signs take up a lot of space. Magazine ads are very popular, but they too can take up space if mounted in protective frames, and hung on the wall. Collectors usually protect their ads by placing them in albums. Small or miniature collectibles have always been most popular, because they can be displayed in a small area.

Lithographed tins are very popular and cover a wide range of automotive products: oil, wax, antifreeze, cleaners of all kinds, talcum powder for clincher tires, light bulbs, auto parts, and spark plugs. Any tin bearing the likeness of a car would have had a current model showing; therefore, this is helpful in dating the can. Simonize and Prestone were excellent examples of tins showing cars. Recently, oilcans have become quite popular, and understandably so. They are very colorful and relatively inexpensive. Even more interesting are the tin banks with oil-company names. They measure approximately three inches high and one-and-a-half inches in diameter. (See color insert.)

Owners' manuals are collected, generally only by people who have the matching cars. There are usually few if any pictures of the car itself in these books. Showroom literature is more colorful and shows the entire line of models for a given year. This literature is extremely helpful to restorers who are looking for those accurate details in paint, trim, or factory-authorized accessories. Postcards, also given out by dealers, are desirable because of their compact size. In fact, postcards are so popular that many new ones with pictures of restored cars can be found at part swaps.

Magazine ads are by far the most popular. They provide historical information, prices and specifications, emblem or logo designs, precise dating, and a good pictorial view of the car. Color was even used as far back as the twenties. Once you get past the propaganda about speed, power, and beauty, you can usually find some pertinent information about the car.

Magazine ads are relatively easy to come by. Attics, basements, and flea markets are good sources for old magazines. *Cosmopolitan, Harper's, Munsey's, Horseless Age, Colliers'*, and *The Scientific American* are good sources for pre- and post-1900 ads. The latter two even printed special issues covering the new horseless carriage. *Post, Look,* and *Colliers'* are good sources for forties and fifties ads. Prior to the thirties, *National Geographic* had many car ads in each issue, but after the thirties it seemed to shy away from an abundance of car ads. Luxury car ads appeared in expensive magazines like *Fortune, New Yorker, Vogue,* etc. Publications like *Motor, Motor Age,* and other auto trade journals were directed to the auto business, and usually sported many ads. Even *Literary Digest* had many car and tire ads in the twenties and thirties. *Hemmings Motor News* of Bennington, Vermont, has a large section each month listing literature for sale. At most part swaps, literature dealers can usually be found displaying a large selection of ads.

Maxwell—From 1923 *National Geographic.* Lists basic features and price range. The words about the "Good Maxwell" and "Domination" have a slight tinge of arrogance. Radiator emblem is shown at bottom.

Flint—From *Literary Digest,* 1926. Shows radiator emblem at top. Notice wide price range, from $1,085 to $2,395.

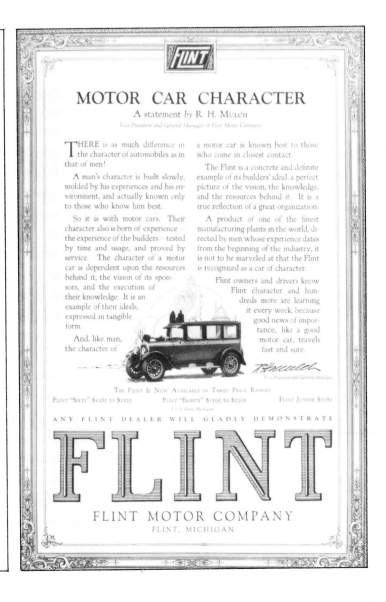

Columbia—From *Motor Age*, 1919. After an abundant use of the word *charm*, some interesting facts about the car's features like Continental motor, Firestone tires, and how about the Atwater Kent ignition, a company known primarily for its fine radios? A very nice detail of the radiator emblem is shown as well.

Ford—From 1955 *Time* magazine. For lovers of the fifties' cars, there are many nice color ads to be found in popular magazines of the fifties.

Hupmobile—From *Literary Digest*, 1926. Some advertisers chose simplicity as opposed to wordy ads.

One of the most interesting and famous forms of advertising was the Burma Shave signs of the thirties, forties, and fifties. The only direct relation to the automobile was their placement along the roadside. These signs first started appearing along the highways and byways in 1925 and soon caught on. By 1930 there were thousands of signs from coast to coast. At the height of their success there were over 7,000 sets of signs boasting over 600 different jingles, and six or more crews spent months each year maintaining old signs and implanting new ones. You may remember as a youngster how while on vacation trips everyone in the car would strain their eyes looking for the next series to appear on the horizon. Then all would quibble over who was to read them aloud. As it usually turned out, everyone in the car read them aloud in unison. Eagerness to reach the next set often found the car's occupants reading backwards signs intended for the opposite side of the road and then recomposing them.

By the early sixties the signs were all but gone from the roadsides, pilfered by souvenir hunters and antique collectors or used by farmers to patch the corncrib.

During the mid-thirties travel by auto was a part of almost everyone's life. Consequently, the accident rate among drivers was skyrocketing. In 1935 the Burma Shave people decided to make a contribution to curbing this highway carnage. Many public service type slogans directed at would-be traffic offenders were added to the roster. Here are but a few.

DON'T STICK / YOUR ELBOW / OUT TOO FAR / IT MIGHT GO HOME / IN ANOTHER CAR.

IT WILL NEVER / COME TO PASS / A BACK SEAT DRIVER / OUT OF GAS.

AT INTERSECTIONS / LOOK EACH WAY / A HARP SOUNDS NICE / BUT IT'S HARD TO PLAY.

DON'T TAKE / A CRUISE / AT 60 PER / WE HATE TO LOSE / A CUSTOMER.

TRAIN APPROACHING / WHISTLE SQUEALING / PAUSE . . . AVOID THAT / RUN DOWN FEELING.

HE SAW THE TRAIN / AND TRIED TO / DUCK IT / KICKED FIRST THE GAS / AND THEN THE BUCKET.

AROUND THE CURVE / LICKETY-SPLIT / IT'S A BEAUTIFUL CAR / WASN'T IT?

IF YOU DON'T KNOW / WHOSE SIGNS THESE ARE / YOU CAN'T HAVE DRIVEN / VERY FAR / BURMA SHAVE!

If Burma Shave jingles were alive today, there would probably be one for antique car collectors. It might read:

WHEN HOME YOU BRING / SOME RUSTY THING / THE WIFE MAY SAY / WHAT A HUNK / WHEN ALL THE TIME / SHE KNOWS IT'S JUNK.

1. Star Cars. A very nice white-on-green porcelain sign, two feet by four feet, from the late twenties.

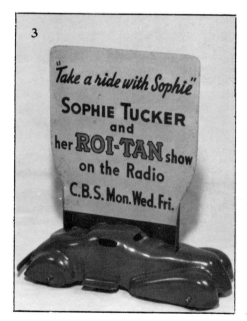

2. Prestone can from the late twenties.
   Prestone, being a new product intended
   to replace the use of alcohol, was
   unfamiliar to the public, hence the
   association with an established Union
   Carbide product Eveready.

3. "Take a ride with Sophie," a rare
   advertisement for a 1939 radio show.
   The other side says, "A 1939 Chevrolet
   given away weekly."

4. Printers and advertising agencies
   sometimes dispose of their letterpress
   cuts. These copper or zinc etchings are
   mounted on cherry or walnut wood
   and make interesting conversation
   pieces. Most can be dated by a
   matching radiator emblem.

5. Gas pumps, batteries, and oil drums
   are all formats for small tin banks less
   than six inches high.

6. Ford was not the only auto maker to
   set up at the 1933 Chicago World's
   Fair. This copper ashtray is from
   Chrysler Corp.

7. Hupmobile offered this battery-
   operated lamp.

8

12

13

9

10

14

8. Matchbook covers usually display colorful advertising.

9. Postcard-size ink blotter, circa 1920.

10. Nash postcard from 1933 World's Fair. Notice how artist's rendering makes the car look huge.

11. 1959 Rambler postcard, a dealer giveaway.

12. 1956 Lincoln Capri postcard, also a dealer giveaway.

13. Desk ornament or paperweight, this pot-metal 50th-anniversary Nash trophy is typical of the type of knick-knacks found in dealer showrooms on desktops.

14. Glass transparent slides about four inches by five inches were used in movie theaters to advertise local dealers. This one shows a 1935 Chevrolet two-door sedan.

15. Gas station trinkets, salt and pepper
shakers in a miniature gas pump
format, Delco coin holder, Standard
Oil crown valve covers, Firestone Clip
on clothes hanger, uniform patches,
Sunoco & DX car coins (a giveaway
premium game), Standard Oil
reproduction political badges (1972),
Texaco wartime gas ration coupon, a
chance ticket on a 1929 Essex Coach,
etc. With a little effort a lot of this
trivia can be uncovered.

16. Road maps are also a form of
advertising. Maps usually show
current-model cars making dating
relatively easy. More recent maps show
a composite no-name vehicle while still

depicting current features. Shown here
are 1931 Conoco Arizona, and 1924
Illinois map from Marland Oil Co.

Brass: Poor Man's Gold

BRASS is often described as *poor man's gold.* Despite its inferior reputation, brass is quite beautiful. Automobiles prior to 1915 were called "brass cars" due to their numerous brass accessories, radiator, headlamps, carbide generator, taillights, instruments, and virtually all exposed unpainted trim. The war in Europe and cost reduction were responsible for the demise of brass. Brass was used for years to come, but in lesser amounts and covered with nickel plating. The pre-1915 brass accessories are quite desirable, as well as scarce. Headlamps and accessories, a popular favorite, are not represented in this book, avoiding repetition, as there are other books on these available. Instead, less popular, but perhaps unthought of collectibles will be shown. These items are relatively easy to find and not too hard on the pocketbook. Some hubcaps and spark plugs were brass but were left in their respective chapters for the sake of continuity.

1. Restored brass carburetors come in many sizes and shapes. Upper left: an interesting Stromberg, with a glass float bowl and add-on moisture injector with glass viewing window. The other three are Schebler.

2

3

2. Unrestored brass carburetors waiting
   for the buffing wheel.
   Left: another Stromberg glass bowl,
   two ports on side are for radiator
   water, a primitive method of
   preheating the fuel/air mixture.
   Unfortunately when pre-heating is
   most needed during warmup, the
   radiator water is cold. Right: a
   Zenith carburetor marked Yellow
   Cab. The brass disc covering the
   float bowl could be marked with any
   auto maker's name.

   Some of the more popular names in
   brass carburetors were:

Ball & Ball	Marvel	Schebler
Carter	Master	Stewart
Holly	Miller	Stromberg
Johnson	Monarch	Tillotson
Kingston	Rayfield	·Zenith

3. Related to the carburetor are these
   early throttle quadrants. These could
   be early auto or tractor.

4. Also related to the fuel system were
   these gasoline primer cups. Many
   varieties exist, as you can see. Some
   have levers; the one in the center even
   has a wooden-tipped handle; some have
   built-in dust covers, while others
   require the cup itself to be rotated.
   One had a two-position lever. One
   position was for gas priming while the
   other position opened a port to a water
   reservoir for water injection.

4

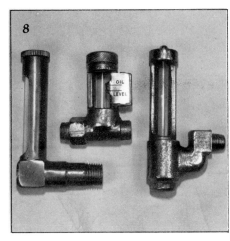

5. Brass radiator drain cocks were made in various shapes.

6 & 7. Grease fittings, grease cups, oil cups, and drip oilers, make interesting displays. These could have been used on cars, tractors, or stationary machinery.

8. Brass and glass oil level indicators were usually for transmissions.

CHAPTER 8

Mascots

THE presence of a mascot is supposed to bring good luck. Mascots on vehicles can be traced back to the days of the Roman Empire. Chariots were adorned with small bronze statuettes, supposedly to please the gods. This lends to the fact that so many Greek and Roman gods have been miniaturized in auto-mascot form; *Atalanta, Adonis, Diana, Griffin, Hermes, Icarus, Mercury, Neptune,* and *Triton,* to name a few of the more popular.

Modern-day use of mascots got its start when England's Lord Montagu equipped his 1896 *Daimler* with a statue of St. Christopher. The idea soon caught on, and many accessory mascots were appearing in European and American shops.

The largest contribution to early mascot design was by the French. Many beautiful works of art emerged from early mascot sculptors. The true state of the art was manifested in crystal glass creations by Rene Lalique. Various animals and birds were made in pastel colors, and an accessory lighting device added a glow to these masterpieces.

Other early mascots were unusual, some having spinning propellers, one with built-in steam whistle, a statue of a Japanese gentleman committing *hara-kiri,* a black youngster smoking a cigarette, a dog jumping through a hoop, a devil thumbing his nose, a skull and crossbones, a nude lady in a saucepan, a pig jumping through a horseshoe, dogs chained to a fireplug, even a statue of Cupid that would urinate when the water in the radiator boiled over, to name a few.

Those who could not afford mascots found other ways to add a personal touch to their cars. Flagpole eagles were quite popular, while others used paperweights, trophy heads, silver cups or chalices, even bookends.

For the first twenty years of motoring, factory mascots were slow in coming. *Thomas Flyer* put a globe on the radiator cap following his victory in the round-the-world race. Rolls-Royce introduced the *"Spirit of Ecstacy"* in 1911, a mascot that has lasted for sixty-nine years with more than twenty minor design changes. At first, mascots were more or less reserved for the affluent by virtue of their price and quality, but American mass-production advocates did not miss a trick when potential profit was in sight. Because of the ever-increasing popularity of quality mascots, the market was ripe for cheap copies for the lower-income bracket. One might say that the birth of the motometer by Boyce in 1912 was the beginning of the cheap mascot. Although a very functional device, they were constructed of pot metal, a zinc die-cast material, and priced to suit everyone's pocket. Not long after that, mini-mascots were offered by a few manufacturers that could be attached to the top of a motometer. Motometers are quite collectible by themselves as Boyce offered over 175 different name discs for their seven sized meters. A couple dozen brand names of meter manufacturers can also be found.

Auto makers were beginning to see the light by the mid-twenties, as more and more cars became equipped with dash-mounted temperature gauges. This left the radiator cap free to support a mascot. Although most factory mascots were made of that terrible pot metal, credit must be given for some beautiful designs. Most notable were the products of Ternstedt Mfg. Co., now a division of General Motors. Much detail work is seen in flowing hair, leaves, and feathers in examples like, '27 Buick, '27 Chevy Quota Trophy, '28 DeSoto, '27–'28 Oakland Eagle, and the copper-faced '29 Pontiac Indian.

Some factory mascots changed every year while others used the same design for many years. Some mascot designs were used by more than one company. *Hudson & Gardner* used a Greek mythological creature called a *Griffin,* half eagle and half lion. *Studebaker* and *Erskine* used the Greek goddess *Atalanta,* a swift-footed maiden who challenged any man to a foot race; the winner could marry her, but losers had to pay with their lives. *Reo, Pierce Arrow,* and *Buick* had at least one version of *Mercury,* the Roman god of commerce. *Hermes* was the Greek counterpart to *Mercury* and was used by the *Hermes* automobile. Likewise, the *Diana* used the Roman god of chase, *Diana,* as a mascot. The use of gods was abundant with still more, *Stutz* using *Ra,* the Egyptian sun god, and Duesenberg using *Pegasus,* a Greek winged horse. *Moon* had a *Centaur,* half horse and half man.

The *Ryan Monoplane* flown by Lindbergh in 1927 was miniaturized by *Chevrolet, Franklin,* and *Hudson.* The popular *Eagle* was adopted by many as a factory symbol, *Coey Flyer, Alvis, Chandler, Peerless, Marmon, Kissel, Duesenberg,* and *Oakland.*

Factory mascots were short-lived from the mid-twenties to about 1934. By 1935 most radiator caps were concealed under the hood and body styles were becoming quite round in the name of streamlining. Mascots were soon replaced by trinket-like ornaments, which gradually reduced in size until World War II, after which they disappeared.

The fifties saw hood and fender decorations reappear in the form of modernized birds, jet planes, rockets, and gun sights. Then the federal government decided that a couple pounds of metal perched on the hood could become a dangerous missile during an accident. Even though stately mascots are gone forever, hood decoration is not dead. For about five years or so, mini-emblems mounted on spring bases have served to accentuate the long smooth hoods of today. This provides the chance for young collectors to get started in some form of auto art.

Quality mascots were made from cast stainless steel, cast brass or bronze, pewter, German silver, silver, crystal glass, and even cast iron. Lack of mold seam lines, attention to detail, and smoothness of surface are also good indicators. Of course, these types of mascots command premium prices.

Cheap aftermarket mascots can be readily recognized by the zinc die-cast construction with evident seam lines, or harsh grinder marks where a hasty mass-production attempt was made to remove them. Surfaces are usually rough and irregular. Pot metal pits very easily even if not exposed to weather. It is extremely hard to restore pot metal, as the surface must be gound and polished to the depth of any pitting; in doing this, much detail is lost. Some die cast will crack all over and crumble with age. Some aftermarket pieces were cast aluminum. Poor quality was evident on some in the form of sand holes, indicating poor castings.

A few factory mascots are available today like *Mercedes, Excalibur, Rolls-Royce,* plus various cheap auto-part store versions like standing horses, steer heads, and eagles. In 1971 a standing *Nixon* was made in stainless steel. There are also quality reproductions of popular mascots like *Ford Quail, Pierce Arrow Archer, Lincoln Greyhound, Packard Adonis,* etc.

Restoring mascots

Not much can be said about restoring mascots because it usually involves stripping the old plating off chemically, polishing, and replating, tasks most collectors are not equipped to perform. Should you elect to have this done by a professional, be sure of whom you select. A valuable specimen can be easily destroyed by a careless plater. A prime example was a fellow restoring a *'29 Chevy.* He took the stamped, fluted brass radiator cap to a plater. A careless polisher bore down on the buffing wheel and buffed right through the tips of the finger flutes. Making matters worse, the plater tried to make repairs by sending the cap out to be brazed. What the man received when he went to pick up his cap was a perfectly round two-pound blob of shiny plated brass, totally useless on a restored car.

A better bet is to collect only mascots in good displayable condition. Then all you need is a little bright metal cleaner.

Displaying mascots

Shelves, glass cases, and wall mounts are a few conventional ways to show off your wares. But you can make an attractive display by using old radiator shells with a backboard in shadowbox fashion. Small brackets mounted off the backboard will give a three-dimensional effect. Very showy bases can be made from wood or small marble trophy bases. Some old floor lamps had several onyx or colored-glass decorative shapes in the upright stem, each with a hole in the center. These make attractive mascot bases.

Very few automotive collectibles have a specialized book available to collectors. Mascot collectors are lucky to have one. Bill Williams's *Motoring Mascots of the World* is an excellent work on the subject. There are 789 mascots pictured, dated, and described in detail. It is available through Motor Books International, Osceola, WI 54020. The following pages tell a pictorial history of radiator adornment from the teens through the thirties.

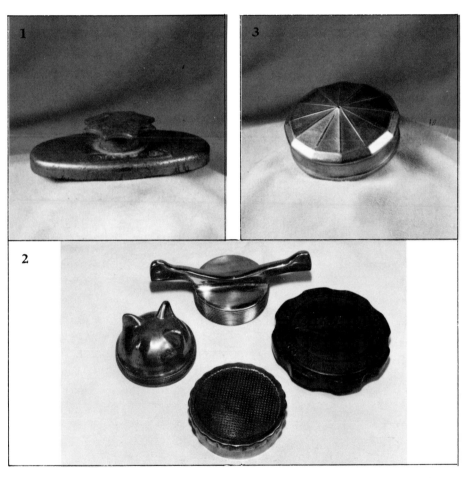

Simple Caps

1. Willys-Overland—early 1920s oval cap.

2. Caps from the teens
   Left: Model T Ford
   Top: early aftermarket brass dog bone for Model T
   Right: hard rubber molded over brass core, this Mitchell being typical of many; bottom, checkerboard pattern on brass is Dodge Brothers from the teens.

3. Evidence of a little styling is seen in this Essex-type cap.

4. Most commercial vehicle caps remained simple; some carried names like this '34 Dodge truck.

5. Very early cast-iron flip top with screw-down dog bone on top bares the name Neva-Lost.

6. Model T accessory cap.

7

10

13

8

11

14

9

12

15

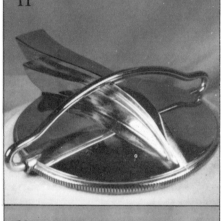

7. Cap with lighted colored-glass jewels.

8. Short of being a stately mascot, but stylish for a radiator cap. A single wing sits atop this unknown cap.

9 & 10. Two versions of aftermarket flip-top caps.

11. Packard accessory cap with bail handle to simulate a flip top.

Motor Meter Types

Many different companies made radiator temperature monitoring devices. The next group of

pictures shows twelve different motor-meter styles.

12. Arro Meter, needle moves from side to side in window.

13. Auto Radiator Meter Co., Seattle, WA.

14. Boyce-Radio Model—Boyce was the largest manufacturer of motor meters.

15. Boyce—Standard with Nash wings on top. Boyce also made Universal, Senior, Junior, and Midget models.

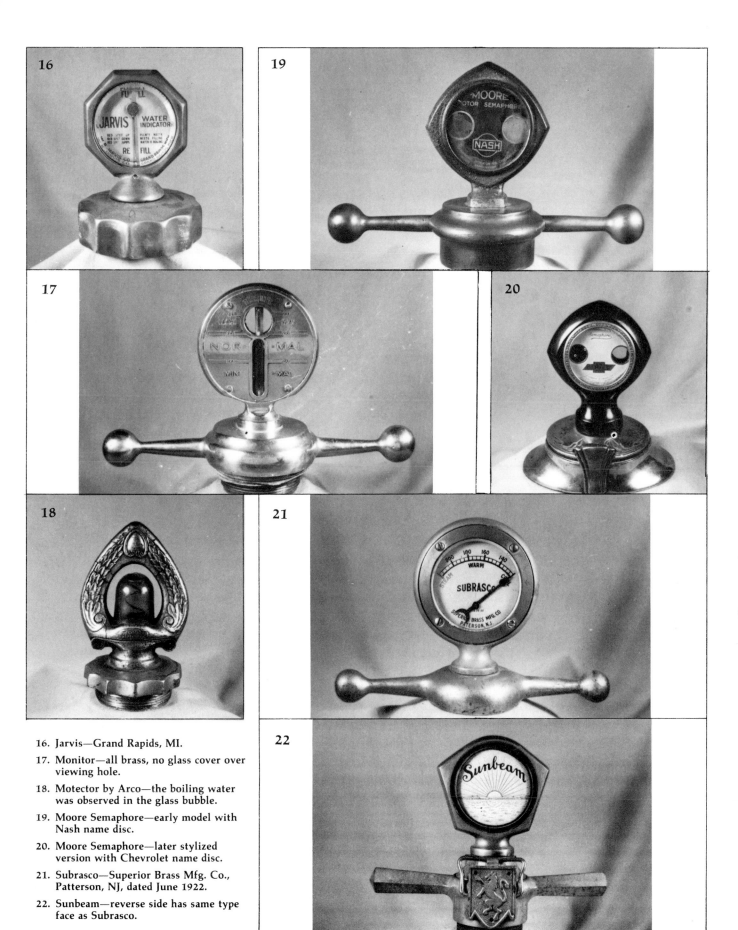

16. Jarvis—Grand Rapids, MI.

17. Monitor—all brass, no glass cover over viewing hole.

18. Motector by Arco—the boiling water was observed in the glass bubble.

19. Moore Semaphore—early model with Nash name disc.

20. Moore Semaphore—later stylized version with Chevrolet name disc.

21. Subrasco—Superior Brass Mfg. Co., Patterson, NJ, dated June 1922.

22. Sunbeam—reverse side has same type face as Subrasco.

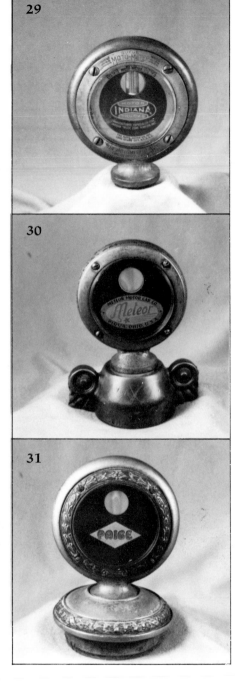

23. Warn-O-Meter.

Most motor meters had a metal name disc bearing the car name or logo. The name side faced forward on the radiator. Here are twelve examples.

24. Auburn.

25. Cole.

26. Haynes.

27. Hudson.

28. Hupmobile.

29. Indiana-Truck.

30. Meteor.

31. Paige.

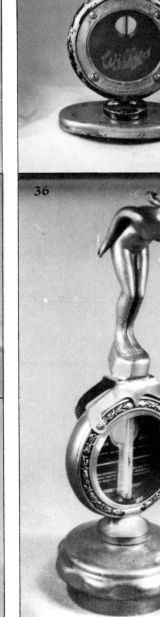

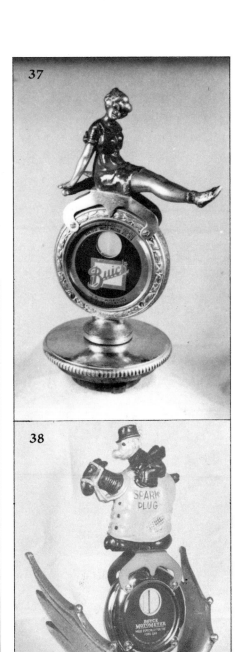

32. Pioneer.

33. Studebaker.

34. Ward LaFrance—Fire Truck.

35. Willys—on early oval cap.

In the early twenties prior to most factory mascots, Boyce and other aftermarket companies, sold mini-mascots that could be attached on top of a motor meter. These figures were about three to four inches high. Vibration and inquisitive children must have taken a heavy toll of these precariously mounted figures.

36. Diving nude.

37. Sitting girl on Buick motor meter.

38. Cartoon character Barney Google and his horse, "Spark Plug," sit atop an Elcar mascot.

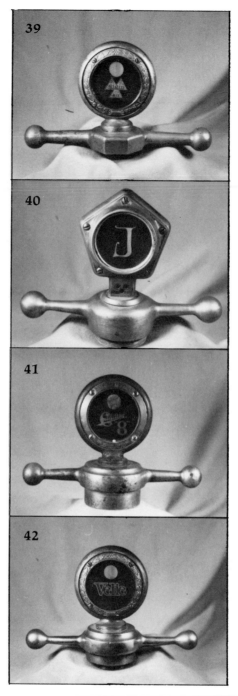

Accessory dog bones were a means of accentuating a radiator cap as well as providing a convenient handle for removal. Hundreds of types abound, as they were sold by dealers, accessory stores, mail-order houses, etc. Most dog bones came with a solid top, but many owners drilled them and mounted a motor meter on top. They were made of cast iron, cast brass, or cast aluminum. The following are but a few of the many once available.

39. Elgin.
40. Warn-O-Meter—probably for Jewett.
41. Cadillac.
42. Velie.
43. Stutz with rare short dog bone.
44. Oldsmobile accessory dog bone.

Some designs omitted the conventional ball on the end.

45. Elcar 8 accessory.
46. Name on dog bone is Thomson of Dayton, Ohio, and this flip top carries a Cleveland meter.

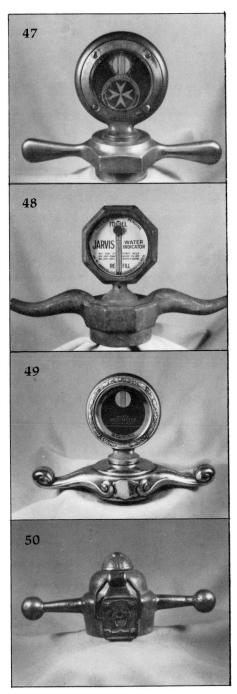

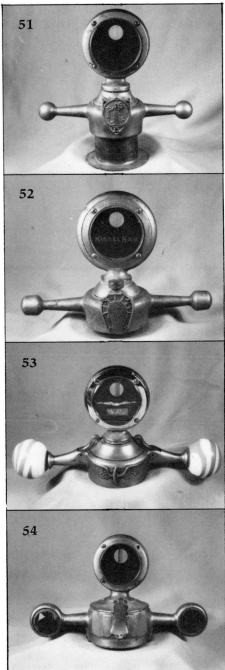

47. Templar motor meter on plain bone.

48. Jarvis motor meter on a steer-horn design.

49. Very stylish dog bone with Boyce universal model motor meter. Not all motor meters were sold with car names on the metal disc.

A more deluxe-style motor meter features a flip-top mechanism for easy water-level fill or check. Most flip tops had some sort of design on the front.

50. Flip top without motor meter shows bulldog and was probably for Mack truck.

51. Design shows lady with flowing gown holding a wreath and winged staff.

52. Kissel Kar on flip top with Statue of Liberty face on dog bone.

53. This flip top has marble balls attached, most likely color coordinated to the car.

54. Flip top with colored-glass jewels.

55. Clear-glass covers protect paper insert in each end; it was used as an advertising gimmick. This one has Diamond Matches insert.

56. Wood or hard rubber was used to make the balls on this one. Even release handle has ball attached.

Accessories were sold that looked somewhat like a motor meter but were actually dummies.

57. Gidelite of Chicago made this lighted version that could be affixed with any car name.

58. Maxwell.

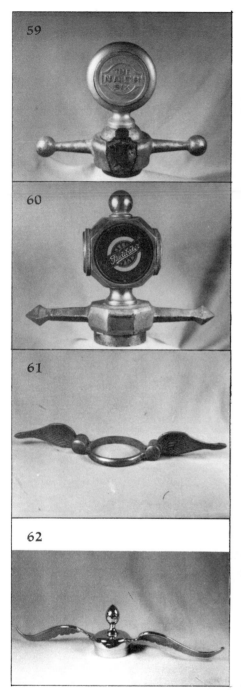

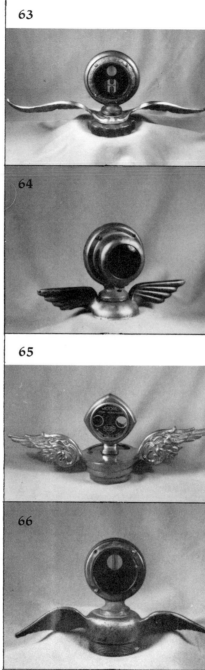

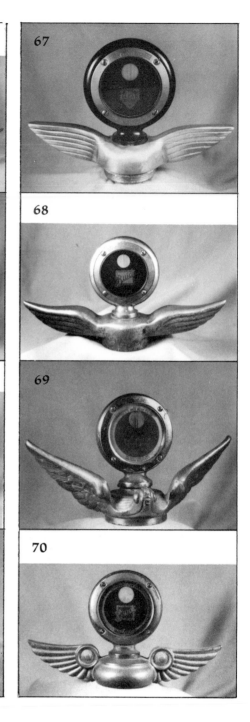

59. Nash.

60. Another lighted ornament—Studebaker.

Equally as popular as dog bones were the winged ornaments available with or without motor meters.

61. Early clamp-on wings designed to fit around radiator filler neck.

62. Wings with small ornament.

63. Add-on wings fit between cap and motor meter.

64. Lighted ornament atop winged cap.

65. Beautiful winged cap with sliding filler port.

66-72. Various common wing caps.

73-75. Three flip-top winged caps.

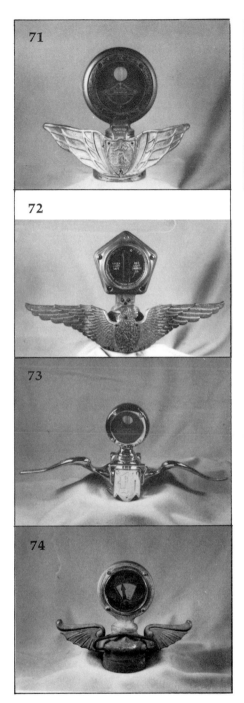

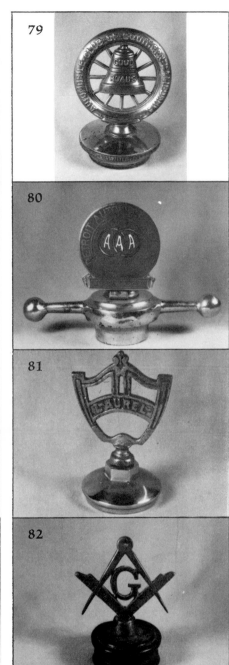

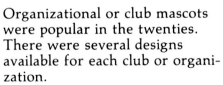

Organizational or club mascots were popular in the twenties. There were several designs available for each club or organization.

76. American Legion.

77 & 78. Two versions of Royal Automobile Club.

79. Southern California Auto Club.

80. Detroit Auto Club—Ribbon on bottom states, "Thieves will be prosecuted." Red, white, and blue enamel.

81. Laurel.

82. Masonic Emblem.

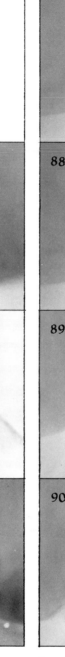

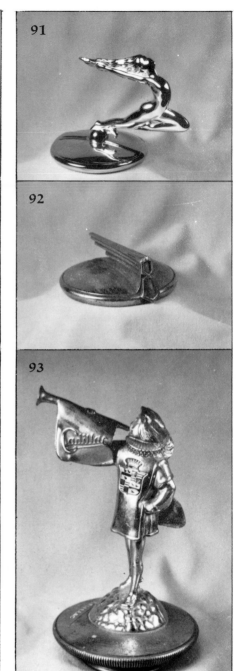

83. Optimist.

84. Wolf in horseshoe, probably a country club.

The following is a representation of factory mascots in alphabetical and chronological order.

85. Apperson Jackrabbit—1921-1923 cast iron.

86. Brockway—Truck.

87. Buick—Goddess 1927.

88. Buick—Goddess 1928.

89. Buick 1931-1932.

90. Buick 1933.

91. Buick 1933 aftermarket—notice differences from factory mascot.

92. Buick 1933.

93. Cadillac 1926-1930.

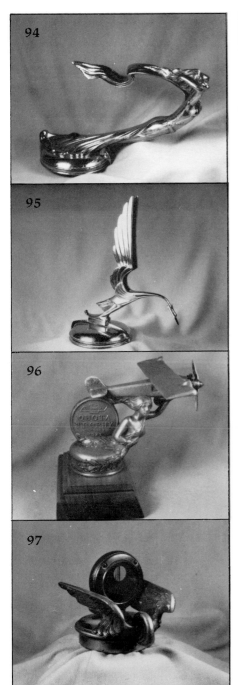

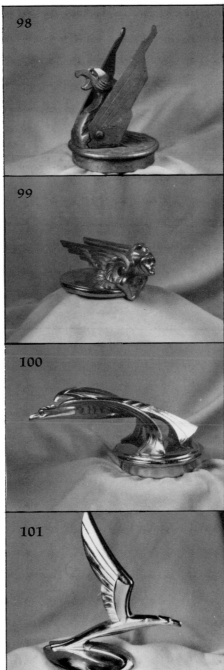

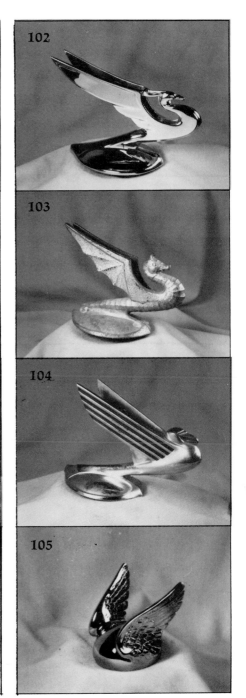

94. Cadillac 1930-1932.

95. Cadillac Heron—1932-1933—Neck of bird is bent, a result of some careless person using neck as handle to remove cap.

96. Chevrolet 1927—Salesmen quota trophy.

97. Chevrolet 1928.

98. Chevrolet 1928.

99. Chevrolet 1929-1930 Viking.

100. Chevrolet 1931-1932.

101. Chevrolet 1933 Eagle.

102. Chevrolet 1934.

103. Chevrolet Truck—1934 Serpent.

104. Chevrolet 1935 Unicorn Bird.

105. Chrysler 1928-1930.

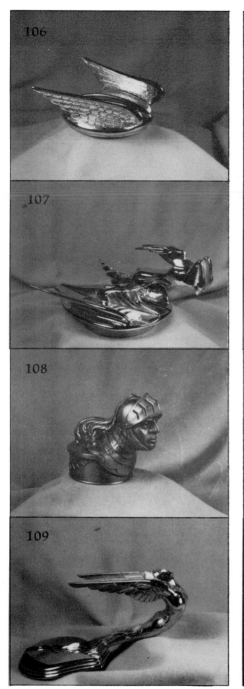

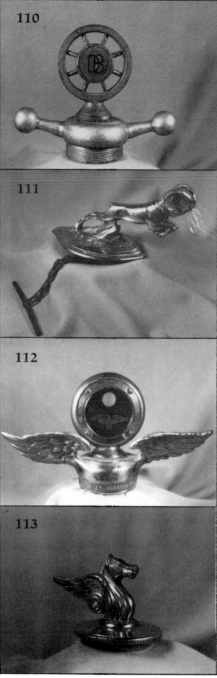

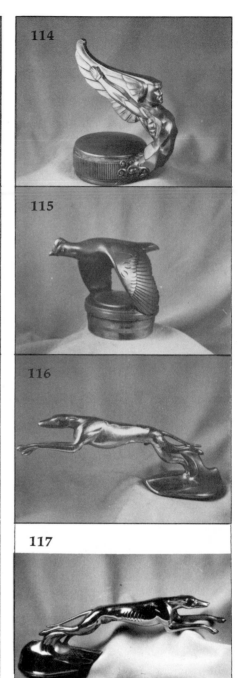

106. Chrysler 1930.

107. Chrysler 1931 Gazelle.

108. Desoto 1928 Head of Hernando DeSoto.

109. Desoto 1933.

110. Dodge 1925–1927.

111. Dodge 1934.

112. Duesenberg 1920–1928 Eagle Wings.

113. Elcar 1930.

114. Essex 1928.

115. Ford 1928–1929 Quail, same mascot for 1930–1931 with different cap.

116. Ford 1933 Greyhound.

117. Ford 1934.

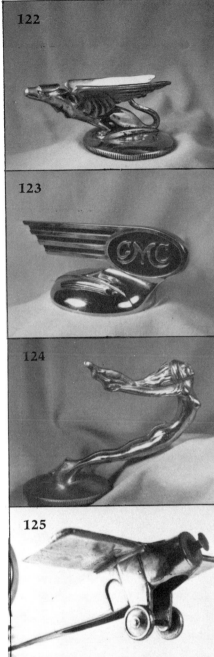

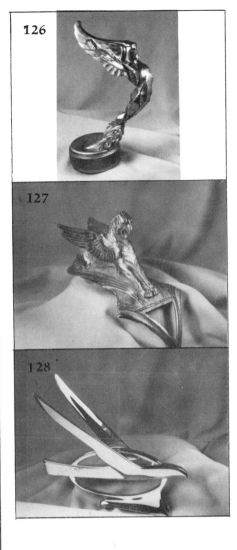

118. Franklin 1917–1923 Lion.

119. Franklin 1925–1928 Lion.

120. Franklin 1928 Ryan Monoplane.

121. Gardner 1926–1927 Griffin.

122. Gardner 1930–1931 Griffin.

123. GMC Truck.

124. Hudson 1927.

125. Hudson 1928 Ryan Monoplane.

126. Hudson 1929 (notice similarity to Essex).

127. Hudson 1933 Griffin (Greek Mythology).

128. Hudson 1934.

129. Jewett 1923-1926.

130. Jewett 1923-1926—Cheap aftermarket copy (compare wing feathers).

131. LaSalle 1927-1928 Sir DeLaSalle.

132. Lincoln 1928.

133. Lincoln 1930.

134. Lincoln 1931—Notice how cap gets progressively larger.

135. Locomobile 1926-1928.

136. Mack Truck 1920s.

137. Mack Truck 1940s-present.

138. Mack Truck—Accessory with lighted eyes.

139. Mack-Bull Dog—Ashtray ornament about half size of actual mascot.

140. Maxwell 1914-1915.

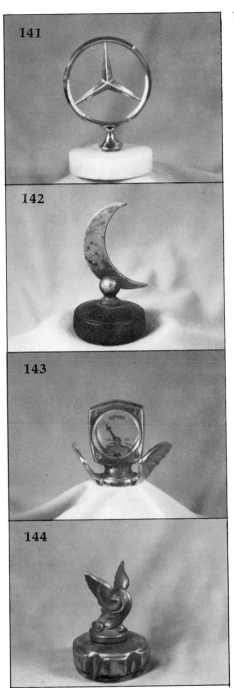

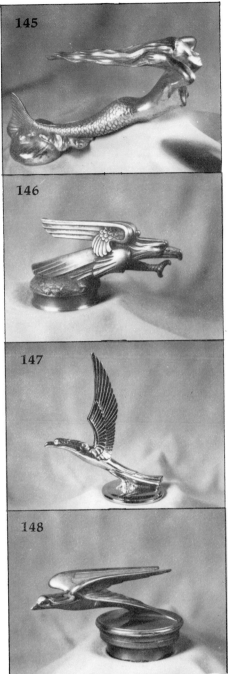

141. Mercedes 1920-present with minor variations.

142. Moon 1912-1928.

143. Morris 1931.

144. Nash 1926-1927.

145. Nash 1929 Mermaid.

146. Oakland 1927-1928.

147. Oakland 1931.

148. Oldsmobile 1931.

149. Oldsmobile 1932.

150. Packard 1926-1928 Goddess of Speed, also nicknamed "Donut Chaser."

151. Packard—through 1928 accessory wings for motor meter.

152. Packard 1930-1931 Adonis.

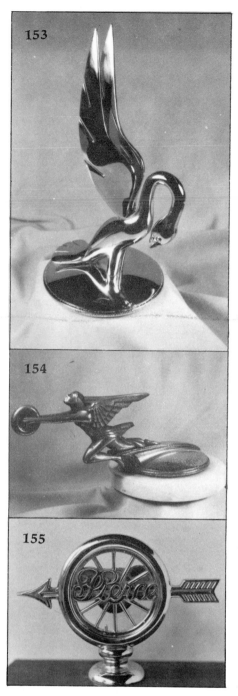

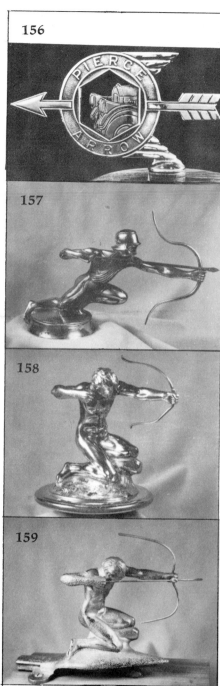

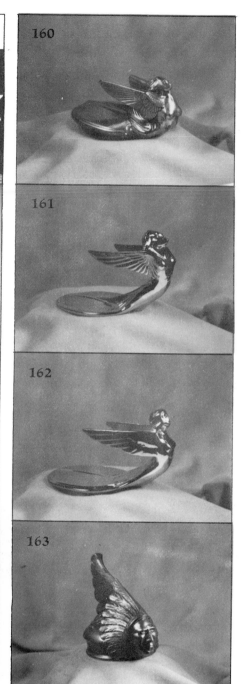

153. Packard 1932.

154. Packard 1932-1937.

155. Pierce Arrow—Teens to early twenties.

156. Pierce Arrow 1924-1926.

157. Pierce Arrow 1928-1929.

158. Pierce Arrow 1931-1932.

159. Pierce Arrow 1934-1937.

160. Plymouth 1931.

161. Plymouth 1933.

162. Plymouth 1934.

163. Pontiac 1927—Very similar to 1926.

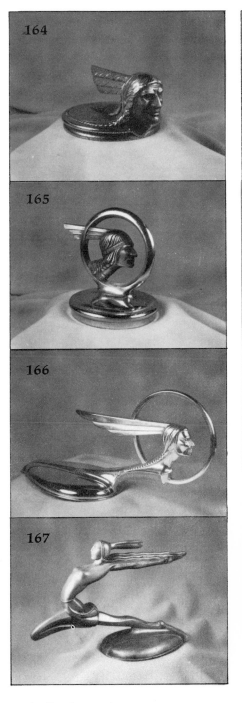

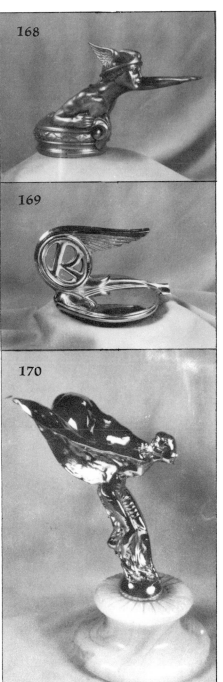

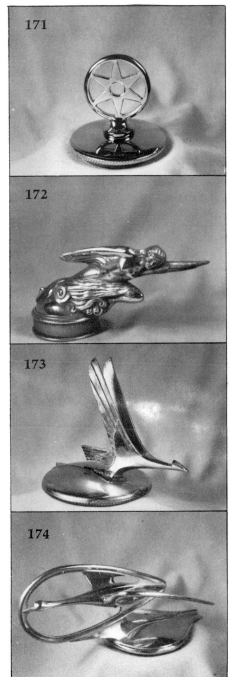

164. Pontiac 1929.

165. Pontiac 1932.

166. Pontiac 1933—Very fragile, many broke off while being used as a handle to remove cap.

167. Pontiac 1934.

168. Reo 1927–1928 Mercury bust.

169. Rockne 1932.

170. Rolls-Royce (Flying Lady) 1911–present with as many as twenty-three minor variations.

171. Star 1920s.

172. Studebaker 1927–1929 Atalanta.

173. Studebaker 1931–1934.

174. Studebaker 1935.

175. Studebaker Truck 1934.

176. Stutz 1926–1935 "Ra," Egyptian sun god.

177. The Pilot 1920s.

178. Toro Tractor 1914 Bull.

179. Whippet 1928.

180. Wills St. Claire 1923–1926.

181. Willys Knight 1923–1926.

182. Willys Knight 1923–1926.

183. Willys Knight 1927–1928.

184. Willys Knight 1928.

185. Willys Knight 1929–1931.

186. Willys Knight—Similar to No. 183, this mascot was cut down and mounted on another radiator cap. Even the broken lance was replaced with a screwdriver blade. Thanks to these crude efforts, another specimen was spared a trip to the scrap pile.

187

188

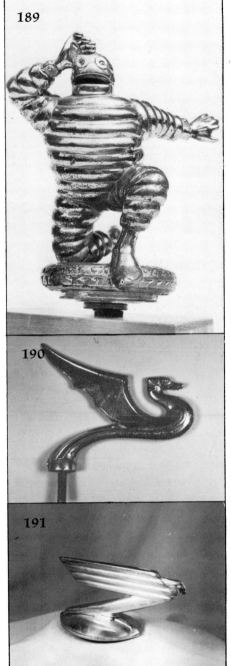

189

190

191

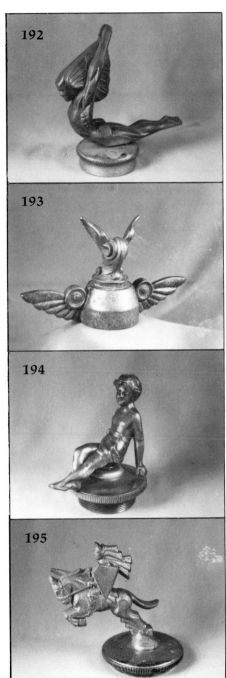

192

193

194

195

Commercial mascots were most interesting. They were used by dealers on their own cars, or given to either salesmen or preferred customers.

187. Dunlop Tires.
188. Esso Oil—England.
189. Michelin Tires (Made in France).

Many aftermarket mascots were made to look like popular factory mascots, but to sell at lesser prices.

190. Chevrolet 1934 copy.
191. Chevrolet 1935 copy.
192. Essex & Hudson 1928 copy.
193. Nash 1924–1928 copy.
194. Packard—Adonis copy.
195. Willys Knight 1928–1931 (similar).

196

197

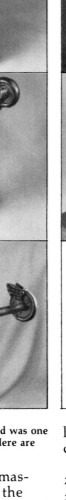
198

199

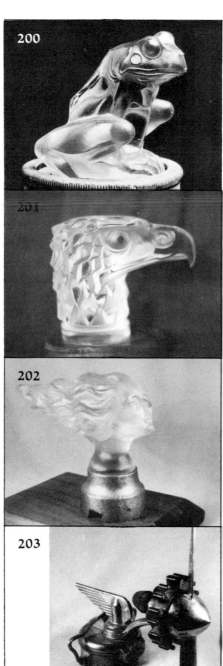

200

201

202

203

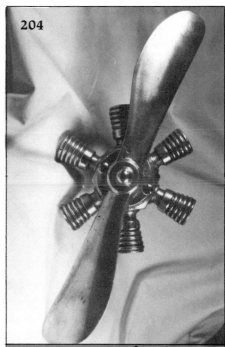
204

205

206

196-199. Packard Goddess of Speed was one of the most copied mascots. Here are four similar examples..

Most desirable accessory mascots among collectors are the glass mascots by Rene Lalique of France. These works of art were made in clear glass and various colors. Two different bases were available, one plain and one equipped with a light and color disc to reflect upward. A deluxe version even had a rotating color disc so that it would change color as you drove along.

200. Frog 1920s-1930s.

201. Eagle Head—Hitler was supposed to have given his officers these for their personal use. 1930 on.

202. Mother by Corning Glass 1920—An American entry into glass mascots.

Another very popular item with mascot collectors is the mechanical ornament. Designed to use airflow to activate some moving device, most were of an airplane- or propeller-type construction.

203. Radial Engine—Small, seven inches. This one was equipped with a light, which shone through slits in a propeller hub.

204. Radial Engine—Large, eleven inches, entire assembly turns.

205. Monoplane.

206. Plane (prop missing)—Defender Auto Lock Co., Detroit, MI.

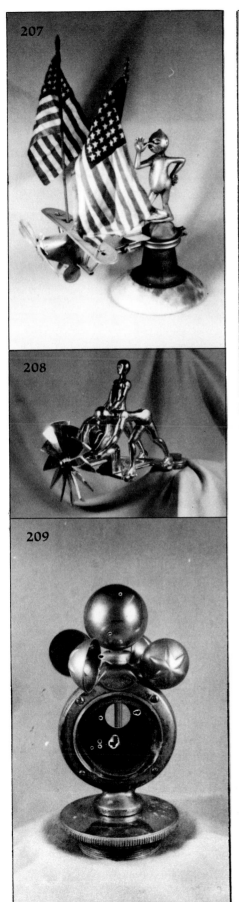

207

210

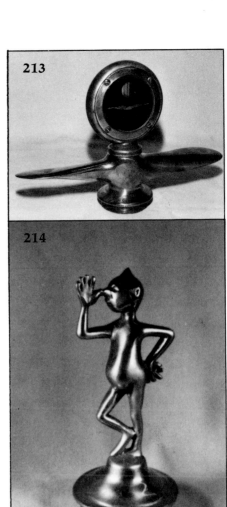

213

214

215

208

211

209

212

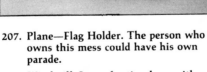

207. Plane—Flag Holder. The person who owns this mess could have his own parade.

208. Windmill. Lots of action here with blades turning and two men cranking.

209. Anemometer. Immitation wind speed indicator. The weatherman must have felt right at home with one of these.

210. Policeman. Arms spin and entire mascot turns around.

211 Rickenbacker 1922–1926. Probably the first of the airplane mascots, as most others jumped on the bandwagon after Lindbergh's famous flight in 1927.

212 & 213. Propellers. No moving parts, but the airplane theme is prevalent.

For motorists with a sense of humor there was an abundance of novelty, hobby related, or occupation related mascots. Of course, there was always the guy who mounted an old water faucet atop the radiator cap.

214. Devil—Thumbing Nose early.

215. Devil—Thumbing Nose later.

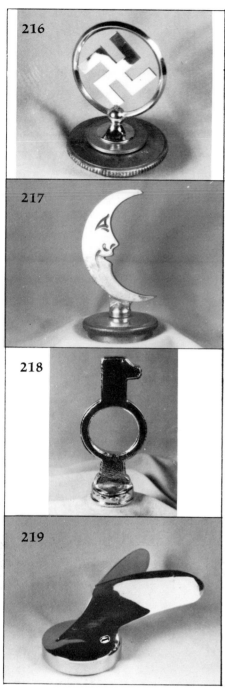

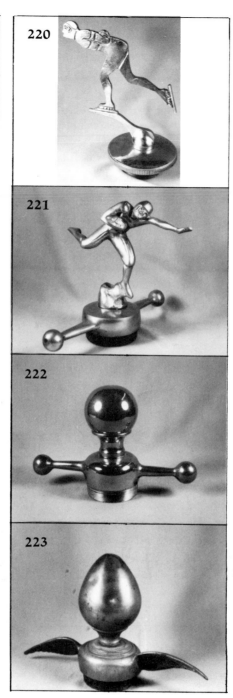

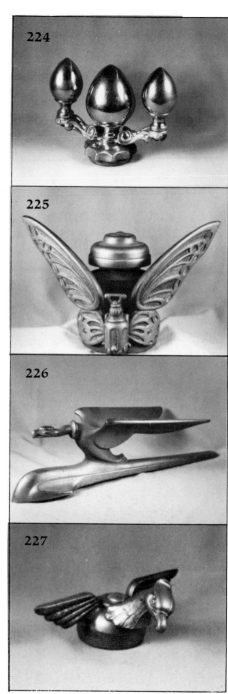

216. Swastika—could have been used on Krit automobile.
217. Man in the Moon.
218. Hole-In-One.
219. Plow Share.
220. Ice Skater.
221. Football Player.
222. Ball.
223. Let's call this one "The Flying Egg."

224. Perhaps an example of one-upmanship. The proud owner of this mascot probably saw the single egg (Figure 223), and decided to out-do the fellow with three eggs, or perhaps somewhere in a hotel lobby an ornate lamp is missing part of its decor.
225. Butterfly 1920s. This mascot has a built-in steam whistle that sounds when water boils.

A substantial share of the accessory market was reserved for birds, and of course, when it comes to birds, the American eagle ranks number one in most people's opinion.

226. This grotesque Buzzard of the 1940s should qualify as a novelty. Undoubtedly its owner must have been chided about it.
227. Mini-Buzzard.

228. Eagle—Flagpole style.

229. Eagle.

230. Eagle.

231. Eagle—Similar to 1913–1916 Coey Flyer.

232 &·233. Eagle on branch, similar to 1927–1928 Marmon.

234. Eagle—Stylized.

235. Goose—Copy of Packard.

236. Goose.

237. Goose—Stylized.

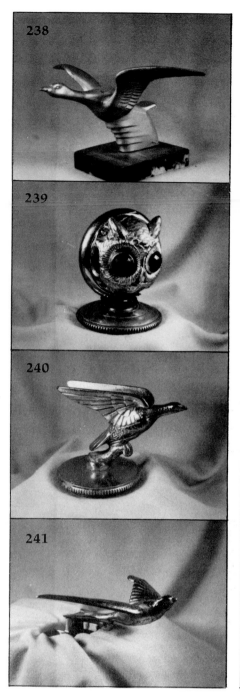

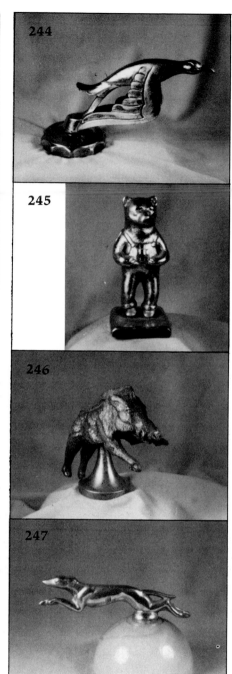

238. Goose—Copy of Wills St. Claire.

239. Owl—with lighted eyes.

240. Quail.

241. Swift.

242. Swan—another Packard copy.

243. Turkey.

244. Unknown bird with penguin head.

The animal lover had his fair share of mascots to choose from.

245. Bear—International Harvester. Dated 1949, issued to herald the new Cub tractor.

246. Bore Hog—England.

247. Dog—like Ford greyhound.

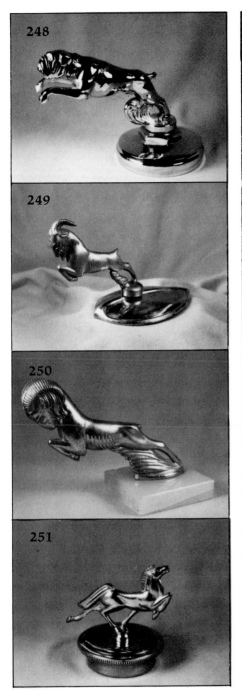

248. Bulldog.
249. Unicorn.
250. Ram—Dodge copy.
251. Horse.
252. Flying Horse—like Elcar or Dover.
253. Jaguar—1950s.
254. Lion.
255. Mustang—like White Truck.

The Pontiac Indian inspired a number of accessory Indians.

256. Chief on dogbone.
257. Chief and wings.
258. Chief large—pot-metal construction.

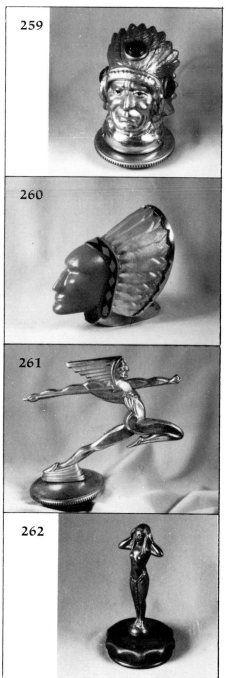

259

260

261

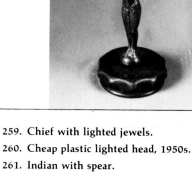

262

263

264

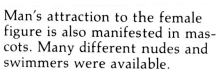

265

266

267

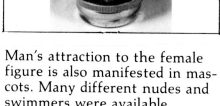

259. Chief with lighted jewels.
260. Cheap plastic lighted head, 1950s.
261. Indian with spear.

Man's attraction to the female figure is also manifested in mascots. Many different nudes and swimmers were available.

262. Indian Maiden.
263. Nude Casual.
264. Nude Dancing.
265. Nude Bodybuilder.
266. Nude Stretching.
267. Nude Winged.

268. Swimmer Diving early 1920s.

269 & 270. Swimmer Diving.

271 & 272. Diving Lady front and rear. One
   wonders how the driver kept his mind
   on the road.

273. Cheap imitation motor meter with
   diving swimmer.

274. Winged Lady.

275. Winged Lady.

276. Draped Nude.

Miscellaneous Mascots

277–283. Variety of winged gods.

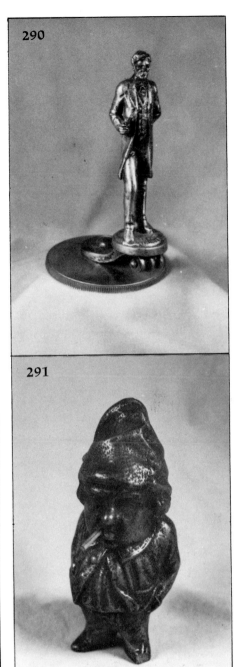

284 & 285. Mercury running.

286. Mercury head.

287. Unknown god.

288. Lady leaning into wind. I wonder if she
stands up straight when the car stops?

289. St. Christopher.

290. Abe Lincoln 1927. Only three hundred
of these made.

291. Dwarf or Munchkin. Three inches
high, was probably motor meter clamp
on.

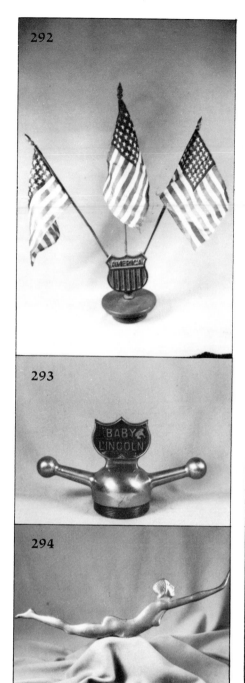

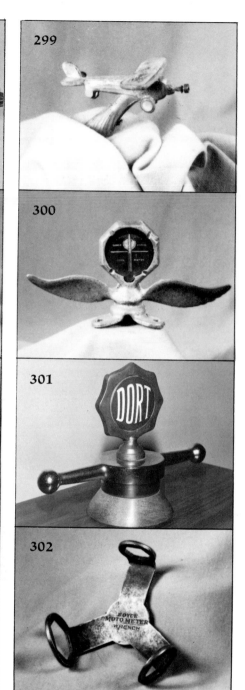

292. America—Flag Holder.

293. Baby Lincoln.

294. Diving Nude. This thin aluminum ornament mounts to face of radiator with bolts through core. About twelve inches long.

295. This 1937 Plymouth hood ornament is typical of what replaced mascots when the radiator cap went under cover beneath the hood.

296-300. Children's pedal cars of the 1930s often had miniature mascots.

301. A cheap aftermarket top that simulates motor meter, with cut-out space to insert the cloisonne emblem from your car.

302. Boyce Moto-Meter wrench.

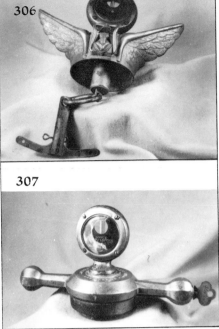

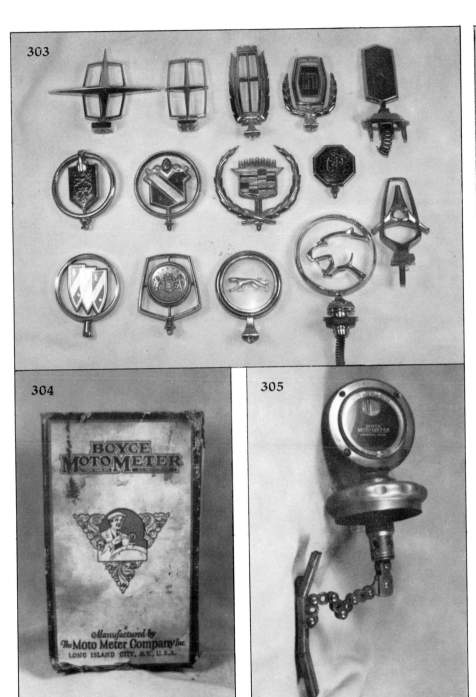

303. Today's reincarnation of the mascot.

304. Boyce Moto-Meter—original box 1920s.

305–307. Three types of antitheft devices.

Photographs

COLLECTING automobile photographs can be interesting and quite educational. No one can deny the truth of the statement, "One picture is worth more than ten thousand words." Perhaps that is why this book has so many pictures: It spares the author from having to write so many words.

Automobile related pictures, especially street scenes, can tell us much about the period, dress modes, advertising signs of the era, building designs, public transportation, street paving, road and information signs, gas-station equipment, the existence or nonexistence of certain familiar buildings, businesses, or landmarks, and much more. The key to all the above is having an accurate date for the photograph. There are several ways of verifying the date. Any vehicle in the photograph may have license plates in view, and unless it is a junkyard or farm-field scene, you can safely assume that the plates were current. A magnifying glass or loupe may be required to read the date. Often, the information and date will be written on the back of the picture. In this case your work has been simplified. It is not very likely, but perhaps a calendar is in view. A building under construction in the background would be a key if you could establish when it was built. A picture showing many cars will most likely contain current models, allowing you to establish a date within a year or two. Some pictures will have a number showing in one corner. Do not confuse this with a date. Company photographers identified all their negatives with a number, and somewhere in that sequence the numbers from 1900 to 1980 appeared, which can be misleading. However, if you recognize this as a company photograph, a little research can establish a date from that photo-identification number. A rather unreliable source for dating is asking the owners, who may have taken the photograph. Memories fade as years pass, and in most cases dating by this method is usually inaccurate.

Old automotive pictures are relatively easy to come by, as photography was well along the way in its development by the early 1900s, and use of the camera was becoming quite common. Many people had their own Kodak cameras and often took photographs of the family car. Because photography was relatively inexpensive, companies used it extensively for record keeping and advertising. These company photographs were usually the work of a professional and, therefore, were sharp and clear in every detail. Most were printed in 8 × 10 size.

Many companies maintain archives open to the public (usually by appointment) and for a small fee will reproduce any old photographs you desire. You may also photograph old ads, sales literature, or manuals, but it is best to seek permission before doing so.

Flea markets, antique shops, and part swaps are other good sources for old photographs. Prices will usually range from fifty cents to five dollars. Unless the photo contains a famous person or is autographed, it should not command any special premium. Picture rarity is directly proportional to the longevity of the particular automobile manufacturer. The longer they were in business and the more cars they produced, the more available photographs will be.

Some collectors specialize in one subject. A Hudson owner will acquire any picture containing Hudson related subject matter; factory pictures, dealer pictures, racing pictures (Hudson was tops on the NASCAR Circuit in the early 1950s), and pictures of the cars themselves.

If your interest lies with an automobile produced by an ongoing company, a letter to the company archives or public relations department with a detailed request of your needs may produce some nice pictures for your library. A little earnest money up front, perhaps a check for five dollars to cover postage and film, may speed up a response to your request. Some companies will probably return your check as a gesture of good will.

Displaying photographs can present problems. First of all, wall space can be rapidly consumed by a few 8 × 10s. Old photographs are sensitive to air and light, each attacking the silver-nitrate base, making it brittle and fading it. Newer photographs have a protective lacquer coating that reduces deterioration, but does not prevent it. Every collector has a desire to show off his favorite photos. Displaying these with the least amount of deterioration can be accomplished by using a glass-covered picture frame and hanging it in an area void of direct sunlight. Adding an extra measure of protection might include hanging a black curtain over the picture, but if you possess the original negative, have no fear, you can always make another print. Three-ring binders with glassine-type protective pages or regular photo albums are the usual places for keeping photographs.

The following photographs will give an idea of what might be found in a photograph collection and examples of what can be learned from them.

1. This 1940 Ford Fordor photograph comes directly from Ford Motor Company (Record No. 71879J) and can be very confusing to an unsuspecting Ford enthusiast who may not be well versed in 1940 Ford features. The 1937 Michigan license plate indicates the key fact, that this car is a mock-up of a 1938 model in preparation for the 1940-model production. Some obvious points are: missing wiper blades and inaccurate wiper-arm location (1940 arms were on the cowl not the roof); 1938–1939-type taillight housings; unmatched hubcaps front and rear; incorrect bumper guards; Ford Deluxe nameplate on the hood should be script, not block letters; crudeness of small louvered panel next to grille; and three distinct seams on the nose of the hood, evidence of a quickie moulding job by the styling department. Perhaps a 1940-Ford expert could find still more errors. This tends to prove that factory photos can sometimes be less accurate than photos taken after the production and sale of a car.

2. Use of a truck as a rolling advertising platform was popular in the 1920s and 1930s. Many trucks were custom fitted with unusual bodies like this eye-catching 1932 International used by the Goodyear Tire Company. Trucks were made up like huge milk bottles, spark plugs, smoking pipes, shoes, radios, etc. A collection of these photos would make a real conversation piece. Accessory driving lights block the view of what appears to be an Ohio license plate. Evidence of slow speed film used then is seen in the blurred fender flags.

3. Hudson factory photograph, pencil dated on the back Oct. 5, 1926, showing hookup for gasoline mileage-testing device similar to one shown in tools and accessories chapter. This picture could be helpful in many ways to someone restoring a 1926 Hudson. Details like hose-clamp style, carburetor type, wire routing, moto meter and dog bone style, etc. are quite visible.

The clarity of these old photographs is remarkable. With a ten-power loupe the fifteen lines of instructions on the small manifold-mounted plate can easily be read. Quite a feat, bearing in mind that on an 8 × 10 photograph that

little four-bolt plate only measures five-sixteenths of an inch square. Further scrutiny shows the car equipped with Goodyear tires, but the loupe reveals Firestone cast into the clincher-type mounting lug.

4. The man seated in this 1911 Stoddard Dayton roadster is a Mr. Carr. He was president of the company and quite proud of his cars as he had the plant photographer take photographs of him poised in each of his new cars. The car carries 1911 Ontario license plates and 1911 New York license plates, indicating that it was operated in both places.

At first, the car was unidentified, but

a careful search of books and magazine articles finally revealed a very similar car. In an April 1972 issue of ARIZONA HIGHWAYS magazine appeared a picture of a 1910 Stoddard Dayton Raceabout. The fenders were exactly the same, and what could be seen of the hubcap was also alike. Although the name on the hubcap could not be read, close examination revealed enough that it could be verified against a full size picture of a Stoddard hubcap. There is a certain satisfaction in successfully identifying an old photograph like this one.

5. A 1926 International two-ton truck bearing 1926 Ontario license plates.

Having access to a company's archives or photography department can reward you with some fine old photographs. Even companies other than automobile makers will have some old photographs showing cars and trucks. One example was the Automatic Transportation Company of Buffalo, New York. Founded in 1906, they were producers of electric powered material handling equipment and baggage carts. In 1929 they relocated in Chicago, Illinois, eventually buying out the Walker Vehicle Company, who were producers of electric powered local delivery trucks. The Chicago plant was closed in 1971, at which time its industrial fork-truck line was taken over by Eaton Yale and Towne. Before old company records were disposed of, some fine automobile related pictures were salvaged. Following are a few examples:

Truck sits by an as yet unidentified body maker. International Harvester Company has a plant in Chatham, Ontario, where this truck was built, after which it was probably sent to this company to have the commercial body attached. The challenge here is to further research the picture and try to determine the carriage maker's name.

6. A 1930 model International displaying a 1930 Illinois license plate makes an interesting photograph for those who think multiple trailers are a recent accomplishment. United Parcel and Consolidated Freightways drivers could really appreciate this photograph. Imagine winding up on a dead-end street with this one.

7. Mr. Carr is seated this time in a 1911 Pierce Arrow touring car. Both the Pierce and Stoddard carry consecutive 1911 New York license plates. The Pierce has no Ontario license plate as it was probably used at the factory in Buffalo to haul VIPs around. If you think cushioned or spring-loaded bumpers are a late model result of government regulations, then take a close look at the spring-loaded front bumper here.

8. Mr. Carr again is seated in a new 1914 Pierce Arrow Coupe. Notice incorporation of the famous Pierce molded-on headlights. This car was also equipped with spring-loaded bumpers.

9. In 1921 the company tried to enter the automobile market with this electric two seater, which would probably qualify as a cycle car. Even though much promotion was done, as demonstrated by this photograph, it was an unsuccessful venture. Vehicles are fitted with 1921 New York Demonstration Plates.

10. This picture shows a size comparison with a full-size car. Here is one of those pictures where the photograph number could be mistaken for the date, but the 1921 license plate and style of background negate that possibility. Notice the on-sidewalk parking. Can you identify the car behind the demonstrator?

11

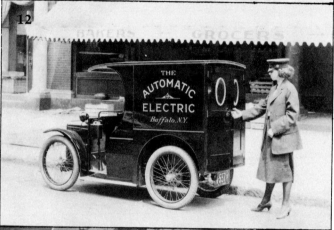

12

15

13

16

11. Automatic Transportation Company photograph number 1948. Clearly a case where the photograph number can confuse the novice. This is actually a chassis view of the 1921 demonstrator car.

12. An enclosed version directed at the postal service market. Notice pair of wood spoke wheels sitting loose.

13. It's Mr. Carr back in the driver's seat again but a step down from the stately Pierce Arrow. Slow speed film caught the lathe operator's curiosity.

14. After the move to Chicago and purchase of the Walker Vehicle Company, photographs like this one started to fill the files. Most manufacturers like a photographic record of successful sales to use in wooing new customers. This truck has 1930 Kentucky license plates (Jefferson County), which means the photograph was probably taken in Louisville.

15. Dairy trucks were very colorfully decorated; unfortunately, there was no color film to record it.

16. True class in a commercial vehicle is seen in this 1930 design for Marshall Field's (an exclusive Chicago department store). Dual side mounts, ample chrome plating, Double Eagle Brand whitewalls on both sides of tire are features just not seen on commercial vehicles. This truck was a gas electric, a six-cylinder Continental engine coupled to a large generator which in turn supplied a variable voltage to an electric drive motor connected to the differential.

17

17. Walker Vehicle production ended in the early 1930s, but Automatic went on building its well-established fork trucks, heavy ram trucks, and as seen in this photograph, platform die-handling trucks. This particular die-handling truck was sold to Oldsmobile, Lansing, Michigan, to handle huge sheet-metal stamping dies. The load of 1949 Oldsmobiles was staged to impress company representatives from Oldsmobile upon their final acceptance of the truck. The four cars and transport weigh approximately thirty thousand pounds.

Auto Album by Tad Burness is a weekly feature appearing in over two hundred syndicated newspapers. Tad started drawing cars at the age of eleven, selecting rare old cars in the neighborhood as his subject. From this evolved the hobby of collecting old-car ads and reference material. His drawings first started appearing in newspapers in 1966, and a new drawing has appeared each week ever since then.

Tad bills this as a free hobby and suggests that you clip and save each drawing. However, if you don't want to wait each week, among the ten old-car books he has written, volume two of *Auto Album* is currently available from Scholastic Books, 900 Sylvan Avenue, Englewood Cliffs, New Jersey 07632 (95¢ postpaid).

These little clippings can be helpful to the collector as seen in the examples shown. Radiator emblems and mascots are clearly shown, plus a variety of specifications.

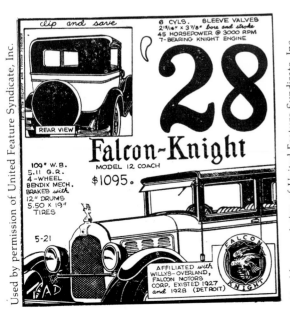

AUTO ALBUM
By TAD BURNESS

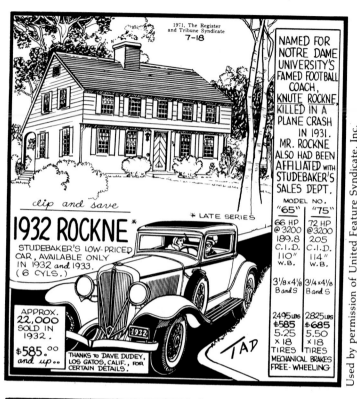

1971, The Register and Tribune Syndicate 7-18

NAMED FOR NOTRE DAME UNIVERSITY'S FAMED FOOTBALL COACH, KNUTE ROCKNE, KILLED IN A PLANE CRASH IN 1931. MR. ROCKNE ALSO HAD BEEN AFFILIATED with STUDEBAKER'S SALES DEPT.

clip and save

1932 ROCKNE *
STUDEBAKER'S LOW-PRICED CAR, AVAILABLE ONLY IN 1932 AND 1933. (6 CYLS.)

* LATE SERIES

APPROX. 22,000 SOLD IN 1932.

$585.00 and up..

THANKS TO DAVE DUDEY, LOS GATOS, CALIF., FOR CERTAIN DETAILS.

MODEL NO.	"65"	"75"
	66 HP @ 3200	72 HP @ 3200
	189.8 C.I.D.	205 C.I.D.
W.B.	110"	114"
B and S	3 1/8 x 4 1/8	3 1/4 x 4 1/8
	2495 LBS	2825 LBS
	$585	$685
TIRES	5.25 x 18	5.50 x 18

MECHANICAL BRAKES
FREE-WHEELING

1941 FORD
85-90 HP
114" W.B.
3.78 G.R.

V-8 (STARTS 9-40)   6 CYL. (STARTS 5-41)
221 C.I.D.   226 C.I.D.
3 1/16" x 3 3/4" BORE and STROKE 3.3" x 4.4"

IDEA = TRY TINTING ADDITIONAL COPIES OF THIS PICTURE, WITH COLOR PENCILS, CRAYONS, ETC.

1972, The Register and Tribune Syndicate

TAD 1-9

1GA-11A

L-HEAD ENGINES IN EITHER TYPE OF 41 FORD.

1926 "SAFETY" STUTZ
STRAIGHT-8   92 H.P. ENGINE
9 MAIN BEARINGS (OVERHEAD CAM) (3 3/16" x 4 1/2")

191" W.B.   TOP SPEED: 70-75   14 M.P.G.
BREWSTER-DESIGNED BODIES BY Phillips on American.
TIMKEN "HYDROSTATIC" (water-alcohol) 4-WHEEL BRAKES and WORM-DRIVE REAR AXLE. STEEL RUNNINGBOARDS A PART OF CHASSIS.

SAFETY GLASS REINFORCED WITH HORIZONTAL STRANDS OF WIRE WAS A UNIQUE FEATURE OF THE SAFETY STUTZ.

TAD 6-3-73

(MASCOT) RA, the EGYPTIAN SUN GOD

The symbol of Safety

HUBBARD VENTILATING EAVES

ONLY 70" HIGH

STUTZ MOTOR CAR CO. OF AMERICA, INC., INDIANAPOLIS, INDIANA

1926 SALES - 5,069 } MODEL "AA"
1927 SALES - 3,298 }

Distributed by King Features Syndicate.

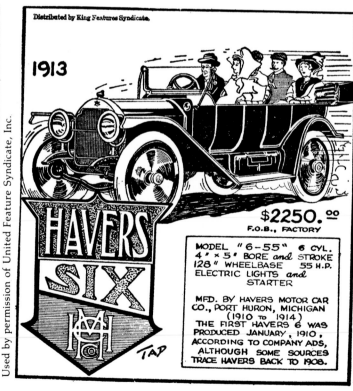

Distributed by King Features Syndicate.

1913

$2250.00
F.O.B., FACTORY

MODEL "6-55"   6 CYL.
4" x 5" BORE and STROKE
128" WHEELBASE   55 H.P.
ELECTRIC LIGHTS and STARTER

MFD. BY HAVERS MOTOR CAR CO., PORT HURON, MICHIGAN (1910 to 1914) THE FIRST HAVERS 6 WAS PRODUCED JANUARY, 1910, ACCORDING TO COMPANY ADS, ALTHOUGH SOME SOURCES TRACE HAVERS BACK TO 1908.

HAVERS SIX

Tools and Accessories

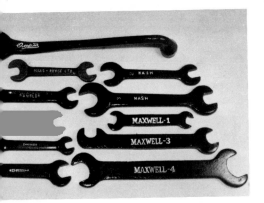

MANY auto tools were embossed with the auto maker's name, but there were just as many interesting aftermarket tools. Tools can be very displayable if sandblasted, painted semi-gloss black to simulate the original dipping enamel, and then accentuated by painting raised or depressed letters white so they may be seen from a distance. Those who feel this detracts from the as is historical appearance are free to leave their tools as they see fit, but it will require close examination to see the name.

Many gas-station tools and accessories exist, but some like gas pumps and floor jacks are quite large. Gas-pump globes make a colorful display, especially when lighted. Many are being reproduced because of increasing popularity.

Today we rely on gauges, dials, and lights, to monitor just about anything. Fifty years ago many fluids were kept track of by glass sight gauges. Today these make interesting collectibles.

When restoring these items, extreme caution must be taken while removing the glass, as most replacement glass is impossible to obtain. Some glass was sealed on each end by a cork gasket, relatively easy to remove. Others, such as gas-pump glasses, are held in by a compound that looks like white lead. It has dried very hard, and will not dissolve with gasoline, alcohol, acetone, or lacquer thinner. Some acids would do it, but are very dangerous to work with, and can produce noxious fumes. The best way to remove these is to tediously scrape the putty away with a ground-down hacksaw blade. It is time consuming but does work and will save a valuable piece of glass. If the glass is broken, there are plexiglass replacements available in some sizes. You might first check your local glass shop to inquire if certain glass-tube sizes are available. If you eventually have to use plexiglass you may be required to buy a full length of tubing (five to ten feet). So take extra care where that old glass is concerned.

1. Almost automobile tools: More research is needed for this Peerless as the back says G.M.Co. Peerless was never part of General Motors, but perhaps GM made tools for Peerless. Studebaker is the same as the car company, but this is a buggy wrench prior to their automobile building days.

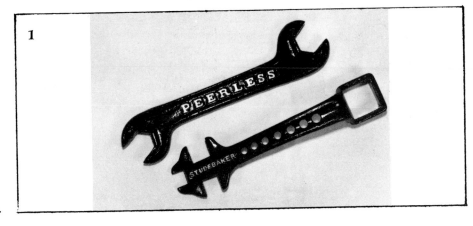

1

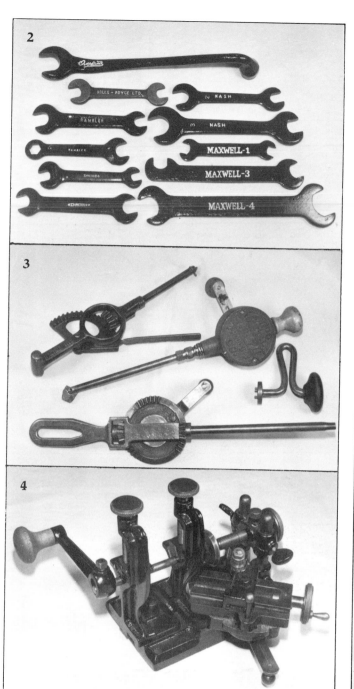

2. Factory supplied wrenches, Overland, Rolls-Royce, Rambler, Pierce Arrow, Nash, and Maxwell. The object here is to find Nash #1 and Maxwell #2 to complete the sets.

3. Many different kinds of valve lapping tools were sold with automatic or manual reversing devices.

4. Very early portable valve grinder dated 1914 was actually a miniature lathe.

5. Early socket and ratchet wrenches. Two on bottom are dated 1914.

6. Gas-pump accessory. Housing a deck of changeable cards, this attached to the gas pump or island support post.

7. Toy lithographed tin gas-station service island, circa 1930, with extra pump and oil tank.

8. Oscillating two-cylinder tire pump dated 1917 is constructed of brass and cast iron.

9. A glass-tube oil dispenser.

10. Gallon counter was attached to pump.

CHAPTER 11

Ford Collectibles

THE year 1978 marked the 75th anniversary of the Ford Motor Company. During that period of time over *100 million* cars were produced. Among car buffs from hot rodders, to dirt-track racers, to antique-car enthusiasts, the Ford has always been most popular. This period of 75 years has produced many collectible items, including car parts, toys, tools, advertising, souvenirs, and books.

At one time nearly every part on the Ford automobile had the familiar Ford script on it, a practice that was dropped in some cases over the years due to cost. Car restorers usually prefer script parts to those not bearing the familiar trademark.

Many aftermarket products were directed right at the Ford owner and, although not sold by Ford, carried the name for one of two reasons. Some products would fit only Ford cars, but in the case of general products such as lubricants, waxes, cooling-system additives, the inference that they were for Ford cars would entice the Ford owner to buy them.

There seemed to be no end to the barrage of products Ford owners could buy to beautify, "soup up," or make driving more pleasurable. Hand starters, extra instruments, a variety of heaters and radiator shutters, several high-compression or overhead-valve conversion kits, trunk racks, special wheels, special tools, cigar lighters, and air cleaners (Ford did not supply air cleaners until 1932). You could even buy a kit to convert your Model T or Model A into a snowmobile, complete with skis on the front and six driving wheels in the rear.

A very good compilation of these can be found in a book by Murray Fahnestock, entitled *Those Wonderful Unauthorized Accessories.*

The ultimate in Ford collectibles was marketed in 1978 by Ford dealers in honor of the 75 years of Ford auto production. It is a $5,000, 13-inch long, 7½-pound replica of the 1903 Model A. (Ford went completely through the alphabet before starting over at *A* in 1928 with the car most are familiar with). Constructed of Sterling silver and 24-karat gold, this model has diamonds and rubies hand set by Cartier. Only 1,708 were produced to equal production of the original car.

An event that produced many Ford keepsakes was the 1933–34 World's Fair held in Chicago. Henry Ford, being a conservative, thought that the fair would not be a success at the height of the depression and did not display in 1933. After seeing what a success 1933 was, he decided to participate in 1934. A small assembly line was set up, and 1934 Fords were actually produced at the fair.

Up until the late forties, most of the tools supplied with each new Ford had Ford script. Many variations of these can be found. Some tools even included the Ford part number. If no script was present, a letter M could be found within a circle which indicated that the tool was made by Moore Drop Forge Co., which made most of Ford's tools.

An extremely good reference for Ford pictures, ads, showroom scenes, and interesting stories was a magazine called *Ford Life.* Unfortunately, it only lasted from November 1970 through June 1974 with a total publication of 22 bimonthly issues. Should you see any of these at part swaps or flea markets, it would be wise to purchase them.

From tools to toys or from cars to cartoons, there seems to be no end to ideas for Ford collectibles. The choice is yours.

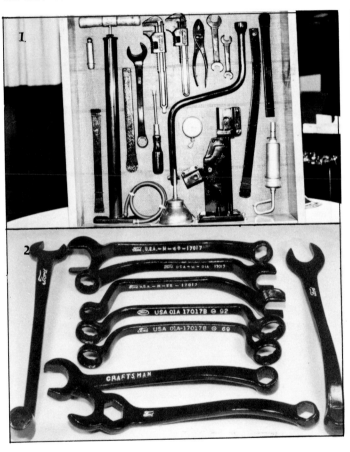

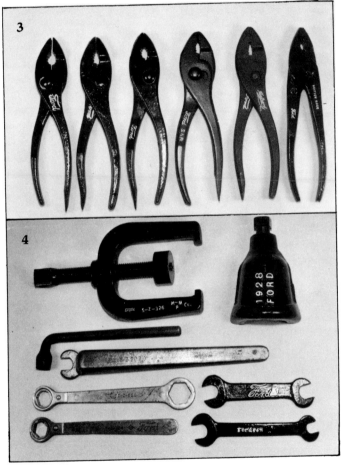

1. A complete set of Ford tools as supplied with the Model A.

2. An assortment of head-nut and spark-plug combination wrenches from Model T to the 1940s. The later ones carry the Ford part number 17017. Popularity of this wrench is demonstrated by the Sears aftermarket version.

3. Pliers left to right: large raised script, small depressed script, small raised script, Ford S & R (probably Sears & Roebuck), Ford by Herbrand, and British Ford.

4. Pullers, special wrenches, ratcheting box wrenches, and a Fordson tractor wrench, lower right. The puller dated 1928 must have been made in that year for if it were made in any succeeding year, it most likely would not have been dated that way because the same puller will work from 1928 to 1948.

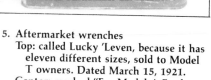

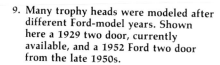

5. Aftermarket wrenches
   Top: called Lucky 'Leven, because it has eleven different sizes, sold to Model T owners. Dated March 15, 1921.
   Center: marked "For Model A Ford Cars," this wrench fit water pump, oil drain plug, brakes, and shock absorbers.
   Bottom: brand name "For-A-Ford." (See spark plug chapter for plug by same company.)

6. Scarce accessory from Model-T and Model-A era.

7. Old part boxes make interesting collectibles.

8. Oil directed at the Ford market.

9. Many trophy heads were modeled after different Ford-model years. Shown here a 1929 two door, currently available, and a 1952 Ford two door from the late 1950s.

10. Ford place setting, an unusual addition to a collection.

11. This plastic bird was given away by dealers to promote the introduction of the Falcon in 1959.

The 1934 Chicago World's Fair produced many collectibles.

12. Rubber coaster set came in four colors—red, yellow, blue, and green.

13. A sample box of materials used to make Ford cars.

14. A group of bronze coins: top, 1935 San Diego Fair; center, front and reverse of 1934 World's Fair coin; bottom, Ford's Thirtieth Anniversary.

15. Cast-iron Model A coupe is desirable, but cast iron is usually expensive. Model A and Model T sedans were abundant. Many reproductions have been made, so be careful of what you purchase. A reproduction has a split pin called a "roll pin" for an axle, where an original has a solid pin.

16. Plastic RCA Television service truck modeled after the 1949 and 1951 Ford Panel Delivery Truck made by Marx.

17. A four-page advertisement was given away. This cover page shows the Ford exhibition building plus other sights at the fair.

18. Center spread of same paper shows full line of 1934 passenger models.

CHAPTER 12

Miscellaneous Pictures

1. Cars on stamps. There are at least 200 world stamps showing automobiles.

2. Headlamp lenses carry many names and designs but are hard to display properly and are very fragile. Example shown: Rickenbacker.

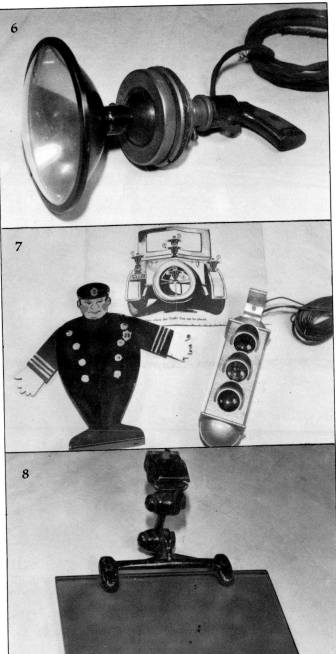

3. Many glass taillight lenses had car names or trademark. An interesting way to display these is to cut out the shape in wood, mount them, and light from behind.

4. Dozens of varieties of stoplight lenses abound in green, red, and yellow.

5. What are light lenses without bulbs? Headlight, taillight, and instrument lights come in many styles. Try a collection of these, they are still plentiful and inexpensive.

6. Accessory windshield mounted spotlight by Fyrac (who also made spark plugs).

7. Two accessory stop indicators. Policeman from 1920s has solenoid-operated arms that swing out to side when brake pedal is depressed. Red, yellow, and green light is 1940s accessory.

8. Cobalt blue sunshade for teens and twenties open cars.

9. Smoking accessories
   Top, left to right: 1937 Ford swing-out ashtray, plated-brass clamp-on ashtray, and marbled-glass stick-on.
   Bottom: 1949 Dodge giveaway, and steering-column cigarette-lighter receptacle.

10. Econometer, gas-mileage minder mounted on dash and measured gallons per hour in flow with a conversion table into M.P.G.

11. Hinckley Myres—mileage measuring device. Holding exactly 1/10 gallon between the full and empty line, this device was an accurate means for factory testing.

12. Article in 1934 Hudson factory newsletter, showing application of mileage device. An earlier version of this is shown in the chapter on photographs.

13 & 14. Avon cars make a nice collection. Shown here is the complete series, except for some smaller-size decanters, Mustang, Porsche, T-Bird, and two more versions of the Volkswagon.

14

17

15

18

16

19

15. Toy version of Oscar Mayer's "Wiener Wagon" that traveled around the country in the 1950s. Those who were old enough in the 1950s probably remember this.

16. Cast iron toys are highly prized but have been degraded somewhat by a flood of reproductions. This original 1933 Pierce Arrow Silver Shadow model was sold at the World's Fair for $1.00 each. This particular one says "Super Salesman" on top as a dealer award.

17. Tin toys were cheaper than cast iron and shared the marketplace with cast iron for a few years until cast iron was dropped in lieu of the cheaper tin. This 1934 vintage Lincoln look-alike has battery-operated headlights. About 9 to 10 inches long.

18. Smaller tin toys about four inches long were geared to a smaller pocket book.
Left is a 1948 Chevrolet wind-up car, made in "Occupied Japan," that in itself makes it quite collectible since the occupied period lasted only three years.
In the middle is a 1934 Chevrolet with white rubber wheels.
The dump truck came in five different sizes.

19. Lithographed tin toys are most desirable as condition is a big factor. These cannot be restored by conventional methods.

20. Hard-rubber and soybean-based toys were popular for a short time from the late 1930s to mid 1940s, obviously a result of the metal shortage during the war.
    Top row: Chrysler Air Flow, 1939 Studebaker.
    Bottom, left to right: 1937 Buick, 1941 Plymouth, 1939 International, Auburn coupe.

21. A new and upcoming collectible is early slot racing cars. These date around 1960. Thunderbird, Austin Healey, and Corvette.

22. Thousands of modeling possibilities exist from 99¢ Matchbox toys to $3,000 working-model ⅛-scale masterpieces. This Model A coupe is a 1/18 Hubley die-cast metal kit with a few modifications to make it look more realistic. Miniature tool kit was scratch built.

CHAPTER 13

Auto Quiz

Questions

1. Who built the first Super Sport? In what year?
2. What year did Chevrolet first introduce its overhead-valve V8 engine?
3. What was the first year Ford produced a Model A?
4. In what year was safety glass introduced and by whom?
5. In what year was the first Mustang built?
6. Who produced the first sixteen-cylinder car in America?
7. What modern rock group adopted the name of an early auto, and what do those initials stand for?
8. Who is credited with producing the first car in America?
9. How many automobiles were registered in America in 1900?
10. How many makes of automobiles were produced in Indiana?
11. From 1909 to 1927 Ford produced its infamous Model T. During that eighteen-year period, how many cars did Ford produce?
12. Since the beginning of powered transportation, how many different names have adorned automobiles, trucks, buses, and motorcycles combined?
13. Who won the first auto race in America, and in what year?
14. Michigan is known today as the automobile capital of the world. What was the first company to establish there?
15. In what year did the post office first try vehicles for delivery?
16. Who introduced the fully automatic transmission and in what year?
17. *True* or *False:* Ford was producing over 9,000 cars a day in 1925.

18. Were license plates ever made from soybeans?
19. What has been the most successful, new-model car ever produced?
20. Was there ever an eight-wheel car? If so, what was its name?

Answers

1. No, it was not Chevrolet. It was Rickenbacker in 1926.
2. In 1917 an overhead valve V8 engine was introduced but lasted only two years. Chevrolet, having had much success with its 6, held out until succumbing to the pressures of the marketplace before producing a successful V8 engine in 1955.
3. The first Model A was produced in 1903, after which Henry Ford ran through the alphabet until 1928 when he started over again at A with the famous Model A most of us remember.

4. In 1926 Stutz made safety glass standard on its cars. Small horizontal ribs of steel, about one inch apart, would prevent shattering on impact. Laminated safety glass came about seven years later.

6. In 1947. However, it was not Ford's famous version. A small Seattle-based company took factory orders only and lasted for two short years.

6. Cadillac in 1930. Several auto makers had V12 engines also: Packard, Lincoln, Auburn, and Cadillac. Marmon had a 16.

7. R.E.O. Speedwagon. R.E.O. stands for Randsom E. Olds.

8. Although Haynes's nameplate heralds it as "America's First Car," Charles Duryea was a year earlier with his Horseless Carriage in 1893. It wasn't until 1896 that Henry Ford emerged with his entry, the Quadracycle.

9. About 8,000.

10. Over 175. At one time Indianapolis could have been called the "Motor City," far exceeding the number of Detroit companies.

11. 15,000,000. That is fifteen percent of Ford's all-time total production.

12. About 10,500.

13. Charles Duryea won a fifty-two-mile race in Chicago, averaging seven-and-a-half miles per hour in 1895.

14. Olds Motor Works in 1897.

15. 1899.

16. Oldsmobile in 1939.

17. *True.* Even in that early year, total production for all manufacturers was 3.7 million cars.

18. Yes, in Illinois from 1943 to 1948. Two other states tried them for a short period.

19. Ford's Mustang, introduced in April 1964. One-and-a-half million were sold in the first three years.

20. Yes. The Reeves Octoauto was built in 1911 but was unsuccessful. So its designer removed two wheels and tried it as a Sextoauto in 1912. But again it was unsuccessful.

After 80 years of motoring, America's care-free love affair with the automobile is seriously threatened. One wonders if O.P.E.C. doesn't stand for *Oil Producers Extortion Cartel!* It is a sad epitaph to our hobby to see cards such as these placed in motel lobbies.

NTGAS

NATIONAL TRAVELERS'
GASOLINE ADVISORY
For instant information on gasoline availability call
800/238-1000
In Tennessee—(800/542-5270)